Selected Chapters From

Clinical Practice of the Dental Hygienist

Selected Chapters From

Clinical Practice of the Dental Hygienist

TWELFTH EDITION

Intraoral Preventive Procedures and Practicum

Esther M. Wilkins, BS, *RDH*, DMD
Department of Periodontology
Tufts University School of Dental Medicine
Boston, Massachusetts

Charlotte J. Wyche, RDH, MS
Department of Periodontics and Oral Medicine
University of Michigan School of Dentistry
Ann Arbor, Michigan

Linda D. Boyd, RDH, RD, EdD
Forsyth School of Dental Hygiene
MCPHS University
Boston, Massachusetts

. Wolters Kluwer

Philadelphia • Baltimore • New York • London
Buenos Aires • Hong Kong • Sydney • Tokyo

Senior Acquisitions Editor: Jonathan Joyce
Custom Product Development Editor: Salimah Perkins
Design Coordinator: Holly McLaughlin
Manufacturing Coordinator: Margie Orzech

Based on the Twelfth Edition of *Clinical Practice of the Dental Hygienist* by Esther M. Wilkins (ISBN 978-1-4511-9311-4).

Printed in the United States of America

Care has been taken to confirm the accuracy of the information presented and to describe gener¬ally accepted practices. However, the authors, editors, and publisher are not responsible for errors or omissions or for any consequences from application of the information in this book and make no warranty, expressed or implied, with respect to the currency, completeness, or accuracy of the contents of the publication. Application of the information in a particular situation remains the professional responsibility of the practitioner.

The authors, editors, and publisher have exerted every effort to ensure that drug selection and dosage set forth in this text are in accordance with current recommendations and practice at the time of publication. However, in view of ongoing research, changes in government regulations, and the constant flow of information relating to drug therapy and drug reactions, the reader is urged to check the package insert for each drug for any change in indications and dosage and for added warnings and precautions. This is particularly important when the recommended agent is a new or infrequently employed drug.

Some drugs and medical devices presented in the publication have Food and Drug Administration (FDA) clearance for limited use in restricted research settings. It is the responsibil¬ity of the health care provider to ascertain the FDA status of each drug or device planned for use in their clinical practice.

To purchase additional copies of this book, call our customer service department at (800) 638-3030 or fax orders to (301) 223-2320. International customers should call (301) 223-2300.

Visit Lippincott Williams & Wilkins on the Internet: at LWW.com.

CONTENTS

Dental Biofilm and Other Soft Deposits

Janis G Keating, RDH, MA, Allyson Ligor, RDH, MS, and Esther M. Wilkins, BS, RDH, DMD

CHAPTER OUTLINE

ACQUIRED PELLICLE
- I. Formation of the Pellicle
- II. Types of Pellicle
- III. Significance of Pellicle
- IV. Removal of Pellicle

DENTAL BIOFILM
- I. Stages in the Formation of Biofilm
- II. Changes in Biofilm Microorganisms
- III. Experimental Gingivitis

SUPRAGINGIVAL AND SUBGINGIVAL DENTAL BIOFILM
- I. Source
- II. Microorganisms
- III. Organization of Subgingival Biofilm

COMPOSITION OF DENTAL BIOFILM
- I. Inorganic Elements
- II. Organic Elements

CLINICAL ASPECTS
- I. Distribution of Biofilm
- II. Detection of Biofilm

SIGNIFICANCE OF DENTAL BIOFILM

DENTAL CARIES
- I. Cariogenic Microorganisms in Biofilm
- II. The pH of Biofilm
- III. Effect of Diet on Biofilm

MATERIA ALBA
- I. Clinical Appearance and Content
- II. Effects
- III. Prevention

FOOD DEBRIS

DOCUMENTATION

EVERYDAY ETHICS

FACTORS TO TEACH THE PATIENT

REFERENCES

LEARNING OBJECTIVES

After studying this chapter, the student will be able to:

1. Define acquired pellicle and discuss the significance and role of the pellicle in the maintenance of oral health.

2. Describe the different stages in biofilm formation and identify the changes in biofilm microorganisms as biofilm matures.

3. Differentiate between the types of soft deposits.

4. Recognize the factors that influence biofilm accumulation.

5. Explain the location, composition, and properties of dental biofilm.

6. Design biofilm control strategies individualized to meet each patient's needs.

During clinical examination of the teeth and surrounding soft tissues, soft and hard deposits are assessed. The presence of dental biofilm is a primary risk factor for gingivitis, inflammatory periodontal diseases, and dental caries.

▶ Assessment is an integral aspect of the dental hygiene diagnosis. On the basis of assessment findings, an individualized preventive care plan can be formulated to meet the needs of the patient.

▶ Key words are defined in Box 15-1.

▶ The soft deposits are acquired pellicle, dental biofilm, materia alba, and food debris.

▶ The hard, calcified deposits on the teeth are dental calculus, which is described in Chapter 21.

▶ A comparison of types of dental deposits, with descriptions, is found in Table 15-1.

ACQUIRED PELLICLE

▶ The acquired pellicle is a thin acellular tenacious film formed of proteins, carbohydrates, and lipids.[1]

▶ Pellicle is uniquely positioned as the interface between the tooth surfaces and the oral environment. It forms over exposed tooth surfaces and prostheses.

▶ Pellicle thickness varies from 100 to 1,000 nm, depending on its location in the mouth; it is thickest near the gingival margin and areas undisturbed by the activities of chewing, swallowing, and speaking.[2]

I. Formation of the Pellicle[1]

▶ Within minutes after eruption or after all soft and hard deposits have been removed from the tooth surfaces

BOX 15-1 KEY WORDS: Dental Biofilm

Acellular: not made up of or containing cells.

Adsorption: attachment of one substance to the surface of another; the action of a substance in attracting and holding other materials or particles on its surface.

Aerobe: heterotrophic microorganism that can live and grow in the presence of free oxygen; some are obligate, others facultative; *adj.* aerobic.

Anaerobe: heterotrophic microorganism that lives and grows in complete (or almost complete) absence of oxygen; some are obligate, others facultative; *adj.* anaerobic.

Biofilm: dynamic, complex, multispecies communities of microorganisms that colonize the oral cavity. Unique characteristics allow biofilms to adapt to a variety of every changing environments; characteristics include: tenacious adherence to surfaces, protective EPS, three-dimensional structures with complex nutrient and communication pathways.

Calculogenic: adjective applied to dental biofilm that is conducive to the formation of calculus.

Cariogenic: adjective to indicate a conduciveness to the initiation of dental caries, such as a cariogenic biofilm or a cariogenic food.

EPS: extracellular polymeric substance are compounds secreted by microorganisms and form a matrix for biofilm.

Facultative: able to live under more than one specific set of environmental conditions; contrast with obligate.

Flora: the collective organisms of a given locale.

   Oral flora: the various bacteria and other microorganisms that inhabit the oral cavity. The mouth has an indigenous flora, meaning those organisms that are native to that area of the body. Certain organisms specifically reside in certain parts, for example, on the tongue, on the mucosa, or in the gingival sulcus.

Food impaction: the forceful wedging of food into the periodontium by occlusal forces.

Heterotrophic: not self-sustaining; feeding on others.

Infection: invasion and multiplication of a microorganism in body tissues.

Iatrogenic dentistry: adverse condition resulting from treatment by a dentist, i.e., over hanging restorations or open margin of a restoration.

Leukocyte: white blood corpuscle capable of amoeboid movement; functions to protect the body against infection and disease.

Materia alba: white or cream-colored "cheesy" mass that can collect over dental biofilm on unclean, neglected teeth; it is composed of food debris, mucin, bacteria sloughed epithelial cells.

Maturation: stage or process of attaining maximal development; become mature.

Microbiota: the microscopic living organisms of a region.

Microorganism: minute living organisms, usually microscopic; includes bacteria, rickettsiae, viruses, fungi, and protozoa.

Mycoplasma: pleomorphic, gram-negative bacteria that lack cell walls; many are regular oral cavity residents; some are pathogenic.

Obligate: ability to survive only in a particular environment; opposite of facultative.

Parasite: plant or animal that lives upon or within another living organism and draws its nourishment therefrom; may be obligate or facultative; *adj.* parasitic.

Pathogen: disease-producing agent or microorganism; *adj.* pathogenic.

Planktonic: free floating single bacteria such as in saliva gingival crevicular fluid.

Pleomorphism: assumption of various distinct forms by a single organism or within a species; *adj.* pleomorphic.

Polymeric: repeating molecular structures; in biofilms the polymers are glycoprotein polysaccharides.

TABLE 15-1	Tooth Deposits		
TOOTH DEPOSIT	**DESCRIPTION**	**DERIVATION**	**REMOVAL METHOD**
Acquired enamel pellicle	Translucent, homogeneous, thin, unstructured film covering and adherent to the surfaces of the teeth, restorations, calculus, and other surfaces.	Supragingival: saliva, oral mucosa, microorganism Subgingival: gingival crevicular fluid	Toothbrush and appropriate interdental aid such as floss.
Microbial (bacterial) biofilm Nonmineralized	Dense, organized bacterial communities embedded in EPS matrix adheres tenaciously to the teeth, calculus, prostheses, and other surfaces in the oral cavity.	Colonization of oral microorganisms	Toothbrush and appropriate interdental aid such as floss.
Materia alba Nonmineralized	Loosely adherent, unstructured, white or grayish-white mass of oral debris and bacteria that lies over dental biofilm	Incidental accumulation	Vigorous rinsing and water irrigation can remove materia alba.
Food debris Nonmineralized	Unstructured, loosely attached particulate matter	Food retention following eating	Self-cleansing activity of tongue and saliva. Rinsing vigorously removes debris. Toothbrushing, flossing, and other aids.
Calculus Mineralized	Calcified dental biofilm; hard, tenacious mass that forms on the clinical crowns of the natural teeth and on dentures and other oral appliances.	Biofilm mineralization	
a. Supragingival	Occurs coronal to the margin of the gingiva; is covered with dental biofilm.	Source of minerals is saliva	Manual instrumentation. Ultrasonic instrumentation.
b. Subgingival	Occurs apical to the margin of the gingiva; is covered with dental biofilm.	Source of minerals is gingival crevicular fluid	Manual instrumentation. Ultrasonic instrumentation.

(such as by rubber cup or air polishing), the pellicle begins to form and is fully formed within 30–90 minutes.[1,2]

▶ Composition: primarily glycoproteins that are selectively adsorbed by the hydroxyapatite of the tooth surface.

  • Protein components are derived from the saliva, oral mucosal cells, gingival crevicular fluid, and microorganisms.[3]

▶ Initial attachment of bacteria to the pellicle is by selective adherence of microorganisms that originate from the oral mucosa.

  • Innate characteristics of the pellicle determine the adhesive interactions that cause planktonic bacteria to aggregate and form clusters to initiate biofilm formation.

  • Salivary proteins have a high affinity for the hydroxyapatite tooth surface and initiate the process of pellicle formation.[3]

▶ The adsorbed material becomes a highly insoluble coating over teeth, existing calculus deposits, restorations, and partial or complete dentures.

II. Types of Pellicle[4]

A. Supragingival Pellicle

▶ The supragingival pellicle is clear, translucent, insoluble, and not readily visible until a disclosing agent has been applied.

▶ Pellicle can take on extrinsic stain and become gradations of brown, gray, or other colors, as described in Chapter 22.

- When stained with a disclosing agent, pellicle appears thin, with a pale staining that contrasts with the thicker, darker staining of dental biofilm.

B. Subgingival Pellicle

▶ Subgingival pellicle is continuous with the supragingival pellicle and can become embedded in tooth structure, particularly where the tooth surface is partially demineralized or rough from iatrogenic dentistry.

III. Significance of Pellicle[1]

The pellicle plays an important role in the maintenance of oral health as it protects, lubricates, and acts as a nidus of attachment for the bacteria and subsequent calculus on the tooth surfaces.

▶ Protective
  - Pellicle appears to provide a barrier against acids; impacting remineralization and demineralization.
▶ Lubrication
  - Pellicle keeps surfaces moist and prevents drying, which in turn enhances the efficiency of speech and mastication.
▶ Nidus for bacteria
  - Pellicle participates in biofilm formation by aiding the adherence of microorganisms.
▶ Attachment of calculus
  - One mode of calculus attachment is to the pellicle (see Chapter 21).

IV. Removal of Pellicle

▶ Pellicle is not resilient enough to withstand rigorous patient oral self-care.[5]
▶ Extrinsic factors that may interfere with pellicle formation and maturation include:[6]
  - Abrasive toothpastes.
  - Whitening products.
  - Intake of acidic foods and beverages.

DENTAL BIOFILM

▶ Dental biofilm is a dynamic, structured community of microorganisms encapsulated in a self-produced extracellular polymeric substance (EPS) form a matrix around microcolonies.
▶ The matrix is composed of polysaccharides, proteins, and other compounds; it acts to protect the biofilm from the host's immune system and from antimicrobial and antibiotic agents.
▶ The microcolonies are separated by a network of open water channels that supply nutrients deep within the biofilm community.

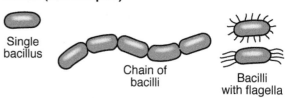

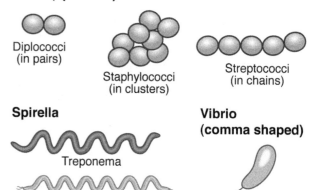

FIGURE 15-1 Bacteria Shapes: Cocci, Bacilli, Spiral. (Adapted from Sakai J. *Practical Pharmacology for the Pharmacy Technician*. Baltimore, MD: Lippincott Williams & Wilkins; 2008.)

▶ The three-dimensional structure of biofilms enhances their ability to communicate with each other, adapt, and respond to their environment.
▶ Dental biofilm adheres tenaciously to any inert or living moist surface; in the oral cavity, biofilms initially adhere to the pellicle on the teeth, existing calculus, fixed, and removable restorations.
▶ Biofilm communities also form on the oral mucosa, surfaces of the tongue, and tonsils; their presence especially on the tongue and tonsils may contribute to malodor.
▶ There are over 700 distinct bacterial species found in the oral cavity along with a variety of other microorganisms including viruses, protozoa, and yeast.[7] Morphologic forms of bacteria that are found within biofilms are shown in Figure 15-1.

I. Stages in the Formation of Biofilm[8]

▶ Biofilm formation does not occur randomly, but involves a series of complex interactions that are predictable and specific to oral biofilm development.
▶ Gene expression controls many of the growth and attachment capabilities and varies depending on species variety within a biofilm community.

A. Stage 1—Formation

▶ Biofilm formation begins with the initial attachment of planktonic bacterial cells to the pellicle on the tooth surface by the way of the bacteria's interactions with the pellicle (physicochemical).

▸ Initially the adherent cells are not yet "committed" to this process, and during this stage of adhesion, the process is reversible. When cells are disrupted (as would occur with oral hygiene activities), they can dislodge from the surface to resume planktonic life and either be eliminated or begin the formation process elsewhere in the oral cavity.

B. Stage 2—Bacterial Multiplication and Colonization

▸ If the planktonic microorganisms are not removed, they will attach themselves more permanently using cell adhesion structures such as fimbriae, pili, flagella, and adhesion proteins.

▸ Microcolonies multiply in layers growing upward and outward, creating the three-dimensional aspect of biofilm structures.

▸ With increased size, colonies produce extracellular polymeric substance (EPS) to firmly attach in an irreversible manner; rough surfaces will result in more rapid irreversible attachment.

▸ Organisms that colonize within the first few hours are primarily gram-positive cocci and rods.

C. Stage 3—Matrix Formation

▸ Bacteria within the aggregate of cells continue to secrete EPS as bacteria multiply to form a matrix.

▸ Components of the EPS are:
  • Polysaccharides, glucans, and fructans or levans produced by certain bacteria within the community and from dietary sucrose.
  • The polysaccharides are sticky and cement the biofilm more firmly to the teeth.

▸ The EPS matrix anchors the bacteria together which increases its adherence to the tooth and other structures; in this way, the bacterial community is protected and continues to grow.

▸ The adhesion and stickiness of the EPS matrix make biofilm disruption challenging; ineffective toothbrushing will not adequately disrupt biofilm for this reason.

▸ The biofilm structure enhances its ability to survive, thrive, and adapt to ever-changing environments within the oral cavity both supragingivally and subgingivally.

▸ The adaptive characteristics, structure, and EPS of the biofilm limit the ability of antibiotic therapy to reduce the virulence of pathogenic bacteria found deep within the biofilm communities.[8]

D. Stage 4—Biofilm Growth

▸ This stage is characterized by further development of the biofilm architecture that enhances a cell-to-cell communication process:

• The process is known as *quorum sensing*.
• Activated by specific genes located on the surface of the bacterial cells within the biofilm.

▸ The mass and thickness of biofilm increases as a result of bacterial multiplication; left undisturbed bacteria continuously adhere to the biofilm community and surrounding surface area.

E. Stage 5—Maturation

▸ Bacterial colonies mature and release planktonic cells to spread and colonize other areas within the oral cavity.

▸ Bacteria can disperse as single cells or in clumps.

II. Changes in Biofilm Microorganisms

▸ Dental biofilm consists of a complex mixture of microorganisms in microcolonies. The microbial density is very high, and it increases as biofilm ages and matures.

▸ The potential for the development of dental caries and/or gingivitis increases with more microorganisms especially as the numbers of pathogenic outnumber non-pathogenic microorganisms.

▸ The pellicle, EPS, biofilm architecture, and resulting environment promote anaerobic gram-negative bacterial growth activity.

▸ With undisrupted biofilm or if the numbers of bacteria increase rapidly, the chance of potential disease activity such as dental caries, gingivitis, and eventually other inflammatory periodontal diseases increases.

▸ The changes in oral flora follow a pattern such as that shown in Figure 15-2 and vary by days of accumulation as described below.[9]

A. Days 1–2

▸ Early biofilm consists primarily of gram-positive cocci.

▸ Streptococci, which dominate the bacterial population, include *Streptococcus mutans* and *Streptococcus sanguis*.

B. Days 2–4

▸ The cocci still dominate, and increasing numbers of gram-positive filamentous form and slender rods join the surface of the cocci colonies.

▸ Gradually, the filamentous forms grow into the cocci layer and replace many of the cocci.

▸ People who form biofilm slowly will exhibit more cocci and fewer filamentous forms.

C. Days 4–7

▸ Filaments increase in numbers, and a mixed flora appears comprised of rods, filamentous forms, and fusobacteria.

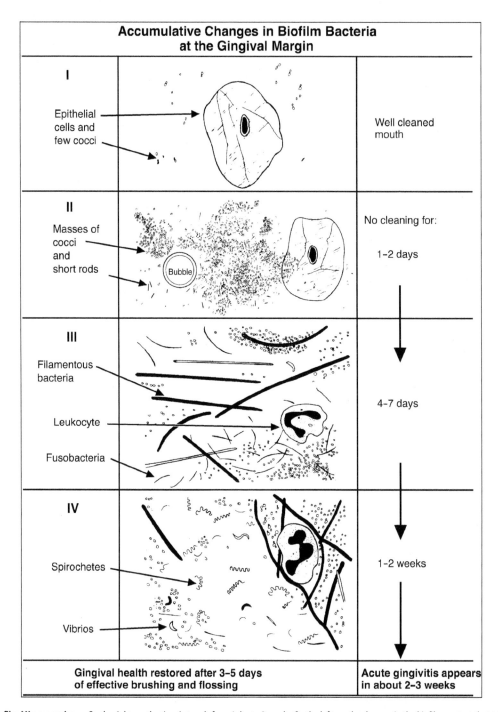

Accumulative Changes in Biofilm Bacteria at the Gingival Margin

I		Well cleaned mouth
Epithelial cells and few cocci		
II		No cleaning for: 1–2 days
Masses of cocci and short rods	Bubble	
III		4–7 days
Filamentous bacteria		
Leukocyte		
Fusobacteria		
IV		1–2 weeks
Spirochetes		
Vibrios		
Gingival health restored after 3–5 days of effective brushing and flossing		**Acute gingivitis appears in about 2–3 weeks**

FIGURE 15-2 **Biofilm Microorganisms.** On the right are the time intervals from 1 day to 3 weeks. On the left are the changes in the biofilm content that take place as biofilm ages. As the numbers of microorganisms increase, the numbers of defense cells (leukocytes) also increase. (From Crawford JJ. Microbiology. In: Barton RE, Matteson SR, Richardson RE (eds.). *The Dental Assistant*. 6th ed. Philadelphia, PA: Lea & Febiger; 1988.)

▶ Biofilm near the gingival margin thickens as a more mature flora develops. Gram-negative spirochetes and vibrios proliferate.

▶ As biofilm spreads coronally, newer/younger biofilm is primarily coccal.

D. Days 7–14

▶ Vibrios and spirochetes appear, and the number of white blood cells increases.

▶ During this period, inflammation develops and can be observed in the gingival tissues.

E. Days 14–21

▶ In older biofilm, vibrios and spirochetes are prevalent, with fewer cocci and filamentous forms.

▶ Densely packed filamentous microorganisms can arrange themselves perpendicular to the tooth surface in a palisade.

BOX 15-2

Steps in Experimental Gingivitis

1. Observe and record characteristics of the healthy gingiva at the outset. Record a gingival index, biofilm index, and bleeding index (see examples in Chapter 23).
2. Withhold all oral hygiene self-care measures (no attempt to control biofilm) for a period of 3 weeks.
3. Repeat clinical observations of tissues and record indices at least weekly during the test period. Note initial evidence of gingivitis.
4. Reinstate oral hygiene self-care measures after final recordings at 3 weeks. Make daily observations relative to gingival bleeding and indications that healing is taking place. In 1 week, repeat gingival and biofilm indices.

Source: Löe H, Theilade E, Jensen SB. Experimental gingivitis in man. *J Periodontol.* 1965;36:177–187.

▶ As biofilm matures and thickens, more gram-negative anaerobic organisms appear, which are protected by the biofilm architecture and environment.

▶ Gingivitis is evident clinically.

III. Experimental Gingivitis[9]

▶ Gingivitis develops in 2–3 weeks when biofilm is left undisturbed on the tooth surfaces.

▶ Most gingivitis is reversible, with mechanical biofilm disruption; healthy gingiva can return within a few days.

▶ An experimental gingivitis program to demonstrate the effect of biofilm can be conducted. The steps are outlined in Box 15-2.

SUPRAGINGIVAL AND SUBGINGIVAL DENTAL BIOFILM

I. Source

▶ Subgingival biofilm results from the apical proliferation and migration of supragingival biofilm.

▶ In the early stages of gingivitis and periodontitis, the supragingival biofilm is a strong influence on the accumulation and pathogenic features of the subgingival biofilm. Characteristics of supragingival and subgingival biofilms are listed in Table 15-2.

II. Microorganisms

▶ Recent technology innovations such as confocal scanning electron microscopy, epifluorescent microscopy, use of DNA probes, and gene amplification sequencing research studies have allowed for a more in-depth understanding of the science of biofilms.[10]

▶ The supragingival flora is predominantly gram-positive aerobic bacteria. Several species populate early "healthy" supragingival biofilm. Both Streptococcus and Actinomyces species are closely aligned with Lactobacillus and Candida species as this flora matures.

▶ Subgingival biofilm includes more predominantly gram-negative anaerobic and motile organisms of periodontal diseases. Actinomyces, *Tannerella forsythia*, *Fusobacterium nucleatum*, and a cluster of B-Cytophaga-Flavo bacterium-bacterodes have been identified.

▶ The study of biofilms has led to an identification of six groups of subgingival bacterial species in undisrupted aging biofilm.

- Early colonizers, depicted as yellow and blue in Figure 15-3, transition to predominantly gram-negative organisms, depicted by orange- and red-colored complexes.

- Older undisrupted biofilms consistently contain more of the orange and red species complexes (see Figure 15-3).[11,12]

III. Organization of Subgingival Biofilm

The biofilm architecture subgingivally arranges itself in layers:

▶ The initial layer is composed of Actinomyces that gives rise to an intermediate layer composed of spindle-shaped cells such as *F. nucleatum*, Tannerella, and *T. forsythia*. The top layer is composed of bacteroides clusters and spirochetes, which form a palisade-like lining.[10]

▶ Many gram-negative microorganisms and numerous white blood cells are loosely attached to the pocket epithelium.

▶ Virulent pathogenic organisms in this layer may be considered a focus for the advancement of periodontal infections.

▶ From this layer, microorganisms may invade the underlying connective tissue.

▶ Figure 15-4 shows bacteria within the connective tissue and on the bone surface.[13]

COMPOSITION OF DENTAL BIOFILM

▶ Microorganisms and EPS comprise 20% of the biofilm that are organic and inorganic solids. The other 80% is water.

▶ Composition differs among individuals and among tooth surfaces.

I. Inorganic Elements[14,15]

A. Calcium and Phosphorus

▶ Calcium, phosphorus, and magnesium are more concentrated in biofilm than in saliva.

▶ Saliva transports the minerals during the mineralization and demineralization processes.

TABLE 15-2	Characteristics of Supragingival and Subgingival Biofilm	
CHARACTERISTIC	**SUPRAGINGIVAL BIOFILM**	**SUBGINGIVAL BIOFILM**
Location	Coronal to the margin of the free gingiva	Apical to the margin of the free gingiva
Origin	Salivary glycoprotein forms acquired enamel pellicle Microorganisms from saliva are selectively attracted to pellicle	Downgrowth of bacteria from supragingival biofilm
Distribution	Starts on proximal surfaces and other protected areas Heaviest collection on areas not cleaned daily by patient Cervical third, especially facial Lingual mandibular molars Proximal surfaces Pit and fissure biofilm	Shallow pocket: similar to supragingival biofilm Undisturbed; held by pocket wall Attached biofilm covers calculus Unattached biofilm extends to the periodontal attachment
Adhesion	Firmly attached to acquired enamel pellicle, other bacteria, and tooth surfaces	Adheres to tooth surface, subgingival pellicle, and calculus
	Surface bacteria (unattached): loose; washed away by saliva or swallowed	Subgingival flora: loose, floating, motile organisms in deep pocket do not adhere; they are between adherent biofilm on tooth and the pocket epithelium
Retention	Rough surfaces of teeth, existing calculus, or restorations Malpositioned teeth Carious lesions	Pocket holds biofilm against tooth Overhanging margins of fillings that extend into pockets hold biofilm
Shape and size	Friction of tongue, cheeks, lips, limits shape and size Thickness: thicker at the cervical third and on proximal surfaces Healthy gingiva: thin biofilm, 15–20 cells thick Chronic gingivitis: thick biofilm, 100–300 cells thick	Molded by pocket wall to shape of the tooth surface Follows form created by subgingival calculus May become thicker as the diseased pocket wall becomes less tight
Structure	Adherent, densely packed microbial layer over acquired enamel pellicle on tooth surface Intermicrobial matrix Onset: small isolated colonies 2–5 d; colonies merge to form a covering of biofilm	Three layers (Figure 15-2) 1. Tooth-surface-attached biofilm: many gram-positive rods and cocci 2. Unattached biofilm in middle: many gram-negative, motile forms; spirochetes; leukocytes 3. Epithelium-attached biofilm: gram-negative, motile forms predominate; many leukocytes migrate through epithelium
Microorganisms	Early biofilm: primarily gram-positive cocci Older biofilm (3–4 d): increased numbers of filaments and fusiforms 4–9 d undisturbed: more complex flora with rods, filamentous forms 7–14 d: vibrios, spirochetes, more gram-negative organisms	Environment conducive to growth of anaerobic population Diseased pocket: primarily gram-negative, motile, spirochetes, rods
Sources of nutrients for bacterial proliferation	Saliva Ingested food Microorganisms metabolites	Tissue fluid (gingival crevicular fluid) Exudate Leukocytes
Significance	Etiology of Gingivitis Supragingival calculus Dental caries (Figure 15-6)	Etiology of Gingivitis Periodontal infections Subgingival calculus

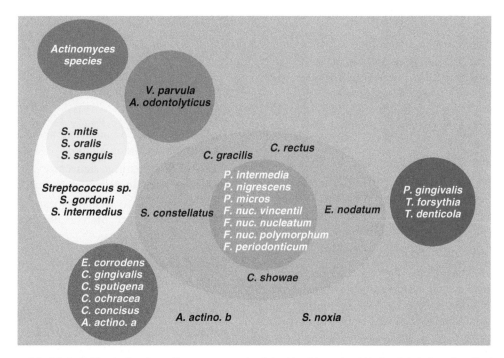

FIGURE 15-3 **Diagram of the Subgingival Species Complexes.** Diagram represents the relationships of the species within the subgingival complexes. The six groups differentiate the subgingival bacterial species in undisrupted aging biofilm. The yellow is early colonies and then progress to the orange then red colonies that are older undisrupted biofilm. (Source: Socransky SS, Haffajee AD, Cugini MA, et al. Microbial complexes in subgingival plaque. *J Clin Periodontol*. 1998;25(2):134–144, at 140.

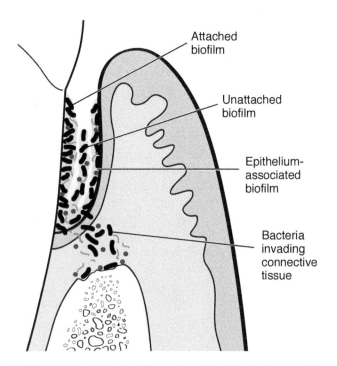

FIGURE 15-4 **Bacterial Invasion.** Diagram of a periodontal pocket shows attached and unattached biofilm bacteria within the pocket epithelium, in the connective tissue, and on the surface of the bone.

B. Fluoride

▶ The concentration of fluoride in biofilm is higher in the presence of fluoridated water and increases following professional topical applications of fluoride and the use of fluoride-containing dentifrices and mouthrinses.

II. Organic Elements

The organic EPS surrounds the microorganisms of biofilm and contains primarily carbohydrates and proteins, with small amounts of lipids.

A. Carbohydrates

▶ Carbohydrates include glucans such as dextran and fructans or levans formed by bacterial metabolism of dietary sucrose.

▶ Carbohydrates contribute to the adherence of microorganisms to each other and to the tooth, adding to biofilm's tenacious adherence to tooth surfaces.

B. Proteins

▶ The proteins of supragingival biofilm originate from the gingival sulcus fluid (crevicular fluid).

CLINICAL ASPECTS

I. Distribution of Biofilm

A. Location

▶ *Supragingival biofilm*: coronal to the gingival margin.
▶ *Gingival biofilm*: forms on the external surfaces of the oral epithelium and attached gingiva.
▶ *Subgingival biofilm*: located between the epithelial attachment and the gingival margin, within the sulcus or pocket.
▶ *Fissure biofilm*: develops in pits and fissures of the teeth.

B. By Surfaces

▶ *During formation*
  • Supragingival biofilm formation begins at the gingival margin, particularly on proximal surfaces, and extends coronally when left undisturbed.
  • It spreads over the gingival third and on toward the middle third of the crown.

▶ *Tooth surfaces involved*
  • Biofilm is the heaviest on proximal surfaces and around the gingival third, associated with protected areas.
  • Palatal surfaces of maxillary teeth may have the least biofilm due to the activity of the tongue during chewing, swallowing, and speaking.

C. Factors Influencing Biofilm Accumulation

▶ *Crowded teeth*: Dental biofilm accumulates readily around crowded mandibular anterior teeth as shown in Figure 15-5. With effective biofilm control, biofilm accumulation around crowded teeth is not greater than that around teeth in good alignment. Special accommodations such as using a toothbrush placed in a vertical position can remove thick biofilm on the lingual of the crowded mandibular anterior.

▶ *Rough surfaces*: Biofilm develops more rapidly on rough tooth surfaces, existing calculus, poorly contoured restorations, and removable appliances; thick dense deposits can be difficult to remove.

▶ *Occlusion*: Deposits may extend over an entire crown of a tooth that is unopposed, out of occlusion, or not actively used during mastication.

D. Removal of Biofilm

▶ Manual or power toothbrushing is the most universal daily mechanical disruption method.

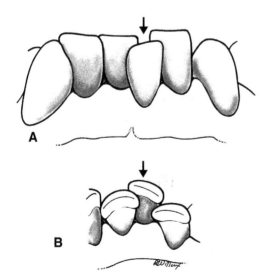

FIGURE 15-5 Biofilm Accumulation in Protected Areas. A: Crowded mandibular anterior teeth demonstrate dental biofilm after use of a disclosing agent. Thickest biofilm is on proximal surfaces and at cervical thirds of teeth; **B:** note central incisors with thick extensive biofilm on the less accessible protected surfaces.

▶ Daily flossing or other proximal surfaces biofilm disruption activities are necessary for the maintenance of optimal oral health.

II. Detection of Biofilm

A. Direct Vision

▶ *Thin biofilm:* May be translucent and therefore not visible without disclosing solution.

▶ *Stained biofilm:* Extrinsic stains may make biofilm more visible, for example, yellow, green, tobacco stains.

▶ *Thick biofilm:* The tooth may appear dull, dingy, with a matted furlike surface. Materia alba or food debris may collect over the biofilm.

B. Use of Explorer or Probe

▶ *Tactile examination:* When calcification has started, biofilm may feel slightly rough; otherwise, the surface may feel slippery from the coating of soft, slimy biofilm.

▶ *Removal of biofilm:* Biofilm may be detected by passing the side of the tip of a probe over the suspected tooth surface. When present, biofilm adheres to the probe tip.

C. Use of Disclosing Agent

▶ When a disclosing agent is applied, biofilm takes on the color and becomes readily visible (Figure 15-5).

▶ Disclosing agent is applied only after the evaluation of the oral mucosa and gingival color has been recorded so that tissue color is discernible.

D. Clinical Record

▶ A specifically designed form with several charts of the complete dentition labeled with space for dates and details can be used for recording to show initial biofilm accumulation, followed by continuing changes over the treatment and follow-up appointments.

▶ Record biofilm by location and thickness (slight, moderate, or heavy). For objective evaluations, an index or a biofilm score is recommended (see Chapter 23 for details on several methods).

▶ Biofilm scores are compared over time and used to develop the biofilm control plan at both current and maintenance appointments.

▶ Biofilm scores are a component of the permanent patient record.

SIGNIFICANCE OF DENTAL BIOFILM

▶ Microbial biofilm plays a major role in the initiation and progression of both dental caries and periodontal infections.

▶ Periodontal diseases and dental caries are infectious, transmissible diseases caused by pathogenic microorganisms found in oral biofilms.

▶ Biofilm is significant in the formation of dental calculus, which is essentially mineralized dental biofilm.

▶ Optimal oral hygiene depends on consistent daily dental biofilm disruption as complete removal of all biofilm is impossible.

▶ Accumulation of dental biofilm on the teeth, tongue, tonsils, and oral mucosa contributes to an unpleasant personal appearance as well as oral malodor.

DENTAL CARIES

▶ Dental caries is a disease of the dental calcified structures (enamel, dentin, and cementum) characterized by demineralization of the mineral components and dissolution of the organic matrix.

▶ Clinical characteristics and types of cavitated dental caries are described in Chapter 16.

▶ The process of dental caries is described in Chapter 27.

▶ The sequence of events leading to demineralization and dental caries is shown in Figure 15-6.

I. Cariogenic Microorganisms in Biofilm[16]

▶ Mutans streptococci (S. mutans and Streptococcus sobrinus, predominantly) and Lactobacilli acid-forming bacteria are the initial etiologic agents.

▶ Mutans streptococci initiate the caries process and Lactobacilli contributes to the progression of a carious lesion.

▶ Xerostomia (decreased salivary flow) and frequent fermentable carbohydrate exposure promote the growth of Streptococcus mutans and Lactobacilli, in dental biofilm.

▶ Biofilm architecture and EPS matrix of the biofilm community helps to maintain the caries causing acidic environment.[17]

II. The pH of Biofilm

▶ Acid formation begins *immediately* when the cariogenic substance is taken into the biofilm.

▶ The pH of the biofilm is lowered quickly, and 1–2 hours are required for the pH to return to a normal level, assuming the biofilm is left undisturbed.

▶ Biofilm pH before eating ranges from 6.2 to 7.0; it is lower in the caries-susceptible person and higher in the caries-resistant person.

▶ Immediately following sucrose intake into biofilm, a rapid drop in the pH of the biofilm occurs.[18]

▶ Critical pH for enamel demineralization averages 4.5–5.5. The critical pH for root surface demineralization is approximately 6.0–6.7, especially relevant for patients with multiple areas of recession and xerostomia.[19]

▶ The amount of demineralization depends on the length of time and frequency the pH is below critical level;

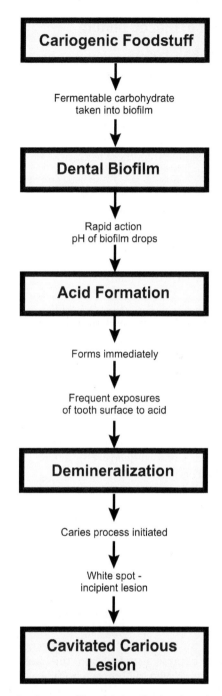

FIGURE 15-6 **Development of Dental Caries.** Flowchart shows the step-by-step action within the microbial biofilm on the tooth surface.

biofilm density and maturity are additional factors that affect the caries process.

▶ With each meal or snack that contains sucrose, the pH of the biofilm is lowered (Figure 35-8 in Chapter 35).

▶ Quantity of sucrose or carbohydrates eaten is less damaging than frequency, sucrose eaten with meals is less damaging than as snacks.[20]

▶ A discussion of dietary sucrose or carbohydrate consumption is part of a total dental caries assessment control program (see Chapter 35).

III. Effect of Diet on Biofilm

A. Cariogenic Foods

▶ Effect of Sucrose on pH of Biofilm

- With a highly cariogenic diet, biofilm forms and grows more profusely when oral hygiene is neglected or inadequately performed.[21]
- Patients fed sucrose by stomach tube have less acidogenic biofilm than those fed sucrose by mouth since oral microbes are avoided.[22]

MATERIA ALBA

▶ Materia alba is a loosely adherent mass of bacteria and cellular debris that frequently occurs over the surface of undisturbed dental biofilm.

I. Clinical Appearance and Content

▶ Materia alba ("white material") is distinguished as a bulky, soft deposit that is clinically visible without application of a disclosing agent. It is white, or grayish white, with a cottage cheeselike texture and appearance.

▶ Materia alba is an unorganized accumulation of living and dead bacteria, desquamated epithelial cells, disintegrating leukocytes, salivary proteins, and possibly a few particles of food debris. This differentiates it from organized oral biofilms

II. Effects

▶ Surface bacteria in contact with the gingiva contribute to gingival inflammation.

▶ Tooth surface demineralization and early noncavitated lesions can be seen under materia alba.

III. Prevention

▶ Materia alba can be removed with a water spray, oral irrigator, or tongue action, whereas only the surface organisms of biofilm can be removed.

▶ Clinical distinction of materia alba, food debris, and dental biofilm is necessary, but patient instruction for the removal of all three involves the same basic biofilm control procedures.

FOOD DEBRIS

▶ Loose food particles collect about the cervical third and proximal embrasures of the teeth.

▶ Cariogenic foods contribute to dental caries because liquefied carbohydrate diffuses rapidly into the biofilm and hence to the acid-forming bacteria.

▶ *Food impaction:* When there are open contact areas, mobility of teeth, or irregularities of occlusion such as plunger cusps, food may be forced between the teeth during mastication. This could result in vertical food impaction.

▶ Horizontal or lateral food impaction occurs in facial and lingual embrasures, particularly when the interdental papillae are reduced or missing.

▶ Food debris adds to a general unsanitary condition of the mouth. Some self-cleansing through the action of the tongue, lips, saliva, and related factors may take place.

EVERYDAY ETHICS

Daria was particularly excited to begin her patient schedule today because a student from the local community college was coming to observe her. Daria had graduated from the same dental hygiene program 6 years earlier and had volunteered to participate in the program for students to observe practitioners.

Roland, a second-year student, presented promptly at the receptionist's window 15 minutes prior to the first patient. Daria was already busily preparing her treatment room, and she quickly introduced herself to the student. She invited Roland to ask her any questions but not in front of a patient. She said she would introduce him to the patient at the beginning of each appointment, and would request verbal approval from the patient for his presence; he would scrub up and assist. Roland was impressed with Daria's professionalism.

After the first appointment was completed, Roland asked Daria why she was still using the term "plaque" during patient instruction instead of "biofilm" and why she didn't disclose the teeth before the providing education and selective polishing procedures. "Oh," Daria replied, "Is this something new you learned in school? I've only been to one continuing education course since I left school but I didn't hear anything about—what is it? Biofilm?"

Questions for Consideration

1. Role-play the dialogue that might take place regarding use of the term "plaque" versus "biofilm," which was a new concept for Daria.

2. Ethically, how is Daria violating/not violating any ethical principles relative to total patient care by not using disclosing agent to identify the biofilm? In what ways may terminology be important in practice?

3. Which of the dental hygiene core values (Table II-1, in Section II) are in action in this scenario? Describe how each one selected was in action.

► Debris removal by toothbrushing, and interproximal biofilm removal techniques constitutes a total biofilm control program. Cleansing of food debris from around fixed prostheses and orthodontic appliances is necessary to prevent disease.

DOCUMENTATION

The permanent records for each patient will include information for the soft deposits including:

► Clinical description of appearance of the teeth relative to the biofilm, materia alba, or food debris as indications of the personal oral care on a daily basis.

► Patient's understanding of biofilm and the significance of various deposits.

► Patient's description of the methods used daily: brush teeth, tongue, floss, rinse, and exactly what products are used at each mouthcare episode (such as in the morning after breakfast, chew xylitol gum after lunch, etc.).

A sample progress note for a patient's appointment may be reviewed in Box 15-3.

BOX 15-3

Example Documentation: Nonsurgical Periodontal Therapy Appointment for Patient with Inadequate Biofilm Removal

S –40-year-old female patient represents for third quadrant nonsurgical periodontal therapy (NSPT) with local anesthesia. Medical history includes an allergy to penicillin. There are no contradictions for treatment or anesthesia.

O –Update today indicates no changes to health history, allergies, or functions status. No changes in oral status indicated by assessment data. Only change is a biofilm score of greater than 60%, which has increased by 10% from last visit.

A –Discuss, review, and demonstrated proper oral self-care instructions and schedule final quadrant of NSPT with local anesthesia.

P –Medical history updated, intra- and extraoral examination performed, biofilm score using disclosing solution, assessed quadrants from last visit, and periodontal probed. Biofilm removal remains inadequate; discussed

and showed her disclosed dentition where most proximal surfaces showed red and bleeding on probing. Demonstrated how to work the power toothbrush in between; she said she doesn't use her power brush much. When asked why, she shrugged and said it was a nuisance to care for it; tried to make some suggestions, with emphasis that it would help her gingiva get healthy sooner; I asked if this week she would use it and include all four quadrants, especially the next one we will do next (max. left) so we can see the difference from my scaling. She said she would try.

Next step: Schedule last quadrant of NSPT with local anesthesia.

Signed: _____, RDH

Date:_____

Factors To Teach The Patient

▷ Location, composition, and properties of dental biofilm, with emphasis on its role in dental caries and periodontal infections.

▷ The cause and prevention of dental caries.

▷ Effects of personal oral care procedures in the prevention of dental biofilm.

▷ Biofilm control procedures with special adaptations for individual needs.

▷ Sources of cariogenic foodstuff in the diet, with suggestions for control.

▷ Relationship of frequency of eating cariogenic foods to dental caries.

References

1. Siqueira WL, Custodio W, McDonald EE. New insights into the composition and functions of the acquired enamel pellicle. *J Dent Res.* 2012;91(12):1110–1118.

2. Hanning M. Ultrastructural investigation of pellicle morphogenesis at two different intraoral sites during a 24-h period. *Clin Oral Investig.* 1999;3:88–95.

3. Hanning M, Joiner A. The structure, function and properties of the acquired pellicle. *Monogr Oral Sci.* 2006;19:26–64.

4. Meckel AH. Formation and properties of organic films on teeth. *Arch Oral Biol.* 1965;10(4):585–598.

5. Kuroiwa M, Kodaka T, Kuroiwa M, et al. Acid resistance of human enamel by brushing with and without abrasive dentifrice. *J Biol Buccale.* 1992;20:175–180.

6. Hara AT, Zero DT. The caries environment: saliva, pellicle, diet, and hard tissue ultrastructure. *Dent Clin North Am.* 2010;54(3):455–467.

7. Aas JA, Paster BJ, Stokes LN, et al. Defining the normal bacterial flora of the oral cavity. *J Clin Microbiol.* 2005;43(11):5721–5732.

8. Stoodley P, Sauer K, Davies DG, et al. Biofilms as complex differentiated communities. *Annu Rev Microbiol.* 2002;56:187–209.

9. Löe H, Theilade E, Jensen SB. Experimental gingivitis in man. *J Periodontol.* 1965;36:177–187.

10. Zijnge V, van Leeuwen M, Degener J, et al. Oral biofilm architecture on natural teeth. *PLoS One.* 2010;5(2):e9321. http://www.plosone.org/article/info:doi/10.1371/journal.pone.0009321.

11. Socransky SS, Haffajee AD, Cugini MA, et al. Microbial complexes in subgingival plaque. *J Clin Periodontol.* 1998;25(2):134–144.

12. Socransky S, Haffajee A. Dental biofilms: difficult therapeutic target. *Periodontol 2000.* 2002;28:12–55.

13. Mandel ID. Relation of saliva and plaque to caries. *J Dent Res.* 1974;53(2):246–266.

14. Grøn P, Yao K, Spinelli M. A study of inorganic constituents in dental plaque. *J Dent Res.* 1969;48(5):799–805.

15. Van Houte J, Sansone C, Joshipura K, et al. Mutans streptococci and non-mutans streptococci acidogenic at low pH, and *in vitro* acidogenic potential of dental plaque in two different areas of the human dentition. *J Dent Res.* 1991;70(12):1503–1507.

16. Rosen S, Weisenstein PR. The effect of sugar solutions on pH of dental plaques from caries-susceptible and caries-free individuals. *J Dent Res.* 1965;44(5):845–849.

17. Koo H, Falsetta ML, Klein MI. The exopolysaccharide matrix: a virulence determinant of cariogenic biofilm. *J Dent Res.* 2013;92(12):1065–1073.

18. Hoppenbrouwers PM, Driessens FC, Borggreven JM. The mineral solubility of human tooth roots. *Arch Oral Biol.* 1987;32(5):319–322.

19. Gustafsson BE, Quensel CE, Lanke LS, et al. The Vipeholm dental caries study: the effect of different levels of carbohydrate intake on caries activity in 436 individuals observed for five years. *Acta Odontol Scand.* 1954;11(3–4):232–264.

20. Carlsson J, Egelberg J. Effect of diet on early plaque formation in man. *Odontol Revy.* 1965;16(1):112–125.

21. Littleton NW, Carter CH, Kelley RT. Studies of oral health in persons nourished by stomach tube. I. Changes in the pH of plaque material after the addition of sucrose. *J Am Dent Assoc.* 1967;74(1):119–123.

22. Egelberg J. Local effect of diet on plaque formation and development of gingivitis in dogs. III. Effect of frequency of meals and tube feeding. *Odontol Revy.* 1965;16(1):50–60.

 ENHANCE YOUR UNDERSTANDING

thePoint **DIGITAL CONNECTIONS**
(see the inside front cover for access information)

- **Audio glossary**
- **Quiz bank**

 SUPPORT FOR LEARNING
(available separately; visit lww.com)

- ***Active Learning Workbook for Clinical Practice of the Dental Hygienist, 12th Edition***

prepU **INDIVIDUALIZED REVIEW**
(available separately; visit lww.com)

- **Adaptive quizzing with *prepU for Wilkins' Clinical Practice of the Dental Hygienist***

Dental Stains and Discolorations

Elizabeth G. Onik, RDH, MEd

CHAPTER OUTLINE

LEARNING OBJECTIVES

After studying this chapter, the student will be able to:

1. Recognize and identify extrinsic and intrinsic dental stains and discolorations.

2. Differentiate between exogenous and endogenous stains.

3. Educate patients regarding the etiology and/or prevention of dental stains.

4. Determine appropriate clinical approaches for stain removal and/or tooth whitening.

Discolorations of the teeth and restorations occur in three general ways[1]:

▸ Adheres directly to the surfaces

▸ Contained within calculus and soft deposits

▸ Incorporated within the tooth structure or the restorative material.

Instructional and clinical procedures apply to all three. The first two types may be removed by scaling or polishing. Certain stains may be prevented by the patient's routine personal care and dietary habits.

SIGNIFICANCE

▸ The significance of stains is primarily the appearance or cosmetic effect.

▸ In general, any detrimental effect on the teeth or gingival tissues is related to the dental biofilm or calculus in which the stain occurs.

▸ Thick deposits of stain conceivably can provide a rough surface on which dental biofilm can collect and irritate the adjacent gingiva.

▸ Certain stains provide a means of evaluating oral cleanliness and the patient's habits of personal care.

▸ Key words that relate to dental stains and discolorations are defined in Box 22-1.

I. Classification of Stains

A. Classified by Location

▸ *Extrinsic*: Extrinsic stains occur on the external surface of the tooth and may be removed by procedures of toothbrushing, scaling, and/or polishing.

▸ *Intrinsic*: Intrinsic stains occur within the tooth surface and cannot be removed by scaling or polishing. Intrinsic stains may be improved by certain whitening procedures.

B. Classified by Source

▸ *Exogenous*: Exogenous stains develop or originate from sources outside the tooth. Exogenous stains may be extrinsic and stay on the outer surface of the tooth or intrinsic and become incorporated within the tooth structure.

▸ *Endogenous*: Endogenous stains develop or originate from within the tooth. Endogenous stains are always intrinsic and usually are discolorations of the dentin reflected through the enamel.

II. Recognition and Identification

More than one type of stain may occur and more than one etiologic factor may cause the stains and discolorations of an individual's dentition. A differential diagnosis may be needed in order to plan whether an appropriate intervention is indicated.

A. Medical and Dental History

▸ Developmental complications, medications, use of tobacco, and fluoride histories all contribute necessary information.

▸ Accurately prepared medical, dental and social histories, and ethnic practices can provide information to supplement clinical observations.

B. Food Diary

▸ Assessment of a patient's food diary may aid in identifying certain contributing factors.
  • Examples of staining from beverages include tea and coffee.

C. Oral Hygiene Habits

▸ The history of personal biofilm removal with the type and frequency of use of toothbrush, floss, and other supplemental materials and devices may help explain the presence of certain stains.

▸ The state of oral hygiene and oral cleanliness is significant to the occurrence of dental stains.

III. Application of Procedures for Stain Removal

A. Stains Occurring Directly on the Tooth Surface

▸ Stains directly associated with the biofilm or pellicle on the surface of the enamel or exposed cementum are

BOX 22-1 KEY WORDS: Dental Stains and Discolorations

Amelogenesis imperfecta: imperfect formation of enamel; hereditary condition in which the ameloblasts fail to lay down the enamel matrix properly or at all.

Chlorophyll: green plant pigment essential to photosynthesis.

Chromogenic: producing color or pigment.

Chronologic: arranged in order of time.

Dentinogenesis imperfecta: hereditary disorder of dentin formation in which the odontoblasts lay down an abnormal matrix; can occur in both primary and permanent dentitions.

Endogenous: produced within or caused by factors within.

Exogenous: originating outside or caused by factors outside.

Extrinsic: derived from or situated on the outside; external.

Hypoplasia: incomplete development or underdevelopment of an organ or a tissue.

Intrinsic: situated entirely within.

removed as much as possible during toothbrushing by the patient.

▶ Certain stains can be removed by scaling, whereas others require scaling and/or polishing (see Chapter 45).

▶ When stains are tenacious, excessive polishing is avoided. As mild an abrasive agent as possible is used. Precautions are taken to prevent the following:
- Abrasion of the tooth surface or gingival margin
- Removal of a layer of fluoride-rich tooth surface
- Overheating with a power-driven polisher.

B. Stains Incorporated Within Tooth Deposits

▶ When stain is included within the substance of a soft deposit or calculus, it is removed with the deposit.

C. Stains Incorporated Within the Tooth

▶ When stain is intrinsic, whether exogenous or endogenous, it cannot be removed by scaling or polishing. Evaluation for possible whitening procedures may be considered. (See Chapter 46.)

EXTRINSIC STAINS

The most frequently observed stains, yellow, green, black line, and tobacco, are described first; descriptions of the less common orange, red, and metallic stains follow.

I. Yellow Stain

A. Clinical Features

▶ Dull, yellowish discoloration of dental biofilm is illustrated in Figure 22-1.

B. Distribution on Tooth Surfaces

▶ Yellow stain can be generalized or localized.

C. Occurrence

▶ Common to all ages.

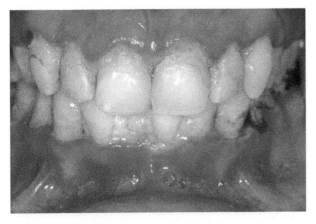

FIGURE 22-1. Yellow Stain. Generalized, dull, yellowish discoloration of dental biofilm. (Photograph used by permission of Dr. Ali Seyedain, University of Pittsburgh.)

▶ More evident when personal oral care procedures are neglected.

D. Etiology

▶ Usually dietary sources.

II. Green Stain

A. Clinical Features

▶ Light or yellowish green to very dark green.

▶ Embedded in dental biofilm.

▶ Occurs in three general forms:
- Small curved line following contour of facial gingival margin.
- Smeared irregularly, may even cover entire facial surface.
- Streaked, following grooves or lines in enamel.

▶ The stain is frequently superimposed by soft yellow or gray debris (materia alba and food debris).

▶ Dark green may become embedded in surface enamel and be observed as an exogenous intrinsic stain when superficial layers of deposit are removed.

▶ Enamel under stain is sometimes demineralized as a result of cariogenic biofilm. The rough demineralized surface encourages biofilm retention, demineralization, and recurrence of green stain.

B. Distribution on Tooth Surfaces

▶ Primarily facial; often extends to proximal.

▶ Most frequently facial gingival third of maxillary anterior teeth.

C. Composition

▶ Chromogenic bacteria and fungi.

▶ Decomposed hemoglobin.

▶ Inorganic elements include calcium, potassium, sodium, silicon, magnesium, phosphorus, and other elements in small amounts.[2]

D. Occurrence

▶ May occur at any age; primarily found in childhood.

▶ Collects on both permanent and primary teeth.

E. Recurrence

▶ Recurrence depends on fastidiousness of personal care procedures.

F. Etiology

▶ Green stain results from poor oral hygiene, dental biofilm retention, chromogenic bacteria, and gingival hemorrhage.

▶ Chromogenic bacteria or fungi are retained and nourished in dental biofilm where the green stain is produced.

▶ Blood pigments from hemoglobin are decomposed by bacteria.

G. Clinical Approach

▶ Do not scale the area. Often, an area of demineralized tooth structure underlies the stain and soft deposits.

▶ Ask the patient to remove the soft deposits with a toothbrush during a dental biofilm control lesson. Initiate a daily fluoride remineralization program.

H. Other Green Stains

▶ In addition to the clinical entity known as "green stain" that was just described, dental biofilm and acquired pellicle may become stained a green color by a variety of substances.

▶ Differential distinction may be determined by questioning the patient or from items in the medical or dental histories. Green discoloration may result from the following:
  • Chlorophyll preparations
  • Metallic dusts of industry
  • Certain drugs. The stain from smoking marijuana may appear grayish-green.

III. Black-Line Stain

▶ Black-line stain is a highly retentive black or dark brown calculus-like stain that forms along the gingival third near the gingival margin. It may occur on primary or permanent teeth.

A. Other Names

▶ Pigmented dental biofilm, brown stain, black stain.

B. Clinical Features

▶ Continuous or interrupted fine line, 1 mm wide (average), no appreciable thickness.

▶ May be a wider band or even occupy entire gingival third in severe cases (rare).

▶ Follows contour of gingival margin about 1 mm from margin.

▶ Usually separated from gingival margin by clear white line of unstained enamel.

▶ Appears black at bases of pits and fissures.

▶ Heavy deposits slightly elevated from the tooth surface may be detected by the gentle application of an explorer. Black-line stain has been compared to a calculus deposit.

▶ Gingiva is firm, with little or no tendency to bleed.

▶ Teeth are frequently clean and shiny, with a tendency to lower incidence of dental caries.[3]

C. Distribution on Tooth Surfaces

▶ Facial and lingual surfaces; follows contour of gingival margin onto proximal surfaces.

▶ Rarely on facial surface of maxillary anterior teeth.

▶ Most frequently: lingual and proximal surfaces of maxillary posterior teeth.

D. Composition and Formation[4,5]

▶ Black-line stain, like calculus, is composed of microorganisms embedded in an intermicrobial substance.

▶ The microorganisms are primarily gram-positive rods, with smaller percentages of cocci.

▶ The composition of black-line stain is different from the composition of supragingival calculus, in which cocci predominate.

▶ Attachment of black-line stain to the tooth is by a pellicle-like structure.

▶ Mineralization in black-line stain is similar to the formation of calculus.

E. Occurrence

▶ All ages; more common in childhood.

▶ More common in female patients.

▶ Frequently found in clean mouths.

F. Recurrence

▶ Black-line stain tends to form again despite regular personal care.

▶ Quantity may be less when biofilm control procedures are meticulous.

G. Predisposing Factors

▶ No definitive etiology.[3]

IV. Tobacco Stain[1]

A. Clinical Features

▶ Light brown to dark leathery brown or black (see Figure 22-2).

▶ Shape
  • Diffuse staining of dental biofilm.

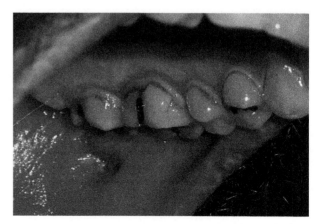

FIGURE 22-2. Tobacco Stain. Dark brown band following contour of gingival crest. (Photograph used by permission of Dr. Julius Manz, San Juan College, NM.)

- Narrow band that follows contour of gingival crest, slightly above the crest.
- Wide, firm, tar-like band may cover cervical third and extend to central third of crown.
▶ Incorporated in calculus deposit.
▶ Heavy deposits (particularly from smokeless tobacco) may penetrate the enamel and become exogenous intrinsic.

B. Distribution on Tooth Surface
▶ Cervical third, primarily. Lingual surfaces, most frequently.
▶ Any surface, including pits and fissures.

C. Composition
▶ Tar and products of combustion.
▶ Brown pigment from smokeless tobacco.

D. Predisposing Factors
▶ Smoking or chewing tobacco, or use of hookah to inhale tobacco. The quantity of stain is not necessarily proportional to the amount of tobacco used.
▶ Personal oral care procedures: increased deposits occur with neglect.
▶ Extent of dental biofilm and calculus available for adherence.

V. Brown Stains

A. Brown Pellicle
▶ The acquired pellicle is smooth and structureless and recurs readily after removal (Figure 22-3).[6]
▶ The pellicle can take on stains of various colors that result from chemical alteration of the pellicle.[7]

B. Stannous Fluoride[8,9]
▶ Light brown, sometimes yellowish, stain forms on the teeth in the pellicle after repeated use of some stannous fluoride products.

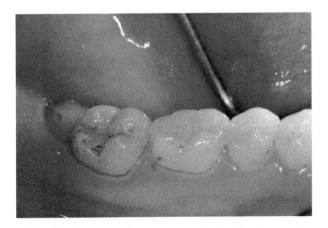

FIGURE 22-3. Brown Stain. Most likely cause by pigmented foods or drinks. (Photograph used by permission of Dr. Ali Seyedain, University of Pittsburgh.)

▶ The brown stain results from the formation of stannous sulfide or brown tin oxide from the reaction of the tin ion in the fluoride compound.

C. Pigmented Foods
▶ Tea, coffee, soy sauce, and other foods are often implicated in the formation of a brownish-stained pellicle.
▶ As with other brown pellicle stains, less stain occurs when the personal oral hygiene and biofilm control are excellent.

D. Anti-Biofilm Agents[10,11]
▶ Chlorhexidine and alexidine are used in mouthrinses and are effective against biofilm formation.
▶ A brownish stain on the tooth surfaces may result, usually more pronounced on proximal and other surfaces less accessible to routine biofilm control procedures.
▶ The stain also tends to form more rapidly on exposed roots than on enamel. Tooth staining has been considered a significant side effect.
▶ Clinical implications: Avoid use of these antimicrobials if enamel defects, porous restorations, or open margins are present. Stain may not be removable from these surfaces.

E. Betel Leaf[12]
▶ Betel leaf chewing is common among people of all ages in eastern countries. Betel has a caries-inhibiting effect.
▶ The discoloration imparted to the teeth is a dark mahogany brown, sometimes almost black. It may become thick and hard, with partly smooth and partly rough surfaces.
▶ Microscopically, the black deposit consists of microorganisms and mineralized material with a laminated pattern characteristic of subgingival calculus. It can be removed by gentle scaling.

F. Swimmer's Stain[13]
▶ Frequent exposure to pools disinfected with chlorine or bromine can cause yellowish or dark brown stains on the facial surfaces of maxillary and mandibular incisor teeth.

VI. Orange and Red Stains

A. Clinical Appearance
▶ Orange or red stains appear at the cervical third.

B. Distribution on Tooth Surfaces
▶ More frequently on anterior than on posterior teeth.

C. Occurrence
▶ Rare (red more rare than orange).

D. Etiology

▶ Chromogenic bacteria.

VII. Metallic Stains[1]

A. Metals or Metallic Salts from Metal-Containing Dust of Industry

▶ Clinical appearance/examples of colors on teeth:
  - Copper or brass: green or bluish-green.
  - Iron: brown to greenish-brown.
  - Nickel: green.
  - Cadmium: yellow or golden brown.
▶ Distribution on tooth surfaces
  - Primarily anterior; may occur on any teeth.
  - Cervical third more commonly affected.
▶ Manner of formation
  - Industrial worker inhales dust through mouth, bringing metallic substance in contact with teeth.
  - Metal imparts color to biofilm.
  - Occasionally, stain may penetrate tooth substance and become exogenous intrinsic stain.
▶ Prevention
  - Workers need to be advised to wear a mask while working.

B. Metallic Substances Contained in Drugs

▶ Clinical appearance/examples of colors on teeth:
  - Iron: black (iron sulfide) or brown.
  - Manganese (from potassium permanganate): black.
▶ Distribution on tooth surfaces
  - Generalized, may occur on all.
▶ Manner of formation
  - Drug enters biofilm substance, imparts color to biofilm and calculus.
  - Pigment from drug may attach directly to tooth enamel.
▶ Prevention
  - Use a medication through a straw or in tablet or capsule form to prevent direct contact with the teeth.

ENDOGENOUS INTRINSIC STAINS

I. Pulpless or Traumatized Teeth

Not all pulpless teeth discolor. Improved endodontic procedures have contributed to the prevention of discolorations. However, traumatized teeth that have not been treated endodontically often discolor.

A. Clinical Appearance

▶ A wide range of colors exists; stains may be light yellow-brown, slate gray, reddish-brown, dark brown, bluish-black, or black. Others have an orange or greenish tinge.

B. Etiology

▶ Blood and other pulp tissue elements may be available for breakdown as a result of hemorrhages in the pulp chamber, root canal treatment, or necrosis and decomposition of the pulp tissue.
▶ Pigments from the decomposed hemoglobin and pulp tissue penetrate and discolor the dentinal tubules.

II. Disturbances in Tooth Development[14]

Stains incorporated within the tooth structure may be related to the period of tooth development. Defective tooth development may result from factors of genetic abnormality or environmental influences during tooth development.

A. Hereditary: Genetic

▶ *Amelogenesis imperfecta*: The enamel is partially or completely missing because of a generalized disturbance of the ameloblasts. Teeth are yellowish-brown or gray-brown.
▶ *Dentinogenesis imperfecta* (*"Opalescent dentin"*): The dentin is abnormal as a result of disturbances in the odontoblastic layer during development. The teeth appear translucent or opalescent and vary in color from gray to bluish-brown.

B. Enamel Hypoplasia

▶ *Generalized hypoplasia* (chronologic hypoplasia resulting from ameloblastic disturbance of short duration): Teeth erupt with white spots or with pits. Over a long period, the white spots may become discolored from food pigments or other substances taken into the mouth.
▶ *Local hypoplasia* (affects single tooth): For example, individual white spots caused by trauma to a primary tooth interferes with development of permanent tooth resulting in "Turner's tooth." White spots may become stained as in generalized hypoplasia.

C. Dental Fluorosis

▶ Dental fluorosis was originally called "brown stain." Later, Dr. Frederick S. McKay, who studied the condition and described it in the dental literature, named it "mottled enamel."
▶ Etiology
  - Enamel hypomineralization results from ingestion of excessive fluoride ion from any source during the period of mineralization. The enamel alterations are a result of toxic damage to the ameloblasts.
  - When the teeth erupt, they have white spots or areas that may later become discolored from oral pigments and appear light to dark brown in color.
  - Severe effects of excess fluoride during development may produce cracks or pitting; the discoloration

concentrates in these. This condition and appearance led to the name mottled enamel.

▶ Classification

• Dean provided the original definitions for five grades of fluorosis (Table 23-2 in Chapter 23). They ranged from "questionable" (a few white flecks or spots) to "severe" (marked brown staining and pitting of the enamel surfaces).[15]

• More specific classifications have been developed for clinical and research purposes, such as the tooth surface index of fluorosis[16,17] (Table 23-3 in Chapter 23).

III. Drug-Induced Stains and Discolorations[18]

A. Tetracylines

▶ Tetracycline antibiotics, used widely for combating many types of infections, have an affinity for mineralized tissues (Figure 46-3 in Chapter 46).

• Are absorbed by the bones and teeth.

• Can be transferred through the placenta and enter fetal circulation.

▶ Discoloration of the teeth of a child can result when the drug is administered to the mother during the third trimester of pregnancy or to the child in infancy and early childhood.

▶ Color of teeth may be light green to dark yellow, or a gray-brown, with or without banding.

▶ The discoloration depends on the dosage, the length of time the drug was used, and the type of tetracycline. After eruption, the teeth may fluoresce under ultraviolet light, but that property is lost with age and exposure.

▶ Discoloration may be generalized or limited to specific parts of individual teeth that were developing at the time of administration of the antibiotic.

▶ Refer to the timing of tooth development for primary teeth (Table 50-4 in Chapter 50) and permanent teeth (Table 16-1 in Chapter 16) to assess the impact of drug administration on tooth discoloration.

▶ The patient's medical history at that age may reveal the illness for which the antibiotic was prescribed.

B. Cipro and Minocycline

▶ Use of these antibiotics can result in a greenish discoloration of teeth.[18]

IV. Other Systemic Causes

▶ Several types of tooth discolorations may result from blood-borne pigments.

▶ Pigments circulating in the blood are transmitted to the dentin from the capillaries of the pulp. For example, prolonged jaundice early in life can impart a yellow or greenish discoloration to the teeth.

▶ Erythroblastosis fetalis (Rh incompatibility) may leave a green, brown, or blue hue to the teeth.

EXOGENOUS INTRINSIC STAINS

▶ When intrinsic stains come from an outside source, not from within the tooth, the stain is called exogenous intrinsic.

▶ Extrinsic stains, such as tobacco, tea, coffee, wine, and green stains, can become intrinsic (see Figure 22-4).

▶ Restorative materials cause staining of teeth, as described in the following section.

▶ Tooth-color restorations may become stained from extrinsic staining sources.

I. Restorative Materials

A. Silver Amalgam

▶ Silver amalgam can impart a gray to black discoloration to the tooth structure around a restoration.

▶ Metallic ions migrate from the amalgam restoration into the enamel and dentin.

▶ Silver, tin, and mercury ions eventually contact debris at the junction of the tooth and the restoration and form sulfides, which are products of corrosion.

B. Copper Amalgam

▶ Copper amalgam used for filling primary teeth may impart a bluish-green color.

II. Endodontic Therapy

Materials used during endodontic therapy can cause intrinsic staining.

▶ Silver nitrate: bluish-black.

▶ Volatile oils: yellowish-brown.

▶ Strong iodine: brown.

▶ Aureomycin: yellow.

▶ Silver-containing root canal sealer: black.

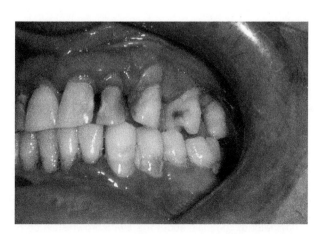

FIGURE 22-4. Intrinsic Stain. Most likely exogenous; likely from an outside source such as tobacco or food and became intrinsic over time. Areas of cervical erosion and recession allow yellow color of underlying dentin to be exposed and become further stained. (Photograph used by permission of Dr. Julius Manz, San Juan College, NM.)

III. Stain in Dentin

▶ Discoloration resulting from a carious lesion is an example.

▶ Arrested decay or secondary dentin can present as black stain on severely decayed teeth. The surface is hard and glossy, and stain cannot be removed.

IV. Other Local Causes

▶ Low pH. The degree and type of tooth discoloration are influenced by both the low pH and the food color rather than dietary pigment alone.[19]

▶ Enamel erosion is the loss of hard tissue by chemical means such as acidic foods (including carbonated drinks), eating disorders (bulimia), and acid reflux disease.

• Resulting thinner enamel allows the yellow color of the underlying dentin to show through and cause the teeth to appear duller grey or yellow (Figure 22-4).

• Age-related erosion is not supported by the literature; erosion a pathologic process.[20]

• Whitening products are ineffective and contraindicated for erosion.

▶ Attrition of occlusal surfaces can result in loss of enamel, allowing a yellow outline of dentin to show through.

DOCUMENTATION

The permanent record of a patient with staining on the teeth contains explanations in the record about the type of stains, location, and other information of a descriptive nature.

▶ Record color, type, extent, and location of stains with the patient's examination and assessment.

▶ Make additions to the dental history as information is gained concerning the origin of stains such as those

related to tooth development, systemic disease, occupations, or medications.

▶ A sample documentation of stain may be found in Box 22-2.

BOX 22-2
Example Documentation: Patient with Dental Stain

S –A 54-year-old female presents for lower left quadrant scaling/planing as indicated in her DH Care Plan. She states that she had difficulty with new brushing technique demonstrated at her last visit. She continues to smoke 1 pack of cigarettes/day.

O –No changes in medical history. BP 131/85; patient took Atenalol today. Generalized heavy extrinsic tobacco stain especially on mandibular anterior lingual surfaces. Plaque-free index is 60%, an improvement of 10%, but still poor.

A –Oral hygiene is poor. Likelihood of continued stain buildup and risk for periodontal complications is increased because of high tobacco use.

P –Scaled and root planed lower left quadrant and removed extrinsic tobacco stain using beaver tail insert of cavitron. Spent 15 minutes reviewing tobacco stain control methods. Reviewed use of power brush and introduced a Tobacco Cessation Plan. She did not act interested. Congratulated patient for returning for this appointment, despite her nervousness.

Next Steps: Review patient's reaction to stain removal today; review recommendations for stain control. Review tobacco cessation steps.

Signed _____, RDH
Date _____

EVERYDAY ETHICS

Daniel returned to the dental office of Dr. Windum after 3 years of working on the East Coast. At the age of 32, Daniel was exhibiting signs of early periodontitis with gingival inflammation and increased subgingival calculus. Ruthie, the dental hygienist, immediately began talking to Daniel about biofilm and suggesting improvements for his personal daily brushing and flossing to change his personal care of his gingival tissues. After she completed a quadrant of scaling with local anesthesia, she suggested that rinsing with chlorhexidine after brushing before going to bed would help the healing.

Dr. Windum confirmed Ruthie's recommendation and wrote the prescription. Daniel left the office only to call a few days later to complain about the "awful brown stain on his teeth and horrible taste of the mouthrinse." He further indicated that he had stopped using the product and wanted to come in and have the stain removed immediately.

Questions for Consideration

1. Which of the dental hygiene core values (in Section II, Introduction, Table II-1) have application in this scenario? How does each core value selected enter the picture?

2. Daniel seems more concerned about the tooth staining and flavor of the chlorhexidine rinse than about the health of his gingival tissues while Ruthie's concerns are for improving his gingival health. What ethical principles may be in effect here?

3. Using the questions in Table VI-1 (in Section VI, Introduction), help Ruthie work out a favorable response explaining her choice of therapy for her patient's poor gingival health.

Factors To Teach The Patient

▷ Etiology of individual's dental stains and discolorations.

▷ Personal care procedures that can aid in the prevention or reduction of stains.

▷ Advantages of starting a smoking cessation program.

▷ Reasons for not using an abrasive dentifrice with vigorous brushing strokes to lessen or remove stain accumulation.

▷ The need to avoid tobacco, coffee, tea, and other beverages or foods that can stain tooth structures or new restorations.

▷ Reasons for the difficulty of removing certain extrinsic stains during scaling and polishing.

▷ Effect of tetracyclines on developing teeth. Need to avoid use during pregnancy and by children to age 12.

References

1. Watts A, Addy M. Tooth discoloration and staining: a review of the literature. *Br Dent J.* 2001;190:309–316.

2. Shay DE, Haddox JH, Richmond JL. An inorganic qualitative and quantitative analysis of green stain. *J Am Dent Assoc.* 1955;50(2):156–160.

3. Żyła T, Kawala B, Antoszewska-Smith J, et al. Black stain and dental caries: a review of the literature. *Biomed Res Int.* 2015;2015:469392.

4. Theilade J, Slots J, Fejerskov O. The ultrastructure of black stain on human primary teeth. *Scand J Dent Res.* 1973;81(7):528–532.

5. Slots J. The microflora of black stain on human primary teeth. *Scand J Dent Res.* 1974;82(7):484–490.

6. Meckel AH. The formation and properties of organic films on teeth. *Arch Oral Biol.* 1965;10(4):585–598.

7. Eriksen HM, Nordbø H. Extrinsic discoloration of teeth. *J Clin Periodontol.* 1978;5(4):229–236.

8. Horowitz HS, Chamberlin SR. Pigmentation of teeth following topical applications of stannous fluoride in a nonfluoridated area. *J Public Health Dent.* 1971;31(1):32–37.

9. Leverett DH, McHugh WD, Jensen OE. Dental caries and staining after twenty-eight months of rinsing with stannous fluoride or sodium fluoride. *J Dent Res.* 1986;65(3): 424–427.

10. Flötra L, Gjermo P, Rölla G, et al. Side effects of chlorhexidine mouth washes. *Scand J Dent Res.* 1971;79(2):119–125.

11. Formicola AJ, Deasy MJ, Johnson DH, et al. Tooth staining effects of an alexidine mouthwash. *J Periodontol.* 1979; 50(4):207–211.

12. Reichart PA, Lenz H, König H, et al. The black layer on the teeth of betel chewers: a light microscopic, microradiographic, and electronmicroscopic study. *J Oral Pathol.* 1985;14(6):466–475.

13. Escartin J, Arnedo A, Pinto V, et al. A study of dental staining among competitive swimmers. *Community Dent Oral Epidemiol.* 2000;28:10–17.

14. Langlais RP, Miller CS. *Color Atlas of Common Oral Diseases.* 3rd ed. Philadelphia, PA: Lippincott Williams & Wilkins; 2003:242.

15. Dean HT. Investigation of physiological effects by epidemiological method. In: Moulton FR, ed. *Fluorine and Dental Health.* Washington, DC: American Association for the Advancement of Science; 1942.

16. Thylstrup A, Fejerskov O. Clinical appearance of dental fluorosis in permanent teeth in relation to histologic changes. *Community Dent Oral Epidemiol.* 1978;6(6):315–328.

17. Horowitz HS, Driscoll WS, Meyers RJ, et al. A new method for assessing the prevalence of dental fluorosis—the Tooth Surface Index of Fluorosis. *J Am Dent Assoc.* 1984; 109(1):37–41.

18. Kumar A, Kumar V, Singh J, et al. Drug-induced discoloration of teeth: an updated review. *Clin Pediatr.* 2012; 51(2):181–185.

19. Azer SS, Hague AL, Johnston WM. Effect of pH on tooth discoloration from food colorant *in vitro. J Dent.* 2010;38 (Suppl 2):e106–e109.

20. Ashcroft AT, Joiner A. Tooth cleaning and tooth wear: a review. *Proc Inst Mech Eng Part J J Eng Tribol.* 2010;224(6): 539–549.

21. Ashcroft AT, Joiner A. Tooth cleaning and tooth wear: a review. *Proc Inst Mech Eng Part J J Eng Tribol.* 2010;224(6): 539–549.

ENHANCE YOUR UNDERSTANDING

thePoint® DIGITAL CONNECTIONS
(see the inside front cover for access information)

- Audio glossary
- Quiz bank

SUPPORT FOR LEARNING
(available separately; visit lww.com)

- *Active Learning Workbook for Clinical Practice of the Dental Hygienist, 12th Edition*

prepU INDIVIDUALIZED REVIEW
(available separately; visit lww.com)

- **Adaptive quizzing with *prepU for Wilkins' Clinical Practice of the Dental Hygienist***

Indices and Scoring Methods

Charlotte J. Wyche, RDH, MS

CHAPTER OUTLINE

LEARNING OBJECTIVES

After studying this chapter, the student will be able to:

1. Identify and define key terms and concepts related to dental indices and scoring methods.

2. Identify the purpose, criteria for measurement, scoring methods, range of scores, and reference or interpretation scales for a variety of dental indices.

3. Select and calculate dental indices for a use in a specific patient or community situation.

This chapter provides an introduction to scoring methods used by clinicians, researchers, and community practitioners to evaluate indicators of oral health status. It is not possible to explain all of the many dental indices that have been used in a variety of settings, but several well-known and widely used indices and scoring methods are described in this chapter. Box 23-1 defines related terminology.

TYPES OF SCORING METHODS

Indices and scoring methods are used in clinical practice and by community programs to determine and record the oral health status of individuals and groups.

I. Individual Assessment Score

A. Purpose

In clinical practice, an index, a biofilm record, or a scoring system for an individual patient can be used for education, motivation, and evaluation.

▶ The effects of personal disease control efforts, the progress of healing following professional treatments, and the maintenance of health over time can be monitored.

▶ An example is the biofilm-free score, in which the dental hygienist is able to measure the effects of a patient's personal daily care efforts.

B. Uses

▶ To provide individual assessment to help a patient recognize an oral problem.

▶ To reveal the degree of effectiveness of oral hygiene practices.

▶ To motivate the patient during preventive and professional care for the elimination and control of oral disease.

▶ To evaluate the success of individual oral self-care and professional treatment over a period of time by comparing index scores.

BOX 23-1 KEY WORDS: Indices and Scoring Methods

Calibration: agreement with a set standard of performance; determination of accuracy and consistency between examiners to standardize procedures and gain reliability of recorded findings. Examiners who collect dental index data for epidemiological research or community health assessment are trained to measure the index in exactly the same way each time.

Community oral health assessment: a multifaceted process of identifying factors that affect the oral health status of a selected population.

Data: pieces of information collected using measurements and/or counts.

Data collection: the process of gathering information (through the use of tools such as dental indices).

Determinant: a factor that can influence the outcome of some process. Health determinants include physical and social factors that influence the health outcomes of an individual or in a community.

Epidemiology: the study of the relationships of various factors that determine the frequency and distribution of diseases in the human community; study of health and disease in populations.

Incidence: the rate at which a certain event occurs, as the number of new cases of a specific disease occurring during a certain period of time.

Index: a graduated, numeric scale with upper and lower limits; scores on the scale correspond to a specific criterion for individuals or populations; *pl.* indices or indexes.

Dental index: describes oral status by expressing clinical observations as numeric values.

Indicator: a factor that typically characterizes a disease or health condition; a factor measured and analyzed to describe health status. Dental indices described in this chapter measure oral health indicators.

Pilot study: a trial run of a planned study using a small sample to pretest an instrument, survey, or questionnaire.

Placebo: an inactive substance or preparation with no intrinsic therapeutic value given to satisfy a patient's symbolic need for drug therapy; used in controlled research studies in a form identical in appearance to the material being tested.

Prevalence: the total number of cases of a specific disease or condition in existence in a given population at a certain time.

Ramfjord index teeth: teeth used for epidemiologic studies of periodontal diseases: the maxillary right and mandibular left first molars, maxillary left and mandibular right first premolars, and maxillary left and mandibular right central incisors.

Reliability: ability of an index or a test procedure to measure consistently at different times and under a variety of conditions; reproducibility; consistency.

Sample: a portion or subset of an entire population.

Screening: assessment of many individuals to disclose certain characteristics or diseases in a population.

Individual screening: brief assessment for initial evaluation and classification of need for additional examination and treatment planning.

Status: refers to the state or condition of an individual or population.

Surveillance: the ongoing systematic collection, analysis, and interpretation of outcome-specific data for use in planning, implementing, and evaluating the effect of public health programs and practices.

Validity: ability of an index or a test procedure to measure what it is intended to measure.

II. Clinical Trial

A. Purpose

A clinical trial is planned to determine the effect of an agent or a procedure on the prevention, progression, or control of a disease.

- The trial is conducted by comparing an experimental group with a control group that is similar to the experimental group in every way except for the variable being studied.
- Examples of indices used for clinical trials are the biofilm index[1] and the patient hygiene performance (PHP).[2]

B. Uses

- To determine baseline data before experimental factors are introduced.
- To measure the effectiveness of specific agents for the prevention, control, or treatment of oral conditions.
- To measure the effectiveness of mechanical devices for personal care, such as toothbrushes, interdental cleaning devices, or irrigators.

III. Epidemiologic Survey

A. Purpose

The word *epidemiology* denotes the study of disease characteristics of populations rather than individuals. Epidemiologic surveys provide information on the trends and patterns of oral health and disease in populations.

- An example is the DMFT (decayed, missing, and filled teeth) index[3] to determine the extent of dental caries.

B. Uses

- To determine the prevalence and incidence of a particular condition occurring within a given population.
- To provide baseline data on indicators that show existing dental health status in populations.
  - The Surgeon General's Report on *Oral Health in America* used epidemiologic data to identify oral health disparities in certain populations.[4]
- To provide data to support recommendations for public health interventions to improve the health status of populations, such as those provided in the United States *Healthy People 2020* document.[5]

IV. Community Surveillance

A. Purpose

Community surveillance of oral health indicators and determinants can be accomplished at many levels.

- Government agencies, local community-based service-providing agencies, and professional associations are examples of groups that collect data to determine oral health status by conducting oral health screenings.

- Information from community-wide oral screenings can be used when planning local community-based oral health services or education.
- An example of a system designed to be used by a community-based group is the Association of State and Territorial Dental Directors' (ASTDD) Basic Screening Survey (BSS).[6]

B. Uses

- To assess the needs of a community.
- To help plan community-based health promotion/disease prevention programs.
- To compare the effects or evaluate the results of community-based programs.

INDICES

An index is a way of expressing clinical observations by using numbers. The use of numbers can provide standardized information to make observations of a health condition consistent and less subjective than a word description of that condition.

I. Descriptive Categories of Indices

A. General Categories

- *Simple index:* measures the presence or absence of a condition. An example is the Biofilm Index that measures the presence of dental biofilm without evaluating its effect on the gingiva.
- *Cumulative index:* measures all the evidence of a condition, past and present. An example is the DMFT index for dental caries.

B. Types of Simple and Cumulative Indices

- *Irreversible:* measures conditions that will not change. An example is an index that measures dental caries experience.
- *Reversible:* measures conditions that can be changed. Examples are indices that measure dental biofilm.

II. Selection Criteria

A useful and effective index:

- is simple to use and calculate
- requires minimal equipment and expense
- uses a minimal amount of time to complete
- does not cause patient discomfort nor is otherwise unacceptable to a patient
- has clear-cut criteria that are readily understandable
- is as free as possible from subjective interpretation
- is reproducible by the same examiner or different examiners
- is amenable to statistical analysis; has validity and reliability.

ORAL HYGIENE STATUS (BIOFILM, DEBRIS, CALCULUS)

Indices that measure oral hygiene status can be used in a clinical setting to educate and motivate an individual patient. When data are collected in a community setting, such as a nursing home, the findings can help determine how daily oral care is being provided and monitor the results of oral hygiene education programs.

I. Biofilm Index

This index was historically known as plaque index (Pl I).[1,7]

A. Purpose

To assess the thickness of biofilm at the gingival area.

B. Selection of Teeth

The entire dentition or selected teeth can be evaluated.

▶ *Areas examined*: Examine four gingival areas (distal, facial, mesial, and lingual) systematically for each tooth.

▶ *Modified procedures:* Examine only the facial, mesial, and lingual areas. Assign double score to the mesial reading, and divide the total by 4.

C. Procedure

▶ Dry the teeth and examine visually using adequate light, mouth mirror, and probe or explorer.

▶ Evaluate dental biofilm on the cervical third; pay no attention to biofilm that has extended to the middle or incisal thirds of the tooth.

▶ Use probe to test the surface when no biofilm is visible. Pass the probe or explorer across the tooth surface in the cervical third and near the entrance to the sulcus. When no biofilm adheres to the probe tip, the area is scored 0. When biofilm adheres, a score of 1 is assigned.

▶ Use a disclosing agent, if necessary, to assist evaluation for the 0–1 scores. When the Pl I is used in conjunction with the gingival index (GI), the GI is completed first because the disclosing agent masks the gingival characteristics.

▶ Include biofilm on the surface of calculus and on dental restorations in the cervical third in the evaluation.

▶ *Criteria*

BIOFILM INDEX

SCORE	CRITERIA
0	No biofilm.
1	A film of biofilm adhering to the free gingival margin and adjacent area of the tooth. The biofilm may be recognized only after application of disclosing agent or by running the explorer across the tooth surface.
2	Moderate accumulation of soft deposits within the gingival pocket that can be seen with the naked eye or on the tooth and gingival margin.
3	Abundance of soft matter within the gingival pocket and/or on the tooth and gingival margin.

D. Scoring

▶ *Pl I for area*
  • Each area of a tooth (distal, facial, mesial, lingual, or palatal) is assigned a score from 0 to 3.

▶ *Pl I for a tooth*
  • Scores for each area are totaled and divided by 4.

▶ *Pl I for groups of teeth*
  • Scores for individual teeth may be grouped and totaled and divided by the number of teeth. For instance, a Pl I may be determined for specific teeth or groups of teeth. The right side of the dentition may be compared with the left.

▶ *Pl I for the individual*
  • Add the scores for each tooth and divide by the number of teeth examined. The Pl I score ranges from 0 to 3.

▶ *Suggested range of scores for patient reference*

RATING	SCORES
Excellent	0
Good	0.1–0.9
Fair	1.0–1.9
Poor	2.0–3.0

▶ *Pl I for a group*
  • Add the scores for each member of a group and divide by the number of individuals.

II. Biofilm Control Record

This index was previously known as the plaque control record.[8]

A. Purpose

To record the presence of dental biofilm on individual tooth surfaces to permit the patient to visualize progress while learning biofilm control.

B. Selection of Teeth and Surfaces

▶ All teeth are included. Missing teeth are identified on the record form by a single thick horizontal line.

▶ Four surfaces are recorded: facial, lingual, mesial, and distal.

▶ Six areas may be recorded. The mesial and distal segments of the diagram may be divided to provide space to record proximal surfaces from the facial separately from the lingual or palatal surfaces (Figure 23-1).[9]

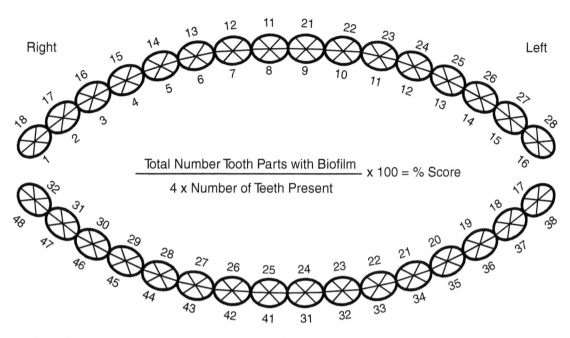

FIGURE 23-1 Biofilm Control Record. Diagrammatic representation of the teeth includes spaces to record biofilm on six areas of each tooth. The facial surfaces are on the outer portion and the lingual and palatal surfaces are on the inner portion of the arches. Teeth are numbered by the American Dental Association (ADA) system on the inside and by the FDI system on the outside. (*Source*: Adapted with permission from Ramfjord SP, Ash MM. *Periodontology and Periodontics*. Philadelphia, PA: WB Saunders Co; 1979:273. and from O'Leary TJ, Drake RB, Naylor JE. The plaque control record. *J Periodontol*. 1972;43:38.)

C. Procedure

▶ Apply disclosing agent or give a chewable tablet. Instruct patient to swish and rub the solution over the tooth surfaces with the tongue before rinsing.

▶ Examine each tooth surface for dental biofilm at the gingival margin. No attempt is made to differentiate quantity of biofilm.

▶ Record by making a dash or coloring in the appropriate spaces on the diagram (Figure 23-1) to indicate biofilm on facial, lingual, palatal, mesial, and/or distal surfaces.

D. Scoring

▶ Total the number of teeth present; multiply by 4 to obtain the number of available surfaces. Count the number of surfaces with biofilm.

▶ Multiply the number of biofilm-stained surfaces by 100 and divide by the total number of available surfaces to derive the percentage of surfaces with biofilm.

▶ Compare scores over subsequent appointments as the patient learns and practices biofilm control. Ten percent or less biofilm-stained surfaces can be considered a good goal, but if the biofilm is regularly left in the same areas, special instruction is indicated.

Calculation: Example for Biofilm Control Record
- Individual findings: 26 teeth scored; 8 surfaces with biofilm
- Multiply the number of teeth by 4: 26 × 4 = 104 surfaces

- Percent with biofilm =

$$\frac{\text{Number of surfaces with biofilm} \times 100}{\text{Number of available tooth surfaces}} = \frac{8 \times 100}{104}$$
$$= \frac{800}{104}$$
$$= 7.6\%$$

Interpretation
- Although 0% is ideal, less than 10% biofilm-stained surfaces has been suggested as a guideline in periodontal therapy. After initial therapy and when the patient has reached a 10% level of biofilm control or better, necessary additional periodontal and restorative procedures may be initiated.[8] In comparison, a similar evaluation using a biofilm-free score would mean that a goal of 90% or better biofilm-free surfaces would have to be reached before the surgical phase of treatment could be undertaken.

III. Biofilm-Free Score

This index was historically called the plaque-free score.[10]

A. Purpose

To determine the location, number, and percentage of biofilm-free surfaces for individual motivation and instruction. Interdental bleeding can also be documented.

B. Selection of Teeth and Surfaces

▶ All erupted teeth are included. Missing teeth are identified on the record form by a single thick horizontal line through the box in the chart form.

▶ Four surfaces are recorded for each tooth: facial, lingual or palatal, mesial, and distal.

C. Procedure

▶ *Biofilm-free score*

• Apply disclosing agent or give chewable tablet. Instruct patient to swish and rub the solution over the tooth surfaces with the tongue before rinsing.

• Examine each tooth surface for evidence of biofilm using adequate light and a mouth mirror.

• The patient needs a hand mirror to see the location of the biofilm missed during personal hygiene procedures.

• Use an appropriate tooth chart form or a diagrammatic form, such as that shown in Figure 23-2. Red ink for recording the biofilm is suggested when a red disclosing agent is used to help the patient associate the location of the biofilm in the mouth with the recording.

▶ *Papillary bleeding on probing*

• The small circles between the diagrammatic tooth blocks in Figure 23-2 are used to record proximal bleeding on probing.

• Improvement in the gingival tissue health will be demonstrated over a period of time as fewer bleeding areas are noted.

D. Scoring: Biofilm-Free Score

▶ Total the number of teeth present.

▶ Total the number of surfaces with biofilm that appear in red on the tooth diagram

▶ To calculate the biofilm-free score

• Multiply the number of teeth by 4 to determine the number of available surfaces.

• Subtract the number of surfaces with biofilm from the total available surfaces to find the number of biofilm-free surfaces.

• Biofilm-free score =

$$\frac{\text{Number of biofilm-free surface} \times 100}{\text{Number of available surfaces}}$$

$$= \text{Percentage of biofilm-free surfaces}$$

▶ Evaluate biofilm-free score: Ideally, 100% is the goal. When a patient maintains a percentage under 85%,

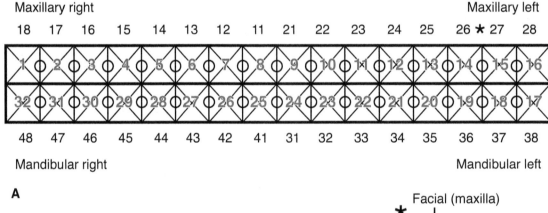

FIGURE 23-2 **Biofilm-Free Score. A:** Diagrammatic representation of the teeth used to record biofilm and papillary bleeding. **B:** Enlargement of one section of the diagram shows tooth surfaces. Teeth are numbered by the ADA system inside each block and by the FDI system outside each block. (*Source:* Adapted with permission from Grant DA, Stern IB, Listgarten MA. *Periodontics.* 6th ed. St. Louis, MO: Mosby; 1988:613.)

check individual surfaces to determine whether biofilm is usually left in the same areas. To prevent the development of specific areas of periodontal infection, remedial instruction in the areas usually missed is indicated.

▶ *Calculation:* Example for Biofilm-Free Score
  • Individual findings: 24 teeth scored and 37 surfaces with biofilm.
  • Multiply the number of teeth by 4: 24 × 4 = 96 available surfaces.
  • Subtract the number of surfaces with biofilm from total available surfaces: 96 − 37 = 59 biofilm-free surfaces.
  • Percentage of biofilm-free surfaces =

$$\frac{59 \times 100}{96} = 61.5\%$$

▶ *Interpretation*
  • On the basis of the ideal 100%, 61.5% is poor. More personal daily oral care instruction is indicated.

E. Scoring: Papillary Bleeding on Probing

▶ Total the number of small circles marked for bleeding. A patient with 32 teeth has 30 interdental areas. The mesial or distal surface of a tooth adjacent to an edentulous area is probed and counted.

▶ Evaluate total interdental bleeding. In health, bleeding on probing does not occur.

IV. Patient Hygiene Performance (PHP)[2]

A. Purpose

To assess the extent of biofilm and debris over a tooth surface. Debris is defined for the PHP as soft foreign material consisting of dental biofilm, materia alba, and food debris loosely attached to tooth surfaces.

B. Selection of Teeth and Surfaces

▶ Teeth examined

MAXILLARY	MANDIBULAR
No. 3 (16)*	No. 19 (36)
Right first molar	Left first molar
No. 8 (11)	No. 24 (31)
Right central incisor	Left central incisor
No. 14 (26)	No. 30 (46)
Left first molar	Right first molar

*Fédération Dentaire Internationale (FDI) system tooth numbers are in parentheses.

▶ Substitutions
  • When a first molar is missing, is less than three-fourths erupted, has a full crown, or is broken down, the second molar is used.

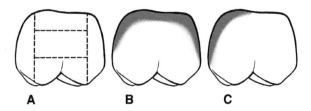

FIGURE 23-3 **PHP. A:** Oral debris is assessed by dividing a tooth into 5 subdivisions, each of which is scored 1 when debris is shown to be present after use of a disclosing agent. **B:** Example of debris score of 3. Shaded portion represents debris stained by disclosing agent. **C:** Example of debris score of 1. (*Source:* Podshadley AG, Haley JV. A method for evaluating oral hygiene performance. *Public Health Rep.* 1968;83(3):259–264.)

  • The third molar is used when the second is missing.
  • The adjacent central incisor is used for a missing incisor.
▶ Surfaces
  • The facial surfaces of incisors and maxillary molars and the lingual surfaces of mandibular molars are examined.

C. Procedure

Apply disclosing agent. Instruct the patient to swish for 30 seconds and expectorate, but not rinse.

▶ Examination is made using a mouth mirror.

▶ Each tooth surface to be evaluated is subdivided (mentally) into five sections (Figure 23-3A) as follows:
  • Vertically: Three divisions—mesial, middle, and distal.
  • Horizontally: The middle third is subdivided into gingival, middle, and occlusal or incisal thirds.

▶ Each of the five subdivisions is scored for the presence of stained debris as follows:

PHP	
SCORE	CRITERIA
0	No debris (or questionable).
1	Debris definitely present.
M	When all three molars or both incisors are missing.
S	When a substitute tooth is used.

D. Scoring

▶ *Debris score for individual tooth*
  • Add the scores for each of the five subdivisions. The scores range from 0 to 5. Examples are shown in Figures 23-3B and C.
▶ *PHP for the individual*
  • Total the scores for the individual teeth and divide by the number of teeth examined. The PHP ranges from 0 to 5.
▶ *Suggested range of scores for evaluation*

RATING	SCORES
Excellent	0 (no debris)
Good	0.1–1.7
Fair	1.8–3.4
Poor	3.5–5.0

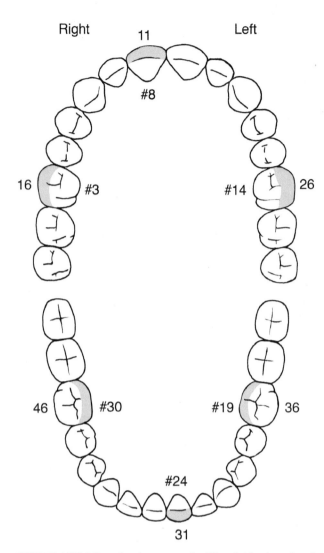

Right   11   Left

#8

16   #3   #14   26

46   #30   #19   36

#24

31

FIGURE 23-4 **OHI-S.** Six tooth surfaces are scored as follows: facial surfaces of maxillary molars and of the maxillary right and mandibular left central incisors, and the lingual surfaces of mandibular molars. Teeth are numbered by the ADA system on the lingual surface and by the FDI system on the facial surface.

Calculation: Example for an Individual

TOOTH	DEBRIS SCORE
No. 3 (16)	5
No. 8 (11)	3
No. 14 (26)	4
No. 19 (36)	5
No. 24 (31)	2
No. 30 (46)	3
Total	**22**

$$\frac{\text{Total debris score}}{\text{Number of teeth scored}} = \frac{22}{6} = 3.66$$

▶ *Interpretation*
  • According to the suggested range of scores, this patient with a PHP of 3.66 would be classified as exhibiting poor hygiene performance.

▶ *PHP for a group*
  • To obtain the average PHP score for a group or population, total the individual scores and divide by the number of people examined.

V. Simplified Oral Hygiene Index (OHI-S)[11,12]

A. Purpose

To assess oral cleanliness by estimating the tooth surfaces covered with debris and/or calculus.

B. Components

The OHI-S has two components, the simplified debris index (DI-S) and the simplified calculus index (CI-S). The two scores may be used separately or may be combined for the OHI-S.

C. Selection of Teeth and Surfaces

▶ *Identify the six specific teeth* (See Figure 23-4)
  • *Posterior:* The facial surfaces of the maxillary molars and the lingual surfaces of the mandibular molars are scored. Although usually the first molars are examined, the first fully erupted molar distal to each second premolar is used if the first molar is missing.
  • *Anterior:* The facial surfaces of the maxillary right and the mandibular left central incisors are scored. When either is missing, the adjacent central incisor is scored.
▶ *Extent*
  • Either the facial or lingual surfaces of the selected teeth are scored, including the proximal surfaces to the contact areas.

D. Procedure

▶ *Qualification:* At least two of the six possible surfaces are examined to calculate an individual score.
▶ *Record six debris scores*
  • Definition of oral debris: Oral debris is soft foreign matter, such as dental biofilm, material alba, and food debris on the surfaces of the teeth.
▶ *Examination:* Run the side of the tip of a probe or an explorer across the tooth surface to estimate the surface area covered by debris.
▶ *Criteria* (Figure 23-5 and Debris Index table on next page)

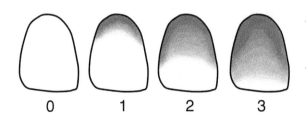

0   1   2   3

FIGURE 23-5 **OHI-S.** For the debris index, six teeth (Figure 23-3) are scored. Scoring of 0–3 is based on tooth surfaces covered by debris as shown.

DEBRIS INDEX (DI-S)

SCORE	CRITERIA
0	No debris or stain present.
1	Soft debris covering not more than one-third of the tooth surface being examined, or presence of extrinsic stains without debris, regardless of surface area covered.
2	Soft debris covering more than one-third but not more than two-thirds of the exposed tooth surface.
3	Soft debris covering more than two-thirds of the exposed tooth surface.

▶ *Record six calculus scores*

• *Definition of calculus*: Dental calculus is a hard deposit of inorganic salts composed primarily of calcium carbonate and phosphate mixed with debris, microorganisms, and desquamated epithelial cells.

▶ *Examination*: Use an explorer to estimate surface area covered by supragingival calculus deposits. Identify subgingival deposits by exploring and/or probing. Record only definite deposits of hard calculus.

• *Criteria*: Location and tooth surface areas scored are illustrated in Figure 23-6.

CALCULUS INDEX (CI-S)

SCORE	CRITERIA
0	No calculus present.
1	Supragingival calculus covering not more than one-third of the exposed tooth surface being examined.
2	Supragingival calculus covering more than one-third but not more than two-thirds of the exposed tooth surface, or the presence of individual flecks of subgingival calculus around the cervical portion of the tooth.
3	Supragingival calculus covering more than two-thirds of the exposed tooth surface or a continuous heavy band of subgingival calculus around the cervical portion of the tooth.

E. Scoring

▶ *OHI-S individual score*

▶ Determine separate DI-S and CI-S.

• Divide each total score by the number of teeth scored (6).

• DI-S and CI-S values range from 0 to 3.

▶ Calculate the OHI-S.

• Combine the DI-S and CI-S.

• OHI-S value ranges from 0 to 6.

▶ *Suggested range of scores for evaluation*[12]

INDIVIDUAL DI-S AND CI-S

RATING	SCORES
Excellent	0
Good	0.1–0.6
Fair	0.7–1.8
Poor	1.9–3.0

OHI-S (COMBINED DI-S AND CI-S)

RATING	SCORES
Excellent	0
Good	0.1–1.2
Fair	1.3–3.0
Poor	3.1–6.0

Calculation: Example for an Individual

TOOTH	DI-S	CI-S SCORE
No. 3 (16)	2	2
No. 8 (11)	1	0
No. 14 (26)	3	2
No. 19 (36)	3	2
No. 24 (31)	2	1
No. 30 (46)	2	2
Total	13	9

$$DI\text{-}S = \frac{\text{Total debris score}}{\text{Number of teeth scored}} = \frac{13}{6} = 2.17$$

$$CI\text{-}S = \frac{\text{Total calculus scores}}{\text{Number of teeth scored}} = \frac{9}{6} = 1.50$$

$$OHI\text{-}S = DI\text{-}S + CI\text{-}S = 2.17 + 1.50 = 3.67$$

▶ *Interpretation*

• According to the suggested range of scores, the score for this individual (3.67) indicates a poor oral hygiene status.

▶ *OHI-S group score*

• Compute the average of the individual scores by totaling the scores and dividing by the number of individuals.

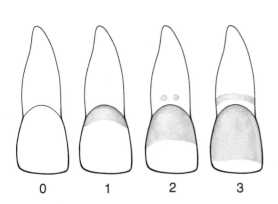

0   1   2   3

FIGURE 23-6 **OHI-S.** For the calculus index, six teeth (Figure 23-3) are scored. Scoring of 0–3 is based on location and tooth surface area with calculus as shown. Note slight subgingival calculus recorded as 2 and more extensive subgingival calculus as 3.

GINGIVAL AND PERIODONTAL HEALTH

Measurements for gingival and periodontal indices have varied over the years. Two indices, not completely described here, are of historic interest.

▶ The papillary-marginal-attached index, attributed to Schour and Massler[13] and later revised by Massler,[14] was used to assess the extent of gingival changes in large groups for epidemiologic studies.

▶ The periodontal index (PI) of Russell,[15] another acclaimed contribution to the study of disease incidence, was a complex index that accounts for both gingival and periodontal changes. Its aim was to survey large populations.

▶ For patient instruction and motivation, several bleeding indices and scoring methods have been developed.

▶ Bleeding on gentle probing or flossing is an early sign of gingival inflammation and precedes color changes and enlargement of gingival tissues.[16,17]

▶ Bleeding on probing is an indicator of the progression of periodontal disease so, testing for bleeding has become a significant procedure for assessment prior to treatment planning, after therapy to show the effects of treatment, and at maintenance appointments to determine continued control of gingival inflammation.

I. Periodontal Screening and Recording (PSR)[18,19]

A. Purpose

To assess the state of periodontal health of an individual patient.

▶ A modified form of the original community periodontal index of treatment needs (CPITN) index.[20]

▶ Designed to indicate periodontal status in a rapid and effective manner and motivate the patient to seek necessary complete periodontal assessment and treatment.

▶ Used as a screening procedure to determine the need for comprehensive periodontal evaluation.

B. Selection of Teeth

The dentition is divided into sextants. Each tooth is examined. Posterior sextants begin distal to the canines.

C. Procedure

▶ *Instrument:* Probe originally designed for World Health Organization (WHO) surveys (Figure 23-7), with markings at intervals from tip: 3.5, 5.5, 8.5, and 11.5 mm.

▶ Color coded between 3.5 and 5.5 mm.

▶ *Working tip:* A ball 0.5 mm in diameter. The functions of the ball are to aid in the detection of calculus, rough overhanging margins of restorations, and other tooth surface irregularities and to facilitate assessment at the probing depth and reduce risk of overmeasurement.

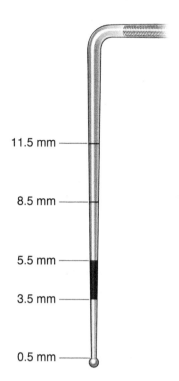

11.5 mm —

8.5 mm —

5.5 mm —

3.5 mm —

0.5 mm —

FIGURE 23-7 WHO Periodontal Probe. The specially designed WHO probe measures 3.5-, 5.5-, 8.5-, and 11.5-mm intervals. This probe is used to make determinations for the PSR and the CPI. (*Source:* Fédération Dentaire Internationale. A simplified periodontal examination for dental practices. Based on the Community Periodontal Index of Treatment Needs—CPITN. *Aust Dent J.* 1985;30(5):368–370.)

▶ *Probe application*
  • Insert probe gently into a sulcus until resistance is felt.
  • Apply a circumferential walking step to probe systematically about each tooth through each sextant.
  • Observe color-coded area of the probe for prompt identification of probing depths.
  • Each sextant receives one code number corresponding to the deepest position of the color-coded portion of the probe.

▶ *Criteria*
  • Five codes and an asterisk are used. Figure 23-8 shows the clinical findings, code significance, and patient management guidelines.
  • Each code may include conditions identified with the preceding codes; for example, Code 3 with probing depth from 3.5 to 5.5 mm may also include calculus, an overhanging restoration, and bleeding on probing.
  • One need not probe the remaining teeth in a sextant when a Code 4 is found. For Codes 0, 1, 2, and 3, the sextant is completely probed.

▶ *Recording*
  • Use a simple six-box form to provide a space for each sextant. The form can be made into peel-off stickers or a rubber stamp to facilitate recording in the patient's permanent record.

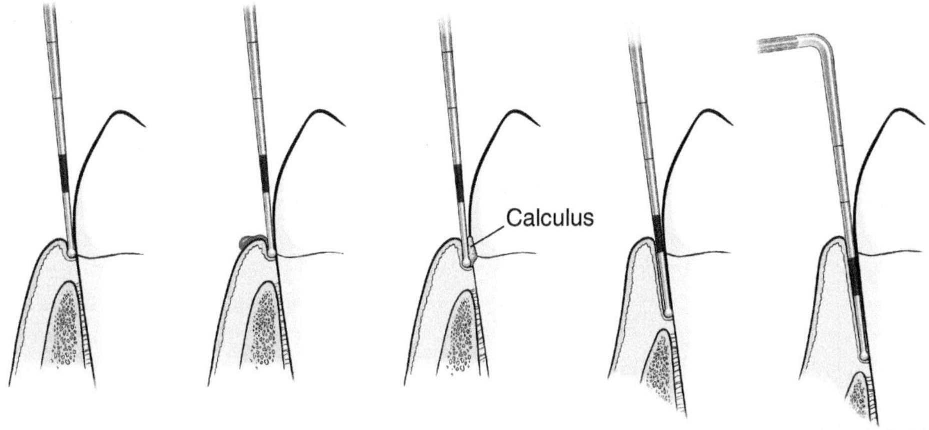

PSR and CPI sextant scores	Code 0	Code 1	Code 2	Code 3	Code 4
CPI description	• Entire black band of the probe is visible	• Entire black band of the probe is visible, but bleeding is present after gentle probin	• Entire black band is visible, but calculus is present • Bleeding may or may not be present.	• 4 to 5 mm pocket depth • Black band on probe partially hidden by gingival margin	• 6 mm or greater pocket depth • Black band of probe completely hidden by gingival margin
PSR sextant code description	• Colored area of probe completely visible • No calculus, defective restoration margins or bleeding	• Colored area of probe completely visible • No calculus or defective restoration margins • Bleeding after gentle probing	• Colored area of probe completely visible • Supra or subgingival rough surface or calculus • Defective restoration margins	• Colored area of probe only partially visible • Calculus, defective restorations, and bleeding may or may not be present	• Colored area of probe completely disappears (probing depth of 5.5 mm or greater)
PSR management guidelines	• Biofilm control instruction • Preventive care	• Biofilm control instruction • Preventive care	• Biofilm control instruction • Complete preventive care • Calculus removal • Correction of defective restoration margins	• Comprehensive periodontal assessment and treatment plan is indicated	• Comprehensive periodontal assessment and treatment plan is indicated

FIGURE 23-8 **Community Periodontal Index (CPI) and Periodontal Screening Record (PSR) Codes.** (*Source:* World Health Organization. *Oral Health Surveys: Basic Methods.* 4th ed. Geneva: WHO; 1997:27, 38 and the American Academy of Periodontology.[18])

- One score is marked for each sextant; the highest code observed is recorded. When indicated, an asterisk is added to the score in the individual space with the sextant code number.

D. Scoring

▶ *Follow-up patient management*

Patients are classified into assessment and treatment planning needs by the highest coded score of their PSR.

Calculation: Example 1: PSR Sextant Score

4*	2	3
3	2*	4*

▶ *Interpretation*
- With Codes 3 and 4, a comprehensive periodontal examination is indicated. The asterisks indicate furcation involvement in two sextants, and a mucogingival involvement in the mandibular anterior sextant. When the patient is not aware of the periodontal involvement, counseling is important if cooperation and compliance are to be obtained.

▶ *Calculation:* Example 2 PSR Sextant Score

2	1	2
2	1*	2*

▶ *Interpretation*
- An overall Code 2 can indicate calculus and overhanging restorations that can be removed. All restorations are checked for recurrent dental caries. Appointments for instruction in dental biofilm control are of primary concern.
  - In this example, the asterisks in two sextants indicate a notable clinical feature such as minimal attached gingiva.

II. Community Periodontal Index (CPI)[21]

A. Purpose

To screen and monitor the periodontal status of populations.

▶ Originally developed as the CPITN index that included a code to indicate an individual and group-summary recording of treatment needs. However, because of changes in management of periodontal disease, the treatment needs portion of the index has been eliminated.

▶ One component of a complete oral health survey[21] designed by the WHO that includes the assessment of many oral health indicators including mucosal lesions, dental caries, fluorosis, prosthetic status, and dentofacial anomalies.

▶ Later modified to form the PSR index for scoring individual patients.

B. Selection of Teeth

▶ The dentition is divided into sextants for recording on the assessment form.

▶ Posterior sextants begin distal to canines.

Adults (20 years and older)

▶ A sextant is examined only if there are two or more teeth present that are not indicated for extraction.

▶ Ten index teeth are examined.

▶ The first and second molars in each posterior sextant. If one is missing, no replacement is selected and the score for the remaining molar is recorded.

▶ The maxillary right central incisor and mandibular left central incisor.

▶ If no index teeth or tooth is present in the sextant, then all remaining teeth in the sextant are examined and the highest score is recorded.

Children and Adolescents (7–19 years of age)

▶ Six index teeth are examined; the first molar in each posterior quadrant and the maxillary right and the mandibular left incisors.

▶ For children under the age of 15, pocket depth is not recorded to avoid the deepened sulci associated with erupting teeth. Only bleeding and calculus are considered.

C. Procedure

▶ *Instrument:* A specially designed probe is used to record both the CPI and PSR. The probe is described in Figure 23-7.

▶ *Criteria:* CPI score.
- Five codes are used to record bleeding, calculus, and pocket depth. Criteria for the CPI codes are similar to the criteria for the PSR, as illustrated in Figure 23-8 and the table below.

COMMUNITY PERIODONTAL INDEX (CPI)	
CODE	**CRITERIA**
0	Healthy periodontal tissues.
1	Bleeding after gentle probing; entire colored band of probe is visible.
2	Supragingival or subgingival calculus present; entire colored band of probe is visible.
3	4- to 5-mm pocket; colored band of probe is partially obscured.
4	6 mm or deeper; colored band on the probe is not visible.

▶ *Criteria:* Loss of attachment (LOA) code.
- In conjunction with the CPI, the WHO probe is also used to record LOA. The five LOA codes used are illustrated in Figure 23-9. LOA is not recorded for individuals less than 15 years of age.

LOA CODE	CRITERIA
0	0–3 mm LOA
1	4–5 mm LOA
2	6–8 mm LOA
3	9–11 mm LOA
4	12 mm or greater LOA

III. Sulcus Bleeding Index (SBI)[16]

A. Purpose

To locate areas of gingival sulcus bleeding and color changes in order to recognize and record the presence of early (initial) inflammatory gingival disease.

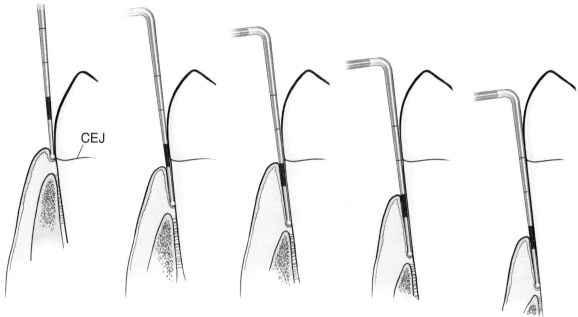

Code 0	Code 1	Code 2	Code 3	Code 4
• 0 to 3 mm loss of attachment • Cementoenamel junction (CEJ) is covered by gingival margin and CPI score is 0 to 3. If CEJ is visible, or if CPI score is 4, LOA codes 1 to 4 are used.	• 3.5 to 5.5 mm loss of attachment • CEJ is within the black band on the probe	• 6 to 8 mm loss of attachment CEJ is between the top of the black band and the 8.5 mm mark on the probe	• 9 to 11 mm loss of attachment • CEJ is between the 8.5 mm and 11.5 mm marks on the probe	• 12 mm or greater loss of attachment • CEJ is beyond the highest (11.5 mm) marks on the probe

FIGURE 23-9 **Loss of Attachement (LOA) Codes.** (*Source:* World Health Organization. *Oral Health Surveys: Basic Methods.* 4th ed. Geneva: WHO; 1997:27, 39.)

B. Areas Examined

Four gingival units are scored systematically for each tooth: the labial and lingual marginal gingiva (M units), and the mesial and distal papillary gingiva (P units).

C. Procedure

▷ Use standardized lighting while probing each of the four areas.

▷ Walk the probe to the base of the sulcus, holding it parallel with the long axis of the tooth for M units, and directed toward the col area for P units.

▷ Wait 30 seconds after probing before scoring apparently healthy gingival units.

▷ Dry the gingiva gently if necessary to observe color changes clearly.

▷ *Criteria*

SULCULAR BLEEDING INDEX (SBI)

CODE	CRITERIA
0	Healthy appearance of P and M, no bleeding on sulcus probing.
1	Apparently healthy P and M showing no change in color and no swelling, but bleeding from sulcus on probing.
2	Bleeding on probing and change of color caused by inflammation. No swelling or macroscopic edema.
3	Bleeding on probing and change in color and slight edematous swelling.
4	• Bleeding on probing and change in color and obvious swelling or • Bleeding on probing and obvious swelling.
5	Bleeding on probing and spontaneous bleeding and change in color, marked swelling with or without ulceration.

D. Scoring

▶ *SBI for area*
  • Score each of the four gingival units (M and P) from 0 to 5.
▶ *SBI for tooth*
  • Total scores for the four units and divide by 4.
▶ *SBI for individual*
  • Total the scores for individual teeth and divide by the number of teeth. SBI scores range from 0 to 5.

IV. Gingival Bleeding Index[22]

A. Purpose

To record the presence or absence of gingival inflammation as determined by bleeding from interproximal gingival sulci.

B. Areas Examined

Each interproximal area has two sulci, which can be scored as one interdental unit or scored separately.

▶ Certain areas may be excluded from scoring because of accessibility, tooth position, diastemata, or other factors, and if exclusions are made, a consistent procedure is followed for an individual and for a group if a study is to be made.

▶ A full complement of teeth has 30 proximal areas. In the original studies, third molars were excluded, and 26 interdental units were recorded.[23]

C. Procedure

▶ *Instrument*
  • Unwaxed dental floss is used. Floss has the advantages of being readily available and disposable
▶ *Steps*
  1. Pass the floss interproximally first on one side of the papilla and then on the other.
  2. Curve the floss around the adjacent tooth, and bring the floss below the gingival margin.
  3. Move the floss up and down for one stroke, with care not to lacerate the gingiva. Adapt finger rests to provide controlled, consistent pressure.
  4. Use a new length of clean floss for each area.
  5. Retract for visibility of bleeding from both facial and lingual aspects.
  6. Allow 30 seconds for reinspection of an area that does not show blood immediately either in the area or on the floss.
▶ *Criteria*
  • Bleeding indicates the presence of disease. No attempt is made to quantify the severity of bleeding.

D. Scoring

The numbers of bleeding areas and scorable units are recorded. Patient participation in observing and recording over a series of appointments can increase motivation.

V. Eastman Interdental Bleeding Index (EIBI)[23,24]

A. Purpose

To assess the presence of inflammation in the interdental area as indicated by the presence or absence of bleeding.

B. Areas Examined

Each interdental area around the entire dentition.

C. Procedure

▶ *Instrument*
  Triangular wooden interdental cleaner.

▶ *Steps*
  1. Insert gently, then immediately remove, a wooden cleaner into each interdental area in such a way as to depress the papilla 1–2 mm (Figure 23-10).
  2. Make the path of insertion horizontal (parallel to the occlusal surface), taking care not to angle the point in an apical direction.
  3. Insert and remove four times; move to next interproximal area.
  4. Record the presence or absence of bleeding within 15 seconds for each area.

D. Scoring

▶ *Number of bleeding sites*
  • The number may be totaled for an individual score for comparison with scores over a series of appointments.

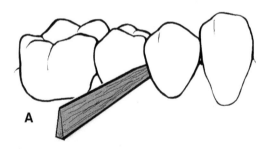

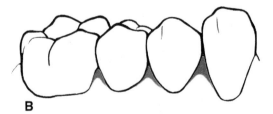

FIGURE 23-10 Eastman Interdental Bleeding Index (EIBI). The test for interdental bleeding is made by inserting a wooden interdental cleaner into each interdental space. **A:** Wooden interdental cleaner inserted in a horizontal path, parallel with the occlusal surfaces. **B:** The presence or absence of bleeding is noted within a quadrant 15 seconds after final insertion. Bleeding indicates the presence of inflammation.

▶ *Percentage scores*
 • Index is expressed as a percentage of the total number of sites evaluated. Calculations can be made for total mouth, quadrants, or maxillary versus mandibular.

▶ *Calculation example*
 • An adult with a complete dentition has 15 maxillary and 15 mandibular interproximal areas. The EIBI revealed 13 areas of bleeding. To calculate percentage:

$$\frac{\text{Number of bleeding areas}}{\text{Total number of areas}} \times 100 = \text{Percent bleeding area}$$

$$\frac{13}{30} \times 100 = 43\%$$

VI. Gingival Index (GI)[7]

A. Purpose

To assess the severity of gingivitis based on color, consistency, and bleeding on probing.

B. Selection of Teeth and Gingival Areas

A GI may be determined for selected teeth or for the entire dentition.

▶ *Areas examined*
 • Four gingival areas (distal, facial, mesial, and lingual) are examined systematically for each tooth.

▶ *Modified procedure*
 • The distal examination for each tooth can be omitted. The score for the mesial area is doubled, and the total score for each tooth is divided by 4.

C. Procedure

▶ Dry the teeth and gingiva; under adequate light, use a mouth mirror and probe.

▶ Use the probe to press on the gingiva to determine the degree of firmness.

▶ Slide the probe along the soft tissue wall near the entrance to the gingival sulcus to evaluate bleeding (Figure 23-11).

▶ *Criteria*

GI CODE	CRITERIA
0	Normal gingiva.
1	Mild inflammation—slight change in color, slight edema. *No bleeding* on probing.
2	Moderate inflammation—redness, edema, and glazing. *Bleeding* on probing.
3	Severe inflammation—marked redness and edema. Ulceration. Tendency to *spontaneous bleeding.*

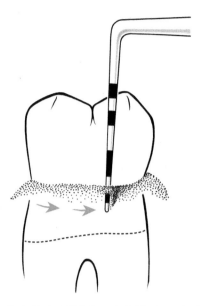

FIGURE 23-11 Gingival Index (GI). Probe stroke for bleeding evaluation. The broken line represents the level of attachment of the periodontal tissues. The probe is inserted a few millimeters and moved along the soft tissue pocket wall with light pressure in a circumferential direction. The stroke shown here is in contrast with the walking stroke used for probing depth evaluation and measurement.

D. Scoring

▶ *GI for area*
 • Each of the four gingival surfaces (distal, facial, mesial, and lingual) is given a score of 0–3.

▶ *GI for a tooth*
 • Scores for each area are totaled and divided by 4.

▶ *GI for groups of teeth*
 • Scores for individual teeth may be grouped and totaled, and divided by the number of teeth. A GI may be determined for specific teeth, group of teeth, quadrant, or side of mouth.

▶ *GI for the individual*
 • Scores for each tooth are added up and divided by the number of teeth examined. Scores range from 0 to 3.

▶ *Suggested range of scores for patient reference*

RATING	SCORES
Excellent (healthy tissue)	0
Good	0.1–1.0
Fair	1.1–2.0
Poor	2.1–3.0

▶ *Calculation:* Example for an Individual
 • Using six teeth for an example of screening; teeth selected are known as the Ramfjord index teeth.[25]

TOOTH NO.	M	F	D	L	
3 (16)	3	1	3	1	
9 (21)	1	0	1	1	
12 (24)	2	1	2	0	
19 (36)	3	1	3	3	
25 (41)	1	1	1	1	
28 (44)	2	1	2	0	
Total	12	5	12	6	= 35

$$\text{Gingival index} = \frac{\text{Total score}}{\text{Number of surfaces}} = \frac{35}{24} = 1.45$$

▶ *Interpretation*
- According to the suggested range of scores, the score for this individual (1.45) indicates only fair gingival health (moderate inflammation).
- The ratings for each gingival area or surface can be used to help the patient compare gingival changes and improve oral hygiene procedures.

▶ *GI for a group*
- Add the individual GI scores and divide by the number of individuals examined.

DENTAL CARIES EXPERIENCE

Dental caries experience data are most useful when measuring the prevalence of dental disease in groups rather than individuals. The population scores can document such information as the number of persons in any age group who are affected by dental caries, the number of teeth that need treatment, or the proportion of teeth that have been treated.

I. Permanent Dentition: Decayed, Missing, and Filled Teeth (DMFT) or Surfaces (DMFS)[3,26]

A. Purpose

To determine total dental caries experience, past and present, by recording either the number of affected teeth or tooth surfaces.

B. Selection of Teeth and Surfaces

▶ The DMFT is based on 28 teeth.
▶ The DMFS is based on surfaces of 28 teeth; 128 surfaces.
- 16 posterior teeth × 5 surfaces (facial, lingual, mesial, distal, and occlusal) = 80 surfaces.
- 12 anterior teeth × 4 surfaces (facial, lingual, mesial, and distal) = 48 surfaces.
- Teeth missing due to dental caries are recorded using 5 surfaces for posterior and 4 surfaces for anterior teeth.

▶ Teeth not counted.
- Third molars.
- Unerupted teeth. A tooth is considered erupted when any part projects through the gingiva. Certain types of research may require differentiation between clinical emergence, partial eruption, and full eruption.
- Congenitally missing and supernumerary teeth.
- Teeth removed for reasons other than dental caries, such as an impaction or during orthodontic treatment.
- Teeth restored for reasons other than dental caries, such as trauma (fracture), cosmetic purposes, or use as a bridge abutment.
- Primary tooth retained with the permanent successor erupted. The permanent tooth is evaluated because a primary tooth is never included in this index.

C. Procedures

▶ *Examination*
- Examine each tooth in a systematic sequence.
- Observe teeth by visual means as much as possible.
- Use adequate light.
- Review the stages of dental caries in Chapter 27.

▶ *Criteria for recording*[26]
- Each tooth is recorded once when using the DMFT index.
- Five surfaces for posterior teeth and 4 surfaces for anterior teeth are recorded when using the DMFS index.
- DMF indices use a dichotomous scale (present or absent) to record decay.

DMF RATING	CRITERIA
Decayed (D)	Visible dental caries is present or both dental caries and a restoration are present.
Missing (M)	A tooth extracted because of dental caries or when it is carious, nonrestorable, and indicated for extraction.
Filled (F)	Any permanent or temporary restoration is present or a defective restoration without evidence of dental caries is present.

D. Scoring

▶ *Individual DMF*
- Total each component separately.
  Total D + M + F = DMF
- *Example:* An individual presents with dental caries on the mesial and occlusal surfaces of a posterior tooth and caries on the mesial surface of an anterior tooth. A molar tooth and an anterior tooth are missing because of dental caries, and there is an amalgam restoration on the mesial–distal–occlusal surfaces of a posterior tooth.
  DMFT = 2 + 2 + 1 = 5
  DMFS = 3 + 9 + 3 = 15

▶ A DMF score may have different interpretations. For example, an individual with a DMF score of 15 who has experienced regular dental care may have a distribution such as D = 0, M = 0, F = 15.

▶ *Group DMF*
  • Total the DMFs for each individual examined.
  • Divide the total DMFs by the number of individuals in the group.

▶ *Calculation:*
  • *Example:* A population of 20 individuals with individual DMF scores of 0,0,0,0,2,2,3,3,3,4,9,9,9,10,10,10,11,11,12, and 16 equals a group total DMF of 124.

$$\frac{124}{20} = 6.2 = \text{the average DMF for the group}$$

  • This DMF average represents accumulated dental caries experience for the group.

▶ The differences in caries experience between two groups of individuals within this population are notable and influence interpretation of the results. For the first 10 individuals, the group average is $\frac{17}{10} = 1.7$. and for the second 10 individuals the average DMF is $\frac{107}{10} = 10.7$.

▶ Scores for these two groups can be presented separately because of the wide difference.

▶ Average DMF scores can also be presented by age group.

▶ *Specific treatment needs of a group*
  • To calculate the percentage of DMF teeth that need to be restored, divide the total D component by the total DMF.

▶ *Calculation:*
  • *Example 1:* To calculate the *percent of DMF teeth* that need to be restored, divide the total D component by the total number of DMF teeth.
  D = 175, M = 55, F = 18
  Total DMFT = 248

$$\frac{D}{DMF} = \frac{175}{248} = 0.70 \text{ or } 70\% \text{ of the teeth need restorations}$$

  • *Example 2:* The same type of calculations can be used to determine the *percent of all teeth* missing in a group of individuals.
  20 individuals have 28 × 20 = 560 permanent teeth.
  D = 175, M = 55, F = 18

$$\frac{M}{\text{Total \# of teeth}} = \frac{55}{560} = 0.098 \text{ or nearly } 10\% \text{ of all}$$

their teeth lost because of dental caries.

II. Primary Dentition: Decayed, Indicated for Extraction, and Filled (df and def)[27]

A. Purpose

To determine the dental caries experience for the primary teeth present in the oral cavity by evaluating teeth or surfaces.

B. Selection of Teeth or Surfaces

▶ deft or dft: 20 teeth evaluated.

▶ defs or dfs: 88 surfaces evaluated.
  • *Posterior teeth:* Each has five surfaces: facial, lingual or palatal, mesial, distal, and occlusal. (8 teeth × 5 surfaces = 40 surfaces.)
  • *Anterior teeth:* Each has four surfaces: facial, lingual or palatal, mesial, and distal. (12 teeth × 4 surfaces = 48 surfaces.)

▶ Teeth not counted
  • Missing teeth, including unerupted and congenitally missing.
  • Supernumerary teeth.
  • Teeth restored for reasons other than dental caries are not counted as f.

C. Procedure

▶ *Instruments and examination*
Same as for DMF.

▶ *Criteria*

DECAYED, INDICATED FOR EXTRACTION, FILLED (df AND def)	
RATING	**CRITERIA**
d	Primary teeth (or surfaces) with dental caries but not restored.
e	Primary teeth (or number of surfaces) that are indicated for extraction because of dental caries.
f	Primary teeth (or surfaces) restored with an amalgam, composite, or temporary filling. Each tooth (or surface) is scored only once, A tooth with recurrent caries around a restoration receives a "d" score.

▶ *Difference between deft/defs and dft/dfs*
  • In the deft and defs, both "d" and "e" are used to describe teeth with dental caries. Thus, d and e are sometimes combined, and the index becomes the dft or dfs.

D. Scoring

▶ *Calculation:*
  • *Example 1:* Individual def A 2½-year-old child has 18 teeth. Teeth A (55) and J (65) are unerupted. There is no sign of dental caries in teeth M (73), N (72), O (71), P (81), Q (82), and R (83). All other teeth have two carious surfaces each, except tooth B (54), which is broken down to the gum line.
  Summary:
  Total number of teeth = 18
  Number of "d" teeth = 11
  Number of "e" teeth = 1
  Number of "f" teeth = 0
  def = d + e + f = 11 + 1 + 0 = 12

▶ *Interpretation*
  • Twelve of 18 teeth (67%) with carious lesions indicates a serious need for dental treatment and a caries management program for the child.

▶ *Calculation*: Example 2: individual dfs
- Using the same 2½-year-old child to calculate dfs: Eleven teeth each have two carious surfaces: $11 \times 2 = 22$ carious surfaces

Tooth B has $1 \times 5 = 5$ carious surfaces

Total dfs: $d + f = 27 + 0 = 27$

▶ *Interpretation*
- The child has 48 total anterior surfaces (12 teeth × 4 surfaces) and 30 total posterior surfaces (6 teeth × 5 surfaces) to total 78 surfaces.

$$\frac{dfs}{\text{Number of surfaces}} = \frac{27}{78}$$
$$= 0.34 \text{ or } 34\% \text{ of the surfaces in need of dental treatment}$$

E. Mixed Dentition

A DMFT or DMFS and a deft or defs are never combined or added together.

III. Primary Dentition: Decayed, Missing, and Filled (dmf)[27]

A. Purpose

To determine dental caries experience for children. Only primary teeth are evaluated.

B. Selection of Teeth or Surfaces

▶ dmft: 12 teeth evaluated (8 primary molars; 4 primary canines).

▶ dmfs: 56 surfaces evaluated.
- *Primary molars*: 8×5 surfaces each $= 40$
- *Primary canines*: 4×4 surfaces each $= 16$

▶ Each tooth is counted only once. When both dental caries and a restoration are present, the tooth or surface is scored as "d."

C. Procedure

▶ Instruments and examination are the same as for DMF.

▶ Criteria for dmft or dmfs

dmf RATING	CRITERIA
d	Primary molars and canines (or surfaces) that are carious.
m	Primary molars and canines (or surfaces) that are missing. A primary molar or canine is presumed missing because of dental caries when it has been lost before normal exfoliation.
f	Primary molars and canines (or surfaces) that have a restoration but are without caries.

D. Scoring

▶ *Calculation*: Example 1: individual dmf

- A 7-year-old boy has all primary molars and canines present. Examination reveals two carious surfaces on one molar tooth, one missing canine tooth, and one two-surface amalgam filling on a molar tooth:

dmft $= 1 + 1 + 1 = 3$

dmfs $= 2 + 4 + 2 = 8$

E. Mixed Dentition

Permanent and primary teeth are evaluated separately. A DMFT or DMFS and a dmft or dmfs are never added together.

IV. Early Childhood Caries (ECC and S-ECC)[28]

A. Purpose

To provide case definitions that determine dental caries experience of children 5 years of age or younger.

B. Selection of Teeth or Surfaces

Each surface (mesial, distal, facial, lingual, and occlusal) of each tooth visible in the child's mouth is evaluated. Only primary teeth are scored.

C. Procedure

▶ Visual examination of all surfaces of each erupted tooth.

▶ Criteria for case definition are included in Table 23-1.

D. Scoring

▶ A designation of ECC or S-ECC (severe early childhood caries) for a particular individual relates the age of the child with the status of DMFT surfaces observed.

▶ Community-based surveys identify the percentage of a population with ECC and/or S-ECC.

V. Root Caries Index (RCI)[29]

A. Purpose

To determine total root caries experience for individuals and groups and provide a direct, simple method for recording and making comparisons.

B. Selection of Teeth

▶ Up to four surfaces (mesial, distal, facial, and lingual/palatal) are counted for each tooth.

▶ Only surfaces with visible gingival recession are counted.

▶ Teeth with multiple roots and extreme recession, though rare, could present with two or three lesions on the same surface. In this case, the most severe lesion is selected for recording and each surface is counted only once.

C. Procedure

▶ *Examination*
- Use adequate retraction and light to examine each tooth. Visible recession is shown in Figure 18-16,

TABLE 23-1	ECC Case Definition			
AGE	BIRTH TO 3 YEARS (0–35 MONTHS)	3–4 YEARS (36–47 MONTHS)	4–5 YEARS (48–59 MONTHS)	5–6 YEARS (60–71 MONTHS)
ECC	1 or more teeth with decayed (either cavitated or noncavitated), missing, or filled surfaces			
S-ECC	■ 1 or more teeth with decay (either cavitated or noncavitated) or fillings present on smooth surface enamel OR ■ 1 or more teeth missing due to caries	■ 1 or more cavitated or filled smooth surfaces in primary maxillary anterior teeth ■ 1 or more missing teeth due to caries OR ■ dmfs[a] score ≥4	■ 1 or more cavitated or filled smooth surfaces in primary maxillary anterior teeth ■ 1 or more missing teeth due to caries OR ■ dmfs[a] score ≥5	■ 1 or more cavitated or filled smooth surfaces in primary maxillary anterior teeth ■ 1 or more missing teeth due to caries OR ■ dmfs[a] score ≥6

[a]dmfs = total number of decayed missing and filled surfaces.

Source: Drury TF, Horowitz AM, Ismail AI, et al. Diagnosing and reporting early childhood caries for research purposes. *J Public Health Dent.* 1999;59(3):192–197.

Chapter 18. An example of root caries is shown in Figure 27-2 in Chapter 27.

* Apply current knowledge of the stages of dental caries to prevent damage to remineralizing areas during examination. Only cavitated lesions are recorded.

▶ *Record a rating for each root surface.*

RCI RATING	CRITERIA
No R	Root surface with a covered cementoenamel junction and no visible recession (R = recession).
R – D	Root surface with recession present and root caries present (D = decay).
R – F	Root surface with recession present and the surface is restored (F = filled).
R – N	Root surface with recession, but no caries or restoration is present.
M	The tooth is missing.

D. Scoring

▶ *Calculation:* Formula

$$\frac{[R-D]+[R-F]}{[R-D]+[R-F]+[R-N]} \times 100 = RCI$$

▶ *Calculation:* Example individual RCI
* A man, aged 70, presents with 23 natural teeth (23 × 4 = 92 surfaces). Clinical examination reveals:

R – D = 26
R – F = 8
R – N = 58

$$RCI = \frac{26+8}{26+8+58} = \frac{37}{92} \times 100 = 36.9\%$$

▶ *Interpretation*
* A score of 36.9% means that of all tooth surfaces with visible gingival recession, 36.9% have a history of root caries (cavitated or restored) carious lesions.

▶ *Group or community RCI*
* The R – D, R – F, and R – N scores for all individuals in the group are added together and the RCI formula is calculated using the total scores.

DENTAL FLUOROSIS

Dental indices such as the Thylstrup–Fejerskov index,[30] the fluorosis risk index,[31] and the developmental defects of dental enamel index[32,33] have been used to investigate the effects of fluoride concentration on dental enamel. The two indices described here are the most commonly used for community-based assessment.

I. Dean's Fluorosis Index[34]

A. Purpose

To measure the prevalence and severity of dental fluorosis.

▶ Originally developed in the 1930s and refined in 1942 to relate the severity of hypomineralization of dental enamel to concentration of fluoride in the water supply.

▶ Considered less sensitive than some other measures of fluorosis, but still recommended for use in community studies.

B. Selection of Teeth

The smooth surface enamel of all teeth is examined.

C. Procedure

Each tooth is visually examined for signs of fluorosis and assigned a numerical score using the descriptive categories listed in Table 23-2.

TABLE 23-2	Scoring System for Dean's Fluorosis Index	
CATEGORY	**DESCRIPTION**	**NUMERICAL SCORE**
Normal	Smooth, creamy white tooth surface	0
Questionable	Slight changes from normal transparency	1
Very mild	Small, scattered opaque areas; less than 25% of tooth surface	2
Mild	Opaque areas; less than 50% of tooth surface	3
Moderate	Significant opaque and/or worn areas; may have brown stains	4
Severe	Widespread, significant hypoplasia, pitting, brown staining, worn areas, and/or a corroded appearance	5

Source: Dean HT. The investigation of physiological effect by the epidemiological method. In: Moulton FR, ed. *Fluorine and Dental Health*. Washington, DC: American Association for the Advancement of Science; 1942:23–71.

D. Scoring

▶ An individual fluorosis score is assigned using the highest numerical score recorded for two or more teeth.

▶ Community levels of fluorosis are indicated by the percentage of individuals in the sample or population that receive scores in each category.

II. Tooth Surface Index of Fluorosis (TSIF)[35]

A. Purpose

▶ To measure the prevalence and severity of dental fluorosis.

▶ More sensitive than Dean's index in identifying the mildest signs of fluorosis.

B. Selection of Teeth

The smooth surface enamel, cusp tips, and incisal edges of all teeth are examined.

C. Procedure

Each tooth is examined visually and assigned a numerical score using the criteria in Table 23-3.

D. Scoring

TSIF data are presented as a distribution citing the percent of the population with each numerical score, rather than as mean scores for the entire group.

TABLE 23-3	Scoring System for TSIF	
DESCRIPTION		**NUMERICAL SCORE**
No evidence of fluorosis		0
Areas with parchment-white color; less than 1/3 of visible tooth surface; includes fluorosis confined to anterior incisal edges and posterior cusp tips		1
Parchment-white color on at least 1/3 but less than 2/3 of visible tooth surface		2
Parchment-white color on at least 2/3 of visible tooth surface		3
Staining (from light to very dark brown) in conjunction with parchment white areas as described above in levels 1, 2, or 3		4
Discrete stained and rough pitted areas, but no staining on intact enamel surfaces		5
Discrete pitting plus staining of intact enamel surfaces		6
Confluent pitting over large areas of tooth surface; anatomy of tooth may be altered; dark-brown stain usually present		7

Source: Horowitz HS, Driscoll WS, Meyers RJ, et al. A new method for assessing the prevalence of dental fluorosis—the tooth surface index of Fluorosis. *J Am Dent Assoc.* 1984;109(1):37–41.

COMMUNITY-BASED ORAL HEALTH SURVEILLANCE

Community oral health screenings can be performed at every level; local, national, and worldwide. Data collected by such screenings are useful for monitoring health status and determining population access to or need for oral health services.

I. WHO Basic Screening Survey (BSS)[21]

The World Health Organization (WHO) screening survey includes the CPI and the LOA indices previously described in this chapter.

A. Purpose

To collect comprehensive data on oral health status and dental treatment needs of a population. This system is suitable for surveying both adults and children.

B. Tissues/Areas Examined

Survey categories include the following:

▶ Orofacial (intraoral and extraoral) lesions and anomalies

▶ Temporomandibular joint status

▶ Periodontal status

▶ Dentition status and treatment need

▶ Prosthetic status and need

▶ Need for immediate care/referral.

C. Procedures

▶ Standardized assessment form with boxes for data entry identifies the codes and descriptive criteria for each data collection category.

▶ Standardized codes facilitate computerized data entry and analysis.

▶ Photographs in the training manual provide examples of criteria for each code.

D. Scoring

▶ Data can be analyzed by survey team or arrangements can be made for data entry forms to be analyzed by the WHO.

II. Association of State and Territorial Dental Directors (ASTDD) Basic Screening Survey (BSS)[6]

A. Purpose

▶ *Developed by the Association of State and Territorial Dental Directors (ASTDD) to provide oral screening for adult, school age, and/or preschool populations.*

• Data levels are consistent with monitoring the United States Public Health Service national health objectives.

• Data collected can easily be compared with data collected by other communities and states using the data collection techniques.

▶ *The system was designed to be used by screeners with or without dental background because:*

• Sometimes nondental personnel have better access to some population groups.

• Some communities have little access to dental public health professionals.

B. Selection of Teeth

All teeth are examined, but each individual patient receives one score for each category.

C. Procedure

▶ Oral screening can be combined with an optional questionnaire that collects additional data on demographics and access to dental care.

▶ Screeners are trained and calibrated. They record oral findings using photographs and detailed descriptions of associated criteria.

D. Scoring

▶ Table 23-4 outlines the scoring criteria and categories recorded for preschool and school children.

▶ Table 23-5 lists the scoring criteria and categories recorded for older adults.

▶ Data from each indicator can be compiled and expressed in frequency graphs or tables as a percentage of the population that exhibits a specific category trait.

DOCUMENTATION

Factors related to dental indices to document in the patient records include:

▶ Name of the index or indices used

▶ Score calculated for the index

▶ Objective statement that provides an interpretation of the index score

▶ Follow-up instructions provided to the patient

▶ An example of documentation for use of a dental index appears in Box 23-2.

TABLE 23-4	ASTDD BSS Scoring Criteria: Preschool and School Children		
CRITERIA	**SCORE**	**PRESCHOOLERS**	**SCHOOL CHILDREN**
Untreated caries (≥½ mm discontinuity in tooth surface)	0 = No untreated caries 1 = Untreated caries	√	√
Treated decay (amalgam, composite, or temporary filling)	0 = No treated decay 1 = Treated decay	√	√
ECC (3 years old with one or more 6 maxillary anterior teeth that were ever decayed, filled, or missing due to caries)	0 = No ECC 1 = ECC	√	
Sealants on permanent molars	0 = No sealants 1 = Sealants		√
Treatment urgency	0 = No obvious problem (routine dental care indicated) 1 = Early dental care (within two wks) 2 = Urgent care (as soon as possible—presents with pain, swelling, etc.)	√	√

A √ mark indicates that the oral condition category is scored in that particular age group. Some categories (i.e., sealants) are not scored in all age groups.
Source: Association of State and Territorial Dental Directors. *Basic Screening Surveys: An Approach to Monitoring Community Oral Health: Preschool and School Children.* Sparks, NV: ASTDD; 2008:36.

EVERYDAY ETHICS

Susanna began practicing in the team clinic at the dental school and found the work to be very challenging. As a hygienist, she was not only providing preventive treatment for patients but was also responsible for data collection for several research projects. Suddenly, the importance of understanding and calculating the various indices became critical. In particular, Susanna found herself reviewing the procedures for the OHI-S, bleeding indices, and the DMFT.

Susanna had always enjoyed her clinical interactions with patients, but now scoring and recording information on each and every tooth was beginning to cause her some stress. Generally Susanna practiced without an assistant and found it difficult to do both examining and recording. Near the end of one day when she was organizing the day's work for Dr. Lowe's caries study, she discovered that she had omitted several surfaces in one quadrant. This was the patient's final visit to the dental school. Susanna contemplated what to do when she realized the data were missing.

Questions for Consideration

1. Discuss how American Dental Hygienists' Association's roles for dental hygienists (Chapter 1) apply to Suzanna's daily duties.

2. Can Susanna "defend" her actions to Dr. Lowe by submitting the data she does have on the patient? Explain your rationale.

3. Which of the core values (Table II-1, Section II Introduction) or principles of ethical behavior come into play in collecting research data such as described in this scenario?

TABLE 23-5	ASTDD BSS Scoring Criteria: Older Adults
CRITERIA	**SCORE**
Removable upper denture	0 = No 1 = Yes
If yes Do you wear upper denture when eating?	0 = No 1 = Yes
Removable lower denture	0 = No 1 = Yes
If yes Do you wear lower denture when eating?	0 = No 1 = Yes
Number of upper natural teeth (include root fragments)	Range 0–16
Number of lower natural teeth (include root fragments)	Range 0–16
Root fragments	0 = No 1 = Yes 9 = Edentulous
Untreated decay	0 = No 1 = Yes 9 = Edentulous
Need for periodontal care	0 = No 1 = Yes 9 = Edentulous
Suspicious soft tissue lesions	0 = No 1 = Yes 9 = Edentulous
Treatment urgency	0 = no obvious problem—next scheduled visit 1 = Early care—within next several weeks 2 = Urgent care—within next week—pain or infection.

Source: Association of State and Territorial Dental Directors. *Basic Screening Surveys: An Approach to Monitoring Community Oral Health:Older Adults*. Sparks, NV: ASTDD; 2010:40–41.

BOX 23-2

Example Documentation: Use of a Dental Index During Patient Assessment

S –Patient presents for reassessment of biofilm and bleeding levels 14 days following oral hygiene instructions that were provided during the previous appointment.

O –Biofilm-free score = 89% compared to previous score of 22%; SBI score = 2 compared to previous score of 5.

A –Significant improvement noted in scores except on maxillary facial surfaces.

P –Patient congratulated on areas of success. Additional instruction provided specifically related to biofilm removal on posterior facial and proximal tooth surfaces. Patient observed while brushing and flossing maxillary molar areas using a mirror.

Next Step: 3 months re-evaluation.

Signed _____, RDH

Date _____

Factors To Teach Patient or Members of the Community

▷ How an index is used and calculated, and what the scores mean.
▷ Purpose for the selection of the particular index being used.
▷ Correlation of index scores with current oral health practices and procedures.
▷ Procedures to follow to improve index scores and bring the oral tissues to health.

References

NOTE: Many of the citations below may seem not to be current or even completely out-of-date, however the reader will note that most are "classic" references, which refer to the development and first use of the index.

1. Silness J, Loe H. Periodontal disease in pregnancy. II. Correlation between oral hygiene and periodontal condition. *Acta Odontol Scand*. 1964;22:121–135.

2. Podshadley AG, Haley JV. A method for evaluating oral hygiene performance. *Public Health Rep*. 1968;83(3):259–264.

3. Klein H, Palmer CE, Knutson JW. Studies on dental caries. I. Dental status and dental needs of elementary school children. *Public Health Rep*. 1938;53(19):751–765.

4. United States Department of Health and Human Services. *Oral Health in America: A Report of the Surgeon General*. Rockville, MD: U.S. Department of Health and Human Services, National Institute of Dental and Craniofacial Research, National Institutes of Health; 2000:63–89.

5. United States Department of Health and Human Services. *Healthy People 2020: Topics and Objectives: Oral Health*. Washington, DC: U.S. Department of Health and Human

Services; 2010. http://www.healthypeople.gov/2020/topics-objectives/topic/oral-health. Accessed May 19, 2015.

6. Association of State and Territorial Dental Directors. *Basic Screening Surveys*. Reno, NV: ASTDD; 2014. http://www.astdd.org/basic-screening-survey-tool/. Accessed March 19, 2014.

7. Löe H. The gingival index, the plaque index and the retention index systems. *J Periodontol*. 1967;38(6, Suppl):610–616.

8. O'Leary TJ, Drake RB, Naylor JE. The plaque control record. *J Periodontol*. 1972;43(1):38.

9. Ramfjord SP, Ash MM. *Periodontology and Periodontics*. Philadelphia, PA: WB Saunders Co; 1979:273.

10. Grant DA, Stern IB, Everett FG. *Periodontics*. 5th ed. St. Louis, MO: Mosby; 1979:529–531.

11. Greene JC, Vermillion JR. The simplified oral hygiene index. *J Am Dent Assoc*. 1964;68:7–13.

12. Greene JC. The Oral Hygiene Index—development and uses. *J Periodontol*. 1967;38(6, Suppl):625–637.

13. Schour I, Massler M. Prevalence of gingivitis in young adults. *J Dent Res*. 1948;27(6):733. Abstract #33 in IADR scientific proceedings.

14. Massler M. The P-M-A index for the assessment of gingivitis. *J Periodontol*. 1967;38(6, Suppl):592–601.

15. Russell AL. A system of classification and scoring for prevalence surveys of periodontal disease. *J Dent Res*. 1956;35(3):350–359.

16. Mühlemann HR, Son, S. Gingival sulcus bleeding—a leading symptom in initial gingivitis. *Helv Odontol Acta*. 1971;15(2):107–113.

17. Meitner SW, Zander HA, Iker HP, et al. Identification of inflamed gingival surfaces. *J Clin Periodontol*. 1979;6(2):93–97.

18. American Academy of Periodontology. Parameter on comprehensive periodontal examination. *J Periodontol*. 2000;71(5, Suppl):847–848.

19. Khocht A, Zohn H, Deasy M, et al. Assessment of periodontal status with PSR and traditional clinical periodontal examination. *J Am Dent Assoc*. 1995;126(12):1658–1665.

20. Ainamo J, Barmes D, Beagrie G, et al. Development of the World Health Organization (WHO) community periodontal index of treatment needs (CPITN). *Int Dent J*. 1982;32(3):281–291.

21. World Health Organization. *Oral Health Surveys: Basic Methods*. Geneva: WHO; 1997:26–39.

22. Carter HG, Barnes GP. The gingival bleeding index. *J Periodontol*. 1974;45(11):801–805.

23. Abrams K, Caton J, Polson A. Histologic comparisons of interproximal gingival tissues related to the presence or absence of bleeding. *J Periodontol*. 1984;55(11):629–632.

24. Caton JG, Polson, AM. The interdental bleeding index: a simplified procedure for monitoring gingival health. *Compend Contin Educ Dent*. 1985;6(2):88, 90–92.

25. Ramfjord SP. Indices for prevalence and incidence of periodontal disease. *J Periodontol*. 1959;30:51–59.

26. United States Department of Health and Human Services, Public Health Service, National Institutes of Health. *Oral Health Surveys of the National Institute of Dental Research, Diagnostic Criteria and Procedures*. Bethesda, MD: National Institute of Dental Research; 1991. NIH Publication No. 91-2870.

27. Gruebbel AO. A measurement of dental caries prevalence and treatment service for deciduous teeth. *J Dent Res*. 1944;23:163–168.

28. Drury TF, Horowitz AM, Ismail AI, et al. Diagnosing and reporting early childhood caries for research purposes. *J Public Health Dent*. 1999;59(3):192–197.

29. Katz RV. Assessing root caries in populations: the evolution of the root caries index. *J Public Health Dent*. 1980;40(1):7–16.

30. Thylstrup A, Fejerskov O. Clinical appearance of dental fluorosis in permanent teeth in relation to histologic changes. *Community Dent Oral Epidemiol*. 1978;6(6):315–328.

31. Pendrys DG. The fluorosis risk index: a method for investigating risk factors. *J Public Health Dent*. 1990;50(5):291–298.

32. Fédération Dentaire Internationale. An epidemiological index of developmental defects of dental enamel (DDE Index). Commission on Oral Health, Research and Epidemiology. *Int Dent J*. 1982;32(2):159–167.

33. Clarkson J, O'Mullane, D. A modified DDE index for use in epidemiological studies of enamel defects. *J Dent Res*. 1989;68(3):445–450.

34. Dean HT. The investigation of physiological effect by the epidemiological method. In: Moulton FR, ed. *Fluorine and Dental Health*. Washington, DC: American Association for the Advancement of Science; 1942:23–71.

35. Horowitz HS, Driscoll WS, Meyers RJ, et al. A new method for assessing the prevalence of dental fluorosis—the tooth surface index of fluorosis. *J Am Dent Assoc*. 1984;109(1):37–41.

ENHANCE YOUR UNDERSTANDING

thePoint® DIGITAL CONNECTIONS
(see the inside front cover for access information)

- **Audio glossary**
- **Quiz bank**

SUPPORT FOR LEARNING
(available separately; visit lww.com)

- ***Active Learning Workbook for Clinical Practice of the Dental Hygienist, 12th Edition***

prepU INDIVIDUALIZED REVIEW
(available separately; visit lww.com)

- **Adaptive quizzing with *prepU for Wilkins' Clinical Practice of the Dental Hygienist***

Oral Infection Control: Toothbrushes and Toothbrushing

Christine Macarelli-Rogers, RDH, MS and Karen A. Raposa, RDH, MBA

CHAPTER OUTLINE

LEARNING OBJECTIVES

After studying this chapter, the student will be able to:

1. Identify characteristics of effective manual and power toothbrushes.

2. Differentiate between the different manual toothbrushing methods including limitations and benefits of each.

3. Describe the different motions of action for powered toothbrushes.

4. Identify the basis for powered toothbrush selection.

5. Describe tongue cleaning and its effect on reducing dental biofilm.

6. Identify negative effects improper toothbrushing can have on hard and soft tissues.

INTRODUCTION

▶ The personal oral healthcare plan for prevention interventions is determined by assessing each patient's oral health needs, dental caries risk factors, periodontal infection risk factors, and the patient's ability to perform self-care procedures.

▶ The dental hygienist has a professional ethical obligation to review current research and select appropriate methods and oral care devices that meets the needs of each patient or parent/caregiver.

▶ An objective for the dental hygienist is to teach and motivate each patient and the caregiver to maintain the oral cavity in a clean healthy state.

▶ Personal daily care requires the following sequence of procedures at least two times each day:
  • Use dental floss first to remove biofilm from proximal surfaces and debris that may have collected in the interproximal embrasures.
  • Flossing before brushing allows access of the proximal tooth surfaces and interdental gingiva to fluoride and other agents in the toothpaste for dental caries prevention and gingival health.
  • Toothbrushing follows flossing to remove the adhering biofilm from tooth surfaces and to apply preventive agents to the gingival tissues and teeth.
  • A final step in oral cleanliness and health is to clean the tongue.

▶ The toothbrush has been the principal instrument in general use for oral care and is a necessary part of oral disease control. Many different designs of both manual and power toothbrushes have been manufactured and promoted. Uses of the toothbrush include the following:
  • Dental biofilm removal
  • Application of preventive agents
  • Contribute to halitosis control
  • Sanitation of oral cavity.

▶ Patients who have not previously received professional advice concerning the best brush for their particular oral conditions may have used brushes selected on the following criteria:
  • Cost
  • Availability
  • Advertising claims
  • Family tradition
  • Habit.

▶ Because of the variety of brushes currently available, and the constant development of new brushes, dental professionals need to maintain a high level of knowledge on these products to advise patients appropriately.

▶ Key words relating to toothbrushes are listed in Box 28-1 with their definitions.

DEVELOPMENT OF TOOTHBRUSHES

▶ Crudely contrived toothpicks, presumably used for relief from food impaction, are believed to be the earliest implements devised for the care of the teeth.

▶ Excavations in Mesopotamia uncovered elaborate gold toothpicks used by the Sumerians about 3000 B.C.

▶ The earliest record of the "chewstick," which has been considered the primitive toothbrush, dates back in the Chinese literature to about 1600 B.C. The care of the mouth was associated with religious training and ritual: the Buddhists had a "toothstick," and the Mohammedans used the "miswak" or "siwak." Chewsticks, made from various types of woods by crushing an end and spreading the fibers in a brush-like manner, are still used in several regions of the world.[1]

▶ The *Ebers Papyrus*, compiled about 1500 B.C. and dating probably to about 4000 B.C., contained reference to oral conditions similar to periodontal diseases and to preparations used as mouthwashes and dentifrices. The writings of Hippocrates (about 300 B.C.) include descriptions of diseased gums related to calculus and of complex preparations for the treatment of unhealthy mouths.[1–4]

I. Early Toothbrushes

▶ It is believed the first tooth brush made of hog's bristles was mentioned in the early Chinese literature.

▶ Pierre Fauchard in 1728 in *Le Chirurgien Dentiste* described many aspects of oral health. He condemned the toothbrush made of horse's hair because it was rough and destructive to the teeth and advised the use of sponges or herb roots.

BOX 28-1 KEY WORDS: Toothbrushes

Abrasion (gingiva): lesion of the gingiva that results from mechanical removal of the surface epithelium.

Abrasion (tooth): loss of tooth structure produced by a mechanical cause (such as a hard-bristled toothbrush used with excessive pressure and an abrasive dentifrice); abrasion contrasts with erosion, which involves a chemical process.

Angled: a nylon filament that is placed in the brush head at an angle.

Bristle: individual short, stiff, natural hair of an animal; historically, toothbrush bristles were taken from a hog or wild boar, but current toothbrush bristles are made of nylon and are called filaments.

End-rounded: characteristic shape of each toothbrush filament; a special manufacturing process removes all sharp edges and provides smooth, rounded ends to prevent injury to gingiva or tooth structure during use.

Filament: individual synthetic fiber; a single element of a tuft fixed into a toothbrush head.

Mechanical biofilm control: oral hygiene methods for removal of dental biofilm from tooth surfaces using a toothbrush and selected devices for interdental cleaning;

contrasts with chemotherapeutic biofilm control in which an antimicrobial agent is used.

Power toothbrush: a brush driven by electricity or battery; also called power-assisted, automatic, electric, or mechanical (in contrast with manual toothbrush).

Sonic: a term used to describe a power toothbrush that operates in the audible range of human hearing.

Stiffness: the reaction force exerted per unit area of the brush during deflection; the term stiffness is used interchangeably with firmness of toothbrush bristles or filaments; the stiffness depends primarily on the length and diameter of the filaments.

Sulcular brushing: a method in which the end-round filament tips are directed into the gingival sulcus at approximately 45° for the purpose of loosening and removing dental biofilm from both the gingival sulcus and the tooth surface just below the gingival margin.

Toothbrush head: the part of the toothbrush composed of the tufts and the stock (extension of the handle where the tufts are attached).

Tuft: a cluster of bristles or filaments secured together in one hole in the head of a toothbrush.

▶ Fauchard recommended scaling of teeth and developed instruments and splints for loose teeth, as well as dentifrices and mouthwashes.

▶ One of the earlier toothbrushes made in England was produced by William Addis about 1780.

- By the early 19th century, craftsmen in various European countries constructed handles of gold, ivory, or ebony in which replaceable brush heads could be fitted.
- The first patent for a toothbrush in the United States was issued to H. N. Wadsworth in the middle of the 19th century.

▶ Many new varieties of toothbrushes were developed around 1,900, when celluloid was available for the manufacture of toothbrush handles.

- In 1919, the American Academy of Periodontology defined specifications for toothbrush design and brushing methods in an attempt to standardize professional recommendations.[5]

▶ Nylon came into use in toothbrush construction in 1938.

- World War II prevented Chinese export of wild boar bristles so synthetic materials were substituted for natural bristles.
- Since then, synthetic materials have been improved and manufacturers' specifications standardized.
- Most toothbrushes are made exclusively of synthetic materials.

▶ Power toothbrushes, although developed earlier, were not actively promoted until the 1960s.

II. Early Brushing Methods

▶ Historically, the purpose of brushing was to provide *massage* to increase the disease resistance of the gingival tissue.

- Massage or friction from a hard-bristled brush was believed to *increase keratinization*, which, in turn, resulted in the resistance to bacterial invasion.[5]

▶ As quoted in Box 28-2, Koecker described, in 1842, a "new" method for daily care of teeth.[6] This early work proved to be a forerunner of contemporary oral care.

BOX 28-2

Historical Perspective on Proper Toothbrushing Instruction

Koecker, in 1842,[6] wrote that after the dentist has scaled off the tartar, the patient will clean the teeth every morning and after every meal with a hard brush and an astringent powder. For the inner surfaces, he recommended a conical-shaped brush of fine hog's bristles. For the outer surfaces, he believed in an oblong brush made of the "best white horsehair." He instructed the patient to press hard against the gums so the bristles go between the teeth and "between the edges of the gums and the roots of the teeth. The pressure of the brush is to be applied in the direction from the crowns of the teeth towards the roots, so that the mucus, which adheres to the roots under the edges of the gums, may be completely detached, and after that, removed by the friction in a direction towards the grinding surfaces."

MANUAL TOOTHBRUSHES

I. Characteristics of an Effective Toothbrush[7]

▶ Conforms to individual patient requirements in size, shape, and texture.

▶ Easily and efficiently manipulated.

▶ Readily cleaned and aerated; impervious to moisture.

▶ Durable and inexpensive.

▶ Functional properties of flexibility, softness, and diameter of the bristles or filaments, and of strength, rigidity, and lightness of the handle.

▶ End-rounded filaments.

▶ Designed for utility, efficiency, and cleanliness.

II. General Description

A. Parts (Figure 28-1)

▶ *Handle*: the part grasped in the hand during toothbrushing.

▶ *Head*: the working end; consists of tufts of bristles or filaments and the stock where the tufts are secured.

▶ *Shank*: the section that connects the head and the handle.

B. Dimensions

▶ *Total brush length*: about 15–19 cm (6–7.5 inches); junior and child sizes are shorter.

▶ *Head*: large enough to accommodate the tufts.

  • Length of brushing plane, 25.4–31.8 mm (1–11/4 inches); width, 7.9–9.5 mm (5/16–3/8 inch).

  • Bristle or filament height, 11 mm (7/16 inch).

III. Handle

A. Composition

▶ *Manufacturing specifications*: Most often a single type of plastic, or a combination of polymers.

▶ *Properties*: Combines durability, imperviousness to moisture, pleasing appearance, low cost, and sufficient maneuverability.

B. Shape

▶ *Preferred characteristics*

  • Easy to grasp.
  • Does not slip or rotate during use.
  • No sharp corners or projections.
  • Lightweight, consistent with strength.

▶ *Variations*

  • A twist, curve, offset, or angle in the shank with or without thumb rests may assist the patient in adaptation of the brush to difficult-to-reach areas.

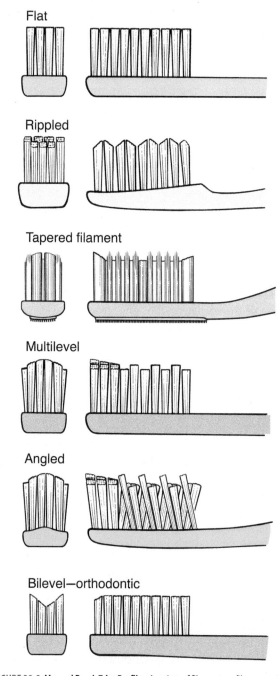

Flat

Rippled

Tapered filament

Multilevel

Angled

Bilevel—orthodontic

FIGURE 28-2 Manual Brush Trim Profiles. A variety of filament profiles are available. In addition to the classic flat planed brush, other trims include the rippled, tapered filaments, bilevel, multilevel, and angled. Brushes for use over orthodontic appliances are made with various bilevel shapes.

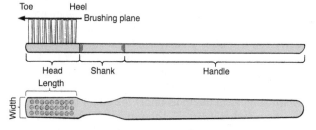

FIGURE 28-1 Parts of a Toothbrush.

- A handle of larger diameter may be useful for patients with limited dexterity, such as children, aging patients, and those with a disability.

IV. Brush Head

A. Design

▶ *Length*: May be 5–12 tufts long and 3–4 rows wide.

▶ *Spacing*: Tufts that are widely spaced allow for easy cleaning. Those closely spaced allow the filaments to support each other.

▶ *Arrangement*: Tufts may be of a consistent shape on the brush head or varied as shown in Figure 28-2.

B. Brushing Plane (Profile)

▶ *Trim*: Variously shaped filament profiles.

▶ *Length*: Range from filaments of equal lengths (flat planes) to those with variable lengths, such as rippled, tapered, bilevel, multilevel, and angled (Figure 28-2).

▶ *Properties*: Soft and end-rounded for safety to oral soft tissues and tooth structure.

▶ *Efficiency in biofilm removal*: Efficiency for cleaning the hard-to-reach areas, such as extension onto proximal surfaces, malpositioned teeth, or exposed root surfaces, depends on individual patient abilities and understanding.

V. Bristles and Filaments

▶ Most current toothbrushes have nylon filaments.

- Natural bristles are relatively unsanitary, and their physical qualifications cannot be standardized.

- A comparison of natural bristles and synthetic filaments is reviewed in Table 28-1.

▶ Many manufacturers of synthetic filaments continue to refer to filaments as "bristles" when communicating with consumers on the toothbrush package and in advertising.

- Dental professionals need to be aware that most manufacturers of toothbrushes today produce brushes using "synthetic filaments" but still refer to these as "bristles."

▶ Companies that produce a toothbrush with "natural bristles" will distinguish themselves by using the word "natural" in the product description.

A. Factors Influencing Stiffness

The stiffness depends on the diameter and length of the filament. Brushes designated as soft, medium, or hard are not comparatively consistent between manufacturers.

▶ *Diameter*: Thinner filaments are softer and more resilient.

▶ *Length*: Shorter filaments are stiffer and have less flexibility.

▶ *Number of filaments in a tuft*: Increased density of filaments and tufts give added support to adjacent filaments, thus increasing the feeling of stiffness.

▶ *Angle of filaments*: Angled filaments may be more flexible and less stiff than straight filaments of equal length and diameter; there is no straight end-line force applied as with the straight filament.

B. End-Rounding

▶ *Process of end-rounding*: Each nylon filament is sealed and rounded by heat treatment. The quality of end-rounding varies depending on manufacturers.[8] Natural bristles cannot be end-rounded.

TABLE 28-1	Comparison of Natural Bristles and Synthetic Filaments	
	NATURAL BRISTLES	**FILAMENTS**
Source	Historically made from hair of hog or wild boar	Synthetic, plastic materials, primarily nylon
Uniformity	No uniformity of texture. Diameter or wearing properties depending upon the breed of animal, geographical location, and season in which the bristles were gathered	Uniformity controlled during manufacturing
Diameter	Varies depending on portion of bristle taken, age, and life of animal	Range from extra soft at 0.075 mm (0.003 inch) to hard at 0.3 mm (0.012 inch)
End shape	Deficient, irregular, frequently open ended	End-rounded to ensure fewer traumas. There is a direct relation between gingival damage and the absence of end-rounding[8,9]; Figure 28-3 shows examples of nonrounded and end-rounded filaments[10]
Advantages and disadvantages	■ Cannot be standardized ■ Wear rapidly and irregularly ■ Hollow ends allow microorganisms and debris to collect inside	■ Rinse clean, dry rapidly ■ Durable and maintain longer ■ End-rounded and closed, repel debris and water ■ More resistant to accumulation of microorganisms

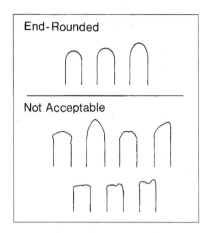

FIGURE 28-3 End-Rounded Filaments. Examples of the shape of acceptable end-rounding and of those that are not acceptable are shown. (Adapted from: Silverstone LM, Featherstone MJ. A scanning electron microscope study of the end rounding of bristles in eight toothbrush types. *Quintessence Int.* 1988;19(2):87–107 and Checchi L, Minguzzi S, Franchi M, et al. Toothbrush filaments end-rounding: stereomicroscope analysis. *J Clin Periodontol.* 2001;28(4):360–364.)

▶ *Effect*: A direct relation exists between gingival damage and the absence of end-rounding.[9,10]

▶ *Examples*: Figure 28-3 shows examples of nonrounded and end-rounded filaments.

TOOTHBRUSH SELECTION FOR THE PATIENT

I. Influencing Factors

Factors influencing the selection of the proper manual or power toothbrush for an individual patient include the following:

A. Patient

▶ Ability of the patient to use the brush and remove dental biofilm from tooth surfaces without damage to the soft tissue or tooth structure.

▶ Manual dexterity of the patient.

▶ The age of the patient and the differences in the dentition and dexterity.

B. Gingiva

▶ Status of gingival and periodontal health.

▶ Anatomic configurations of the gingiva.

C. Position of Teeth

Displaced teeth require variations in brush placement:

▶ Crowded teeth

▶ Open contacts.

D. Compliance

▶ Patient preference may dictate which method and which brush is recommended.

▶ Patient may have preferences and may resist change.

▶ Patient may lack motivation, ability, or willingness to follow the prescribed procedure.

E. Method Selected

Professional personnel may prefer to instruct patients in certain methods and with certain brushes.

II. Toothbrush Size and Shape

▶ Brush head selection is dependent on the patient's ability to maneuver and adapt the brush correctly to all facial, lingual, palatal, and occlusal surfaces for dental biofilm removal.

▶ Multilevel brush heads have been shown to be beneficial and were developed on the basis of their ability to improve cleaning performance and to reach critical sites easier (i.e., interproximal and at the gingival margin).[11]

III. Soft Nylon Brush

The following are suggested as advantages for the appropriate use of a soft end-rounded brush.

▶ More effective in cleaning the cervical areas, both proximal and marginal.

▶ Less traumatic to the gingival tissue; therefore, patients can brush the cervical areas without fear of discomfort or soft tissue laceration.

▶ Can be directed into the sulcus for sulcular brushing and into interproximal areas for partially cleaning of the proximal surfaces.

▶ Applicable around fixed orthodontic appliances or fixation appliances used to treat a fractured jaw.

▶ Tooth abrasion and/or gingival recession can be prevented or may be less severe in an overvigorous brusher.

▶ More effective for sensitive gingiva in such conditions such as necrotizing ulcerative gingivitis or severe gingivitis, or during healing stages following scaling and debridement or periodontal surgery.

▶ Small size is ideal for a young child as a first brush on primary teeth.

GUIDELINES FOR MANUAL TOOTHBRUSHING

▶ Comprehensive toothbrushing instruction for a patient involves teaching what, when, where, and how.

▶ In addition to description of specific toothbrushing methods, the succeeding sections consider the grasp of the brush, the sequence and amount of brushing, the areas of limited access, and supplementary brushing for the occlusal surfaces and the tongue.

▶ The possible detrimental effects from improper toothbrushing and variations for special conditions are described.

I. Grasp of Brush

A. Objectives

▶ Grasp and manipulate the brush for successful removal of dental biofilm.

▶ Provide patients with specific instruction in how to hold and place the brush.

▶ Remove dental biofilm that has been colored with a disclosing agent to show the tenaciousness of the biofilm and the need for controlled pressure.

▶ Using a light, comfortable grasp, the following can be expected:

- Control of the brush during all movements.
- Effective positioning at the beginning of each brushing stroke, follow-through during the complete stroke, and repositioning for the next stroke.
- Sensitivity to the amount of pressure applied.

B. Procedure

▶ Grasp toothbrush handle in the palm of the hand with thumb against the shank.

- Near enough to the head of the brush so it can be controlled effectively.
- Not so close to the head of the brush that manipulation of the brush is hindered or fingers can touch the anterior teeth when reaching the brush head to molar regions.

▶ Position filaments in the proper direction for placement on the teeth; direction depends on the brushing method to be used.

▶ Adapt grasp for the various positions of the brush head on the teeth throughout the procedure; adjust to permit unrestricted movement of the wrist and arm.

▶ Apply appropriate pressure for removal of the dental biofilm. Too much pressure, however, bends the filaments and curves them away from the area where brushing is needed.

II. Sequence

▶ The procedure in brushing, for any method, needs to ensure complete coverage for each tooth surface.

▶ Divide the mouth into quadrants.

▶ Start brushing from a molar region of one arch around to the midline facial then lingual.

▶ Use brush in vertical position for narrow anterior teeth.

▶ Repeat in the opposing arch.

▶ Each brush placement will overlap the previous one for thorough coverage as shown in Figure 28-4.

▶ Encourage the patient to begin by brushing one of the areas of greatest individual need as shown by disclosing agent.

- Areas most frequently missed.
- Areas most difficult for brush placement and/or manipulation, such as the right side for the right-handed brusher or the left side for the left-handed brusher.

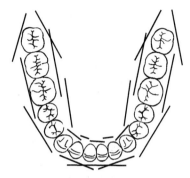

FIGURE 28-4 **Brushing Positions.** Each brush position, as represented by a black line, will overlap the previous position. Note placement at canines, where the distal aspect of the canine is brushed with the premolars and the mesial aspect is brushed with the incisors. Short lines on the lingual anterior aspect indicate brush placed vertically. The maxillary teeth require a similar number of brushing positions.

▶ Suggest the sequence be varied at least once each day so that the same areas are not always brushed last when time may be limited and biofilm removal may be less complete.

III. Amount of Brushing

▶ The main consideration is the removal of the dental biofilm. For infection control, dental biofilm needs to be removed from all surfaces of all teeth as completely as possible daily.

▶ The number of strokes and length of time spent depend on the patient's ability and efficiency in accomplishing the task.

A. The Count System

To ensure thorough coverage with an even distribution in the amount of brushing and to help the patient concentrate on the performance, a system of counting can be useful.

▶ Count the number of strokes in each area (or 5 or 10, whichever is most appropriate for the particular patient) for modified Stillman or other method in which a stroke is used.

▶ Count slowly to 10 for each brush position while brush is vibrated and filament ends are held in position for the Bass, Charters, or other vibratory method.

B. The Clock System

Some patients brush thoroughly while watching a clock or an egg timer for 3 or 4 minutes. Timed procedures cannot guarantee thorough coverage, because single areas that are most accessible may get more brushing time.

C. Combination

For many patients, the use of the "count" system in combination with the "clock" system produces the most complete removal of dental biofilm.

D. Built-in Timers

▶ Many power toothbrushes have built-in timers that signal lapsed time.

▶ Signals may be set for 30 seconds, 1 or 2 minutes.

▶ Timers can motivate patients to increase the total time spent brushing.

IV. Frequency of Brushing

▶ Because of individual variations, one set rule for frequency cannot be applied. The emphasis in patient education is placed on complete biofilm removal daily rather than on the number of brushings.

▶ For the control of dental biofilm, and for oral sanitation and halitosis control, at least two brushings, accompanied by appropriate interdental care, are recommended as a *minimum* for each day.

▶ The longer the bacteria remain undisturbed, the greater the pathogenic potential of the biofilm bacteria.

▶ A clean mouth before going to sleep is encouraged. Bacteria thrive in the dark, warm, moist climate of the oral environment.

▶ Patients who use a chewable fluoride tablet, mouthrinse, or gel application before going to bed need to complete their biofilm removal before fluoride application.

METHODS FOR MANUAL TOOTHBRUSHING

▶ Most toothbrushing methods can be classified based on the position and motion of the brush.

▶ Some of these methods are recorded for descriptive, comparative, or historic purposes only and are not currently recommended. A few may have been shown to be detrimental.

▶ Methods include the following:
- Sulcular: Bass
- Roll: Rolling stroke, modified Stillman
- Vibratory: Stillman, Charters, Bass
- Circular: Fones
- Vertical: Leonard
- Horizontal
- Physiologic: Smith
- Scrub-brush

THE BASS METHOD: SULCULAR BRUSHING

The Bass method is widely accepted as an effective method for dental biofilm removal adjacent to and directly beneath the gingival margin. The areas at the gingival margin and in the col are the most significant in the control of gingival and periodontal infections.

I. Purposes and Indications

▶ For all patients for dental biofilm removal adjacent to and directly beneath the gingival margin.

▶ For open embrasures, cervical areas beneath the height of contour of the enamel, and exposed root surfaces.

▶ For the patient who has had periodontal surgery.

▶ For adaptation to abutment teeth, under the gingival border of a fixed partial denture.

II. Procedure

A. Position the Brush

▶ Direct the filaments apically (up for maxillary, down for mandibular teeth).

▶ First position the sides of the filaments parallel with the long axis of the tooth (Figure 28-5A).

▶ From that position, turn the brush head toward the gingival margin to make approximately a 45° angle to the long axis of the tooth (Figure 28-6B).

▶ Direct the filament tips into the gingival sulcus (Figure 28-5A and B).

B. Strokes

▶ Press lightly so the filament tips enter the gingival sulci and embrasures and cover the gingival margin. Do not bend the filaments with excess pressure.

▶ Vibrate the brush back and forth with very short strokes without disengaging the tips of the filaments from the sulci.

▶ Count at least 10 vibrations.

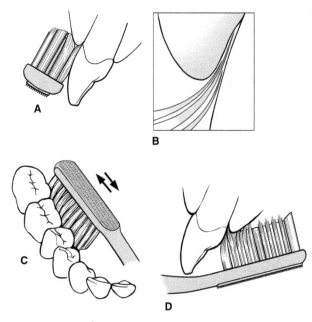

FIGURE 28-5 Sulcular Brushing. A: Filament tips are directed into the gingival sulcus at approximately 45° to the long axis of the tooth. **B:** Brushes designed with tapered filaments reach below the gingival margin with ease. **C:** Brush in position for lingual surfaces of mandibular posterior teeth. **D:** Position for palatal surface of maxillary anterior teeth.

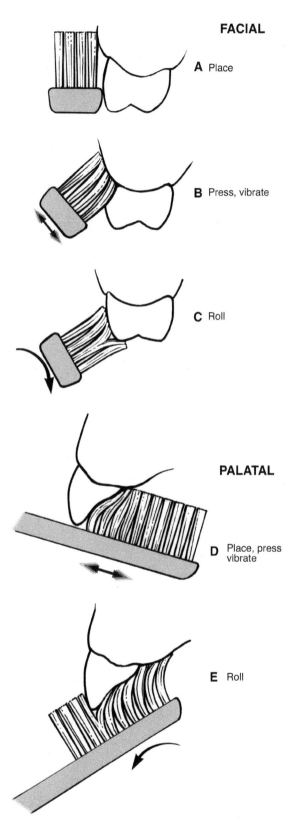

FACIAL

A Place

B Press, vibrate

C Roll

PALATAL

D Place, press
vibrate

E Roll

FIGURE 28-6 **Modified Stillman Method of Brushing. A:** Initial brush placement with sides of bristles or filaments against the attached gingiva. **B:** The brush is pressed and angled, then vibrated. **C:** Vibrating is continued as the brush is rolled slowly over the crown. **D:** Maxillary anterior lingual placement with the brush applied the long way. **E:** Vibrating continues as the brush is rolled over the crown and interdental areas. Placement is similar for the lingual surfaces of the mandibular anterior teeth. The roll or rolling stroke brushing method has the same brush positions.

C. Reposition the Brush

Apply the brush to the next group of two or three teeth. Take care to overlap placement, as shown in Figure 28-4.

D. Repeat Stroke

The entire stroke (steps A–C) is repeated at each position around the maxillary and mandibular arches, both facially and lingually.

E. Position Brush for Lingual and Palatal Anterior Surfaces (Figure 28-5D)

Hold the brush the long narrow way for the anterior components. The filaments are kept straight and directed into the sulci.[12]

III. Limitations

▷ An overeager brusher may convert the previously mentioned "very short strokes" into a vigorous scrub that can cause injury to the gingival margin.

▷ Dexterity requirement may be difficult for certain patients. Because a 45° angle can be difficult to visualize, emphasis is on placing the tips of the filaments into the sulcus.

▷ Rolling stroke procedure may precede the sulcular brushing when a patient believes it helps to clean the teeth. The two methods are performed separately rather than trying to combine them in what has been referred to as a "modified Bass."

▷ The procedure of rolling the brush down over the crown after the vibratory part of the sulcular brush stroke has several disadvantages:
  • Too often the brush is hastily and carelessly replaced into the sulcus position, or the opposite is true, and considerable time is consumed in the attempt to replace the brush carefully.
  • Gingival margin injury by the constant replacement of the brush can result.
  • The patient may tend to roll the brush down over the crown prematurely, thereby accomplishing very little sulcular brushing.

THE ROLL OR ROLLING STROKE METHOD

I. Purposes and Indications

▷ Removing biofilm, materia alba, and food debris from the teeth without emphasis on gingival sulcus.
  • Used for children with relatively healthy gingiva and normal tissue contour, or when a sulcular technique may seem difficult for the patient of any age to master.
  • Intended for general cleaning in conjunction with the use of a vibratory technique (Bass, Charters, Stillman).

▶ Useful for preparatory instruction (first lesson) for modified Stillman method because the initial brush placement is the same.

▶ Can be particularly helpful when there is a question about the patient's ability to master and practice a more complex method.

II. Procedure[4,13]

A. Position the Brush

▶ *Filaments*: Direct filaments apically (up for maxillary, down for mandibular teeth).

▶ *Place side of brush on the attached gingiva*: The filaments are directed apically. When the plastic portion of the brush head is level with the occlusal or incisal plane, generally the brush is at the proper height, as shown in Figure 28-6A.

B. Strokes

▶ *Press to flex the filaments*: The sides of the filaments are pressed lightly against the gingiva. The gingiva will blanch.

▶ *Roll the brush slowly over the teeth*: As the brush is rolled, the wrist is turned slightly. The filaments remain flexed and follow the contours of the teeth, thereby permitting cleaning of the cervical areas. Some filaments may reach interdentally.

C. Replace and Repeat Five Times or More

▶ *Repeat the entire stroke*: The entire stroke (steps A and B) is repeated at least five times for each tooth or group of teeth.

▶ *Rotate the wrist*: When the brush is removed and repositioned, the wrist is rotated.

▶ *Stretch the cheek*: The brush is moved away from the teeth, and the cheek is stretched facially with the back of the brush head. Care is taken not to drag the filament tips over the gingival margin when the brush is returned to the initial position (Figure 28-6A).

D. Overlap Strokes

When moving the brush to an adjacent position, overlap the brush position, as shown in Figure 28-4.

E. Position Brush for Anterior Lingual or Palatal Surfaces

▶ Use the brush the long, narrow way.

▶ Hook the heel of the brush on the incisal edge (Figure 28-6D).

▶ Press (down for maxillary, up for mandibular) until the filaments lie flat against the teeth and gingiva.

▶ Press and roll (curve up for mandibular, down for maxillary teeth).

▶ Replace and repeat five times for each brush width.

III. Limitations

▶ Brushing too high during initial placement can lacerate the alveolar mucosa.

▶ Tendency to use quick, sweeping strokes results in no brushing for the cervical third of the tooth because the brush tips pass over rather than into the area; likewise for the interproximal areas.

▶ Replacing brush with filament tips directed into the gingiva can produce punctate lesions.

THE STILLMAN METHOD

▶ *Purpose*: As originally described by Stillman,[14] the method is designed for massage and stimulation, as well as for cleaning the cervical areas.

▶ *Brush position*: The brush ends are placed partly on the gingiva and partly on the cervical areas of the tooth and directed slightly apically.

▶ *Pressure*: As the tips are pressed lightly, blanching of the tissue occurs.

▶ *Movement*: The handle is given a slight rotary motion, and the brush ends are maintained in position on the tooth surface.

▶ *Repeated*: After several applications, the brush is moved to the adjacent tooth.

THE MODIFIED STILLMAN METHOD

A modified Stillman, which incorporates a rolling stroke after the vibratory (rotary) phase, frequently is used. The modifications minimize the possibility of gingival trauma and increase the biofilm removal effects.[15]

I. Purposes and Indications

▶ Dental biofilm removal from cervical areas below the height of contour of the crown and from exposed proximal surfaces.

▶ General application for cleaning tooth surfaces and massage of the gingiva.

II. Procedure (Figure 28-6)

A. Position the Brush

▶ *Filaments*: Direct filaments apically (up for maxillary, down for mandibular teeth).

▶ *Place side of brush on the attached gingiva*: The filaments are directed apically. When the plastic portion of the brush head is level with the occlusal or incisal plane, generally the brush is at the proper height, as shown in Figure 28-6A.

B. Strokes

▸ *Press to flex the filaments:* The sides of the filaments are pressed lightly against the gingiva. The gingiva will blanch.

▸ *Angle the filaments:* Turn the handle by rotating the wrist so that the filaments are directed at an angle of approximately 45° with the long axis of the tooth.

▸ *Activate the brush:* Use a slight rotary motion. Maintain light pressure on the filaments, and keep the tips of the filaments in position with constant contact. Count to 10 slowly as the brush is vibrated by a rotary motion of the handle.

▸ *Roll and vibrate the brush:* Turn the wrist and work the vibrating brush slowly down over the gingiva and tooth. Make some of the filaments reach interdentally.

C. Replace Brush for Repeat Stroke

Reposition the brush by rotating the wrist. Avoid dragging the filaments back over the free gingival margin by holding the brush out, slightly away from the tooth.

D. Repeat Stroke Five Times or More

The entire stroke (steps A–C) is repeated at least five times for each tooth or group of teeth. When moving the brush to an adjacent position, overlap the brush position, as shown in Figure 28-4.

E. Position Brush for Anterior Lingual and Palatal Surfaces

▸ Position the brush the long, narrow way for the anterior components, as described for the rolling stroke technique and shown in Figure 28-6D and E.

▸ Press and vibrate, roll, and repeat.

III. Limitations

▸ Careful placement of a brush with end-rounded filaments is necessary to prevent tissue laceration. Light pressure is needed.

▸ Patient may try to move the brush into the rolling stroke too quickly, and the vibratory aspect may be ineffective for biofilm removal at the gingival margin.

THE CHARTERS METHOD

▸ *History:* During his long and productive dental career, Dr. W. J. Charters emphasized the importance of prevention.

▸ *Purpose:* The interproximal toothbrushing method he taught had as its objectives cleanliness through removal of the "film and mucin" from the proximal surfaces and gingival massage through mechanical stimulation.

▸ *Brush position:* Among his many published papers, Charters described two brush positions, one at a right angle to the long axis of the tooth[16] and another at a 45-degree angle with the tips of the bristles toward the occlusal plane. The right-angle position might have been intended primarily for patients with interdental periodontal tissue loss, where access permitted the bristles to enter the embrasure.

▸ *Method:* For either brush position, the instructions were to force the tips into the interproximal area.

▸ *Pressure:* "With the bristles between the teeth, as much pressure as possible is exerted, giving the brush several slight rotary or vibratory movements. This causes the sides of the bristles to come in contact with the gum margin, producing an ideal massage."[17]

▸ *Bristle position:* The classic periodontal textbooks[18] have described the Charters method with the bristles directed toward the occlusal plane at a 45-degree angle with the long axis of the tooth.

I. Purposes and Indications

▸ Loosen debris and dental biofilm.

▸ Massage and stimulate marginal and interdental gingiva.

▸ Aid in biofilm removal from proximal tooth surfaces when interproximal tissue is missing, for example, following periodontal surgery.

▸ Adapt to cervical areas below the height of contour of the crown and to exposed root surfaces.

▸ Remove dental biofilm from abutment teeth and under the gingival border of a fixed partial denture (bridge) or from the undersurface of a sanitary bridge.

II. Procedure[16]

A. Apply Rolling Stroke Procedure

Instruct in a basic rolling stroke for general cleaning to be accomplished first.

B. Position the Brush

▸ Hold brush (outside the oral cavity) with filaments directed toward the occlusal or incisal plane of the teeth to be brushed.

▸ Point tips down for application to the maxillary and up for application to the mandibular arch.

▸ Insert the brush held in the direction it will be used.

▸ Place the sides of the filaments against the enamel with the brush tips toward the occlusal or incisal plane.

▸ Angle the filaments at approximately 45° to the occlusal or incisal plane.

▸ Slide the brush to a position at the junction of the free gingival margin and the tooth surface (Figure 28-7B).

▸ Note contrast with position for the Stillman method (Figure 28-7A).

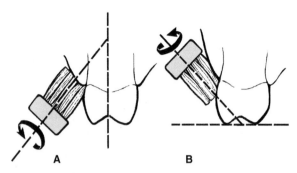

FIGURE 28-7 **Stillman and Charters Methods Compared. A:** Stillman: The brush is angled at approximately 45° to the long axis of the tooth. **B:** Charters: The brush is angled at approximately 45° to the occlusal plane, with brush tips directed toward the occlusal or incisal surfaces.

C. Strokes

▶ Press lightly to flex the filaments and force the tips between the teeth.

▶ Press the sides of the filaments against the gingival margin.

▶ Vibrate the brush gently but firmly, keeping the tips of the filaments in contact with the tooth surface.

▶ Count to 10 slowly as the brush is vibrated with a rotary motion of the handle.

D. Reposition the Brush and Repeat

Repeat steps B and C, as described, several times in each position around the dental arches.

E. Overlap Strokes

When moving the brush to an adjacent position, overlap the brush position, as shown in Figure 28-4.

F. Position Brush for Anterior Lingual and Palatal Surfaces

Because the Charters brush position is difficult to accomplish on the lingual surfaces, a modified Stillman technique is frequently advised. When the Charters method is preferred, the positions are as follows:

▶ *Posterior*
  • With brush tips pointed toward the occlusal surfaces, extend the brush handle across the incisal edge of the canine of the opposing side to be brushed.
  • Place the sides of the toe-end filaments against the distal surface of the most posterior tooth and subsequently at each embrasure.
  • Press and vibrate.

▶ *Anterior*
  • With brush handle parallel with the long axis of the tooth, place the sides of the toe-end filaments over the interproximal embrasure.
  • Press and vibrate.

G. Application of Brush for Fixed Partial Denture

When placing the brush, check to ensure the filament tips are directed under the gingival border of the pontic.

III. Limitations

▶ Brush ends do not engage the gingival sulcus to remove subgingival bacterial accumulations.

▶ In some areas, the correct brush placement is limited or impossible; modifications become necessary, consequently adding to the complexity of the procedure.

▶ Requirements in digital dexterity are high.

OTHER TOOTHBRUSHING METHODS

▶ The rolling stroke, modified Stillman, and Bass are the methods used most often for patient instruction either directly or as guidelines with variations.

▶ Other methods that have been used are included here. The technique and intent of some of the methods overlap.

▶ Assessment before special instruction may reveal a mixture of techniques may be in use by a patient.

I. Historical Methods

▶ Circular: Fones method (Table 28-2 and Figure 28-8)

▶ Vertical: Leonard method (Table 28-2)

▶ Physiologic: Smith's method (Table 28-2).

II. Methods Considered Detrimental

A. Horizontal

▶ An unlimited sweep with a horizontal scrubbing motion bears pressure on teeth that are most facially inclined or prominent.

▶ With the use of an abrasive dentifrice, such brushing may produce tooth abrasion.

▶ Because the interdental areas are not touched by this method, dental biofilm can remain undisturbed on proximal surfaces.

B. Scrub-Brush

▶ A scrub-brush procedure consists of vigorously combined horizontal, vertical, and circular strokes, with some vibratory motions for certain areas.

▶ Without caution, vigorous scrubbing can encourage gingival recession and, with a dentifrice of sufficient abrasiveness, can create areas of tooth abrasion.

POWER TOOTHBRUSHES

Power brushes are also known as power-assisted, automatic, mechanical, or electric brushes. The American Dental Association Council on Scientific Affairs evaluates power brushes for the reduction of dental biofilm and gingivitis.[24]

TABLE 28-2	Historical Toothbrushing Methods		
METHOD	**FONES**	**LEONARD**	**SMITH**
Alternate description	Circular	Vertical	Physiologic
History	Advocated by Alfred C. Fones	As described by Hirschfeld,[19] the up-and-down stroke was employed when teeth were cleaned with a primitive crude twig toothbrush.	Described by Smith[20] and advocated later by Bell.[21] Based on the principle that the toothbrush follows a physiologic pathway and traverses over the tissues in a "natural" masticating act.
Type of brush	A soft brush with 0.006–0.008-inch filament diameter	A soft brush with 0.006–0.008-inch filament diameter	A soft brush with "small tufts of fine bristles arranged in four parallel rows and trimmed to an even length."
Stroke	In abbreviated form, the technique described by Dr. Fones includes the following:[22] 1. With the teeth closed, place the brush inside the cheek over the last maxillary molar, lightly contacting the gingiva. 2. Use a fast, wide, circular motion with light pressure sweeping from the maxillary to the mandibular gingiva. 3. Bring anterior teeth in edge-to-edge contact holding lip out when necessary to make continuous circular strokes. 4. Lingual and palatal tooth surfaces require an in-and-out stroke. Brush sweeps across palate and back and forth to the molars on the mandibular arch (see Figure 28-8).	Paraphrased, Leonard's method is described as follows:[23] 1. With the teeth edge to edge, place the brush filaments against the teeth at right angles to the long axes of the teeth. 2. Brush vigorously with light pressure and mostly up-and-down strokes with a slight rotation or circular motion after striking the gingival margin with force. 3. Use enough pressure to force the filaments into the embrasures, but not enough to damage the brush. 4. The upper and lower teeth are not brushed in the same series of strokes. The teeth are placed edge to edge to keep the brush from slipping over the occlusal or incisal surfaces.	Direct the brush down over the lower teeth onto the gingiva and upward over the teeth for the maxillary. It is also suggested that a few gentle horizontal strokes be used to clean the portion of the sulci directly over the bifurcations of the roots.
Recommendations	An easy-to-learn first technique for young children.	Use when maxillary and mandibular teeth are to be brushed separately surfaces.	
Limitations	Possibly detrimental for adults, particularly when used by a vigorous brusher.		

I. Effectiveness

A. Evolution

▶ Current power brushes move at speeds and motions that cannot be duplicated by manual brushes.

▶ Power toothbrushes have evolved through time due to improved designs and features.

▶ Power toothbrushes of the 1960–1980 era mimicked the motions of manual brushing.

B. Power Versus Manual

▶ Research showed equivalence for power and manual brushes in biofilm removal and reduction of gingivitis.[25,26]

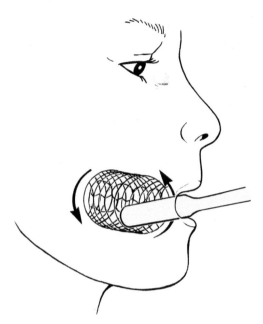

FIGURE 28-8 **Fones Method of Brushing.** With the teeth closed, a circular motion extends from the maxillary gingiva to the mandibular gingiva using a light pressure.

▶ Rotating oscillating action toothbrushes have been shown to be the most effective powered toothbrush for reducing plaque and gingivitis.[27,28]

  • Rotating oscillating action toothbrushes have been shown to be more effective in removing plaque and reducing gingivitis than manual toothbrushes.[28]

▶ Some patients may demonstrate better plaque removal with a manual toothbrush; therefore, patient education must be based on the individual's needs.

▶ The safety of power brushes as compared to manual has been well established.[29–32]

II. Purposes and Indications

A. General Application

▶ Recommended for physically able patients with ineffective manual biofilm removal techniques.

▶ To facilitate mechanical removal of dental biofilm and food debris from the teeth and the gingiva.

▶ Reduce calculus and stain buildup.[32]

B. Patients with Oral Health Challenges

Power brushes can be useful for many patients, including:

▶ Those with a history of failed attempts at more traditional biofilm removal methods.

▶ Those undergoing orthodontic treatment.

▶ Those undergoing complex restorative and prosthodontic treatment.

▶ Those with dental implants.

▶ Aggressive brushers: tendency to use less pressure when using a power brush than with a manual brush.[33–35]

  • Many models of powerbrushes will shut off automatically if too much pressure is applied during brushing, which can be a benefit for those who with tendency to apply too much pressure.

▶ Patients with disabilities or limited dexterity.

▶ The large handles of power brushes can be of benefit.

▶ Handle weight needs to be considered for these patients.

▶ Patients unable to brush.

▶ A power brush may be readily used by a parent or caregiver.

III. Description

A. Motion

There is great variety in the manner in which power brushes move, for example:

▶ The entire brush head moves as a unit in one type of motion.

▶ Groups of tufts on the same brush head may move differently.

▶ The entire brush head moves as a unit, but in different, yet simultaneous motions.

▶ Different-shaped brush heads move separately, and in different, yet simultaneous motions.

▶ A synopsis of the types of motions of power brushes is seen in Table 28-3.

TABLE 28-3	Power Toothbrush Motions
MOTION	**DESCRIPTION**
Rotational	Moves in a 360° circular motion.
Counter-rotational	Each tuft of filaments moves in a rotational motion; each tuft moves counter-directional to the adjacent tuft.
Oscillating	Rotates from center to the left, then to the right; degree of rotation varies from 25° to 55°.
Pulsating	When brush head is on the tooth, direct pulsations toward the interproximal.
Cradle or twist	Side to side with an arc.
Side to side	Side-to-side perpendicular to the long axis of the brush handle.
Translating	Up-and-down parallel to the long axis of the brush handle.
Combination	Combination of simultaneous yet different type of movement.
Ultrasonic	Brush head vibrates at ultrasonic frequency (>250 kHz).

B. Speeds

▶ Vary from low to high.

▶ Generally, power brushes with replaceable batteries move slower than those with rechargeable batteries.

▶ Movement varies from 3,800 to 40,000 movements per minute depending on the manufacturer and type.

C. Brush Head Design

▶ *Adult*: The variety of shapes is illustrated in Figure 28-9. They may be small and round, conical, or like traditional manual heads. Trim profiles include flat, bilevel, rippled, or angled.

▶ *Child*: A child's power brush head can be specially designed to accommodate a smaller mouth and the development of the dentition, as shown in Figure 28-10.

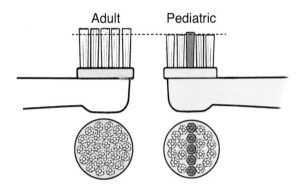

FIGURE 28-10 Child Power Brush Profile. Power brushes for children could necessitate smaller head sizes and shorter filaments to allow for distal reach in tight posterior areas. Raised blue filaments allow for better access to occlusal pits and fissures.

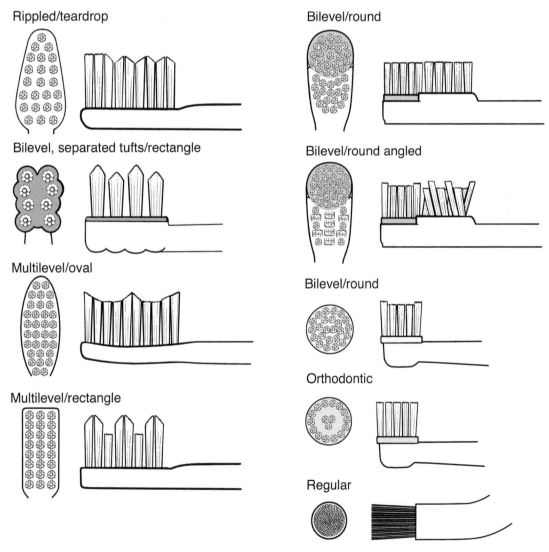

FIGURE 28-9 Power Brush Trim Profiles. Power brushes are made in a variety of brush head shapes, such as oval, teardrop, rectangular, and round. Some power brushes have two different-shaped heads on the same brush. In addition, there are a variety of brush head trims on power brushes, including, flat, bilevel, and multilevel.

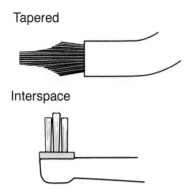

Tapered

Interspace

FIGURE 28-11 Interdental Power Brush Trim Profiles. Some power brushes offer brush heads especially for interdental and proximal surface dental biofilm removal and difficult-access areas such as around implants, orthodontic appliances, and exposed furcations.

▶ *Interdental:* The interdental brush heads pictured in Figure 28-11 are designed to fit a standard power brush handle and are similar in shape to manual interdental brushes, as shown in Figure 29-10 in Chapter 29.

D. Filaments

▶ Made of soft, end-rounded nylon.
▶ Diameters: from extra soft, 0.075 mm (0.003 inch), to soft, 0.15 mm (0.006 inch).
▶ Some children's power brush heads feature specially manufactured filaments for extra softness.

E. Power Source

▶ *Direct*
   • Connects to electrical outlet.
▶ *Replaceable batteries*
   • Relatively inexpensive and convenient.
   • As most batteries lose their power, brush speed is reduced.
   • Advise patients to select a brush that has a water-tight handle to avoid corrosion of batteries.
▶ *Rechargeable*
   • Rechargeable, nonreplaceable battery.
   • Recharges via a stand connected to an electrical outlet.
▶ *Disposable*
   • Batteries cannot be replaced nor recharged.

IV. Instruction

A. Basis for Brush Selection

▶ Quality of clinical research supporting the efficacy and safety of the brush.
▶ Dental professional's experience with the product.
▶ Patient circumstances and preferences.
▶ Dexterity of the patient: detailed hand motion by patient is not a key requirement as it is with manual brushes.

▶ Brush head and batteries that can be replaced for maximum efficiency.
▶ Features that include a timer and pressure sensor.
▶ Patient affordability.
   • Battery-operated models are often less expensive and may be a good way for the patient to try out a powerbrush before investing in a more expensive rechargeable model.

B. Preparation for Instructing Patient

▶ Review manufacturer's instructions as they can differ.
▶ The dental hygienist needs to become familiar with the product before providing patient education.

C. Hands-on Instruction

▶ Provide a demonstration model of the brush and a video of the brushing instructions, when available.
▶ Teach the patient that the use of a power brush requires practice.
▶ Have patient bring toothbrush to appointment for hands-on demonstration and practice.
   • Observe the patient's technique and refine as needed to show the patient how to adapt the brush head to reach difficult areas.

V. Procedure

▶ Follow standard flossing procedure.
▶ Select brush with soft end-rounded filaments.
▶ Select dentifrice with minimum abrasivity.
▶ Place a small amount of dentifrice on the brush and spread the dentifrice over the teeth.
▶ Place brush in the mouth before turning power on to prevent splatter.
▶ Vary the brush position for each tooth surface. Brush each tooth and surrounding gingiva separately.
   • Apply the brush for sulcular brushing to the distal, facial, mesial, and lingual surfaces of each tooth as the brush is moved from the most posterior teeth toward the anterior, quadrant by quadrant.
   • Turn the brush to reach each proximal area.
   • Angulate for access to surfaces of rotated, crowded, or otherwise displaced teeth.
▶ Use light steady pressure. Pressure is not great enough at any time to bend the filaments.

SUPPLEMENTAL BRUSHING

I. Problem Areas

A. Adaptations

▶ Each surface of each tooth is brushed.
▶ Initial instruction may be limited to a basic procedure, particularly when it varies from the patient's present procedures.

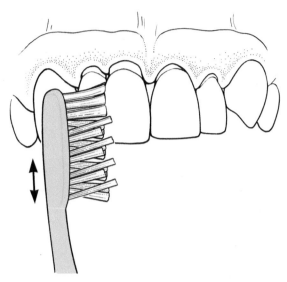

FIGURE 28-12 **Brush in Vertical Position.** For overlapped teeth, open embrasures, and selected areas of recession, the dental biofilm on proximal tooth surfaces can be removed with the brush held in a vertical position.

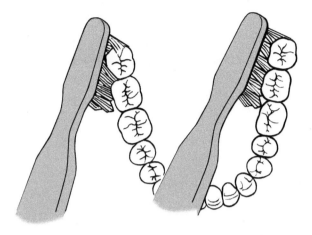

FIGURE 28-13 **Brushing Problems.** Brush placement to remove biofilm from the distal surfaces of the most posterior teeth. The distobuccal surface is approached by stretching the cheek; the distolingual surface is approached by directing the brush across from the canine of the opposite side.

▶ At succeeding lessons, the special hard-to-get areas can be reviewed.

▶ Suggestions are made and demonstrated for brush adaptation for areas missed.

B. Areas for Special Attention

▶ Facially displaced teeth, especially canines and premolars, where the zone of attached gingiva on the facial may be minimal and where toothbrush abrasion may occur.

▶ Inclined teeth, for example, lingual surfaces of mandibular molars that are inclined lingually.

▶ Exposed root surfaces; cemental and dentinal surfaces.

▶ Overlapped teeth or wide embrasures, which require use of vertical brush position (Figure 28-12).

▶ Surfaces of teeth next to edentulous areas.

▶ Exposed furcation areas.

▶ Right canine and lateral incisor, both maxillary and mandibular, which are commonly missed by right-handed brushers; the opposite is true for left-handed brushers.

▶ Distal surfaces of most posterior teeth (Figure 28-13). At best, the brush may reach only the distal line angles. Supplementation with dental floss or textured dental floss is needed for the distal surface (Figures 29-4G and 29-7).

II. Occlusal Brushing

A. Objectives

▶ Loosen biofilm microorganisms packed in pits and fissures.

▶ Remove biofilm deposits from occlusal surfaces of teeth out of occlusion or not used during mastication.

▶ Remove biofilm from the margins of restorations.

▶ Clean pits and fissures to prepare for sealants.

B. Procedure

▶ Place brush on occlusal surfaces of molar teeth with filament tips pointed into the occlusal pits at a right angle.

▶ Position the handle parallel with the occlusal surface.

▶ Extend the toe of the brush to cover the distal grooves of the most posterior tooth (Figure 28-14A).

▶ Strokes: Two acceptable strokes are suggested.

  • Vibrate the brush in a slight circular movement while maintaining the filament tips on the occlusal surface throughout a count of 10. Press moderately so filaments do not bend but go straight into the pits and fissures (Figure 28-14C).

  • Force the filaments against the occlusal surface with sharp, quick strokes; lift the brush off each time to dislodge debris; repeat 10 times.

▶ Move brush to premolar area, overlapping previous brush position.

C. Precaution

Long scrubbing strokes from anterior to posterior on an occlusal surface may contact only the prominent parts of the cusps (Figure 28-14B).

III. Tongue Cleaning

Total mouth cleanliness includes tongue care.

A. Microorganisms of the Tongue

▶ Main foci for oral microorganisms are:

  • Dorsum of tongue
  • Gingival sulci and pockets
  • Dental biofilm on all teeth.

▶ Microorganisms in saliva are principally from the tongue.

▶ The microflora of the tongue is not constant, but changes frequently.[36]

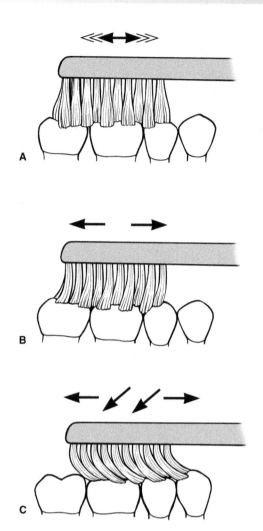

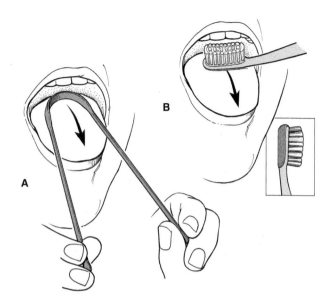

FIGURE 28-15 **Tongue Cleaners. A:** A variety of plastic or flexible metal cleaners are available to clean the dorsal surface of the tongue. **B:** An example of a toothbrush with a rubber tongue cleaner behind the brush head. The cleaner is pressed over the tongue with a light but firm stroke.

FIGURE 28-14 **Occlusal Brushing. A:** Vibrating brush with light pressure while maintaining filament tips on the occlusal surface permits tips to work their way into pits and fissures. **B:** Long horizontal strokes contact only the cusp tips. **C:** Excess pressure curves the filaments so that tips cannot get into the pits and fissures.

B. Purpose of Cleaning the Tongue

▶ Slows dental biofilm formation and total biofilm accumulation.

▶ Reduces number of microorganisms.

▶ Reduces potential for halitosis.

▶ Contributes to overall cleanliness.

▶ Improvements for the patient who has xerostomia, a coated tongue, deep fissures, or who uses tobacco products.

C. Anatomic Features of Tongue Conducive to Debris Retention

▶ *Surface papillae:* Numerous filiform papillae extend as minute projections, whereas fungiform papillae are not as high and create elevations and depressions that entrap debris and microorganisms (Figure 12-5, Chapter 12).

▶ *Fissured tongue:* Fissures may be several millimeters deep and retain debris.

D. Brushing Procedure

1. Hold the brush handle at a right angle to the midline of the tongue and direct the brush tips toward the throat.

2. With the tongue extruded, the sides of the filaments are placed on the posterior part of the tongue surface.

3. With light pressure, draw the brush forward and over the tip of the tongue. Repeat three or four times. Do not scrub the papillae.

4. A power brush can only be used for tongue cleaning when the switch is in the "off" position.

E. Tongue Cleaner

Tongue cleaners may be made of plastic, rubber, stainless steel, or other flexible metal. They are curved or raised, textured pads wide enough to fit over the tongue surface without hitting the teeth.

▶ *Types*

• Curved with a single handle

• Curved with two ends to hold (Figure 28-15A)

• Raised, textured rubber pad on the back side of the brush head (Figure 28-15B).

▶ *Procedure*

• Place the cleaner toward the most posterior area of the dorsal surface (Figure 28-15).

• Press with a light but firm stroke, and pull forward.

- Repeat several times, covering the entire surface of the tongue.
- Wash the tongue cleaner under running water.

TOOTHBRUSHING FOR SPECIAL CONDITIONS

Even when an unusual oral condition develops, a patient is encouraged to brush wherever possible to reduce the possibility of infection and promote healing. Prolonged omission of biofilm removal is never indicated. Examples of conditions that may require a temporary departure from personal care routines are included here.

I. Acute Oral Inflammatory or Traumatic Lesions

When an acute oral condition precludes normal brushing, instruct the patient to:

▶ Brush all areas of the mouth not affected.

▶ Rinse with a warm, mild saline solution to encourage healing and debris removal.

▶ Resume regular biofilm control measures on the affected area as soon as possible.

II. Following Periodontal Surgery

Provide specific instructions concerning brushing while sutures and/or a dressing are in place.

▶ Brush the occlusal surfaces of the teeth and use light strokes over the dressing.

▶ Avoid direct, vigorous brushing to prevent displacement of a dressing.

▶ Brush other teeth and gingiva, not involved in the surgery, as usual.

▶ Additional instructions appear in Table 43-2 in Chapter 43.

III. Acute Stage of Necrotizing Ulcerative Gingivitis

▶ Lack of oral cleanliness can be a major contributing factor (see Chapter 42).

▶ Oral tissues are sensitive to touch during the acute stage, and toothbrushing therefore is neglected.

▶ Careful brush placement and an extra soft brush are indicated to avoid trauma.

IV. Following Dental Extraction

▶ Brush all teeth and gingiva except the surgical wound area.

▶ Clean the teeth adjacent to the extraction site the day following surgery.

▶ Brush areas not involved in the surgery as usual to reduce biofilm and promote healing.

▶ Detailed instructions for pre- and postsurgery are found in Chapter 55.

V. Following Dental Restorations

▶ Patients tend to avoid brushing a new crown, implant, newly placed fixed partial denture, or other prosthesis.

▶ Specific instructions are provided at the time of insertion with review at continuing care appointment.

EFFECTS OF TOOTHBRUSHING

I. The Gingiva

▶ Trauma occurs most frequently on the facial surfaces over prominent teeth in the dental arch.

▶ Lesions are frequently found over canines and premolars.

▶ Lesions occur most often immediately following initial instruction in the use of a new method of brushing; patient may be overzealous or may have misunderstood correct brush placement.

▶ Examination of patient's gingiva within a few days after instruction may be indicated.

A. Acute Alterations

Acute lesions are usually lacerations or ulcerations. The severity of the lesion may depend on the frequency and extent of brushing, as well as on the stiffness of the filaments and the force applied.

▶ Appearance
- Scuffed epithelial surface with denuded underlying connective tissue.
- Punctate lesions that appear as red pinpoint spots.
- Diffuse redness and denuded attached gingiva.

▶ Precipitating factors
- Horizontal or vertical scrub toothbrushing method.
- Excess pressure applied using firm palm grasp of handle.[37]
- Use of abrasive dentifrice.[38]
- Overvigorous placement and application of the toothbrush.
- Penetration of gingiva by filament ends.
- Use of a toothbrush with frayed, broken bristles or filaments.
- Application of filaments beyond attached gingiva.

B. Chronic Alterations

▶ Changes in gingival contour
- Appearance
  1. Rolled, bulbous, hard, firm marginal gingiva, in "piled up" or festoon shape ("McCall's festoon," Figure 18-12 in Chapter 18).

2. Gingival cleft, which is a narrow groove or slit that extends from the crest of the gingiva to the attached gingiva ("Stillman's cleft," Figure 18-13 in Chapter 18).
- Location
    1. May appear only on the facial gingiva, because of the vigor with which toothbrush is used.
    2. Frequently gingival trauma is inversely related to the right-or left-handedness of the patient.
    3. Areas most often involved are around canines or teeth in labioversion or buccoversion.
▶ Gingival recession
- *Appearance*: Margin has moved apically and root surface is exposed.
- *Predisposing factors*
    1. Anatomic: Narrow band of attached gingiva and thin facial bone over teeth malposed in labioversion.
    2. Toothbrushing habits: Vigorous brushing with abrasive dentifrice.
▶ Suggested corrective measures
- Recommend use of a soft toothbrush with end-rounded filaments.
- Correct the patient's toothbrushing method; demonstrate a toothbrushing method better suited to the oral condition.

II. Dental Abrasion

Appearance: Wedge-shaped indentations with smooth, shiny surfaces, as seen in Figure 16-5 in Chapter 16.

A. Definition

▶ Abrasion is the wearing away of tooth structure that results from a repetitive mechanical habit.
▶ Incorrect toothbrushing, especially with an abrasive dentifrice is the most common cause.

B. Location

▶ Primarily on facial surfaces, especially of canines, premolars, and sometimes first molars, or, on any tooth in buccoversion or labioversion, those most available to the pressure of the toothbrush.
▶ Canines are susceptible because of their prominence on the curvature of the dental arches.
▶ Most abraded areas are on the cervical areas of exposed root surfaces, but occasionally they may occur on the enamel.
▶ When adjacent teeth are involved, the lesions appear in a linear pattern across the quadrant or sextant.

C. Contributing Factors

▶ Brushing with abrasive agent in the dentifrice.
▶ Horizontal brushing with excessive pressure.
▶ Form of filament ends: abrasion is less frequent when filaments are end-rounded.
▶ Prominence of the tooth surface labially or buccally.

D. Corrective Measures

▶ Explain the problem to the patient to ensure full cooperation.
▶ Advise use of a toothbrush with end-rounded filaments.
▶ Change the toothbrushing procedure.
▶ Recommend a less abrasive dentifrice.
▶ Use a smaller amount of dentifrice.
- Start brushing in the area of the dentition where the most biofilm and calculus are noted.
- Avoid applying the dentifrice vigorously to the same tooth surfaces.

III. Bacteremia

Evidence suggests toothbrushing and scaling can produce a detectable bacteremia.[39–41]

▶ The incidence and magnitude of bacteremia after scaling is significantly higher in patients with periodontitis than in gingivitis and healthy patients.[40]
▶ There is no definitive data on the relative risks of using manual or electric toothbrushes in patients who are predisposed to infective endocarditis.
▶ The mere fact that bacterial endocarditis can be produced through toothbrushing makes the need for maintaining proper oral hygiene a priority.[41]

CARE OF TOOTHBRUSHES

When discussing the type and features of the brush selected for an individual patient, the number of brushes needed and the frequency of replacement is included. An ideal time to teach cleaning and daily care of brushes would be after a practice session.

The condition of a brush depends on many factors, including the amount and manner of use, the type of care, and the quality of the brush at the start.

I. Supply of Brushes

▶ Recommend at least two brushes for home use and a third in a portable container for use at work, school, or travel.
▶ Purchase of brushes needs to be staggered so that all brushes are not new at the same time and, more importantly, so that they are all not old at the same time, thereby resulting in less than optimum maintenance of the gingival condition.

II. Brush Replacement

▶ Frequent replacement recommended; at least every 2–3 months.
▶ Brushes need to be replaced before filaments become splayed or frayed or lose resiliency. Duration of a brush is influenced by many factors, including frequency and method of use.

▶ Brush contamination occurs with use.[42,43] Contamination has the potential for causing systemic or localized infection.

▶ Patients who are debilitated, immunosuppressed, have a known infection, or are about to undergo surgery for any reason can be advised to disinfect their brushes or use disposable brushes.[43]

III. Cleaning Toothbrushes

▶ Clean thoroughly after each use.

▶ Hold brush head under strong stream of warm water from faucet to force particles, dentifrice, and bacteria from between the filaments.

▶ Tap the handle on edge of sink to remove remaining particles.

▶ Use one toothbrush to clean another brush; filaments can be worked between those of the other brush to remove resistant debris.

▶ Rinse completely and tap out excess water.

IV. Brush Storage

▶ Brushes need to be kept in open air with head in an upright position, apart from contact with other brushes, particularly those of another person to avoid cross contamination.

▶ Portable brush container needs sufficient holes to give air temporarily until the brush can be completely exposed for drying. A closed container encourages bacterial growth.

DOCUMENTATION

In the permanent record, the documentation for initial instruction will include the following:

▶ Type of toothbrush patient has used to date: manual versus power.

▶ Recommended changes in type of brush or method of use.

▶ Identify needs or changes in the soft tissue and teeth from a "plaque score" using a disclosing agent.

▶ Record areas patient has difficulty reaching with suggestions for follow-up.

▶ Tongue cleaning method instructed.

▶ Box 28-3 shows a sample documentation for toothbrush selection and toothbrushing method.

BOX 28-3

Example Documentation: Toothbrush Selection and Toothbrushing Method

S –A 30-year-old male presents for his 6-month preventive appointment with a chief complaint of gums bleeding during toothbrushing. Patient has a negative medical history and reports taking no medications. Patient reports brushing 1× day with a hard manual toothbrush and uses a back and forth "scrubbing" method.

O–Intraoral assessment reveals generalized moderate edema, marginal erythema, and moderate bleeding on probing. Moderate plaque is noted along the gingival margin of posterior teeth. Ulcerations and denuded gingiva noted, particularly on left side maxillary facial and mandibular molar lingual surfaces. Biofilm-free score 63%.

A –Acute tissue trauma related to use of hard toothbrush and scrubbing method.

P–Oral Self-Care—Oral self-care instructions given using a soft toothbrush, recommend twice daily using the modified Stillman method. Flossers were introduced to patient for removal of interdental plaque biofilm. Patient demonstrated modified Stillman method intraorally with some challenges on the lingual of mandibular molars. Patient demonstrated successfully the use of flossers. Patient committed to try the following behavior modifications: increase frequency of brushing from 1 to 2×'s a day, and floss at least 4×'s a week. Increase biofilm-free score to 85% at re-evaluation appointment. Next Visit—6–8 weeks re-evaluation of gingival condition, plaque-free score, evaluate biofilm removal, and assess patient's toothbrushing and flossing technique. Modify as needed. Determine appropriate continue care visit for patient.

Signed _____, RDH
Date _____

EVERYDAY ETHICS

Karen, a long-standing patient of the dental office, presents for her six-month continuing care visit. She has always been consistent with her preventive appointments and has a history of maintaining good oral self-care. A medical history update indicates that that Karen was recently diagnosed with rheumatoid arthritis. The condition is affecting her hands, limiting her dexterity and tactile sensitivity. She reports moderate joint pain especially in the morning hours. She presents with a chief complaint to Jennifer, the dental hygienist, "my gums bleed when I brush. I am worried something is wrong."

The oral examination indicates generalized moderate marginal biofilm and moderate bleeding on probing. It is clear that her oral health status has declined since her last continuing care appointment. Jennifer is new to the practice and running behind schedule so she decided to skip the oral hygiene instructions.

Questions for Consideration

1. Which core ethical values did Jennifer violate with regard to patient education? Explain how each applies to this scenario.

2. How could the information on the patient's health history been used to provide a patient-centered approach to oral self-care?

3. Given the client's physical challenges, list intervention strategies that could have been recommended to assist her with maintaining optimal oral health (e.g., toothbrush, interdental aids). Explain the rationale for each in relation to the Dental Hygiene Standard of Care (see Chapter 1)

4. What would be the best continuing care interval for Karen (2 months, 3 months, 6 months, or yearly)? How can you find evidence to support your choice?

Factors To Teach The Patient

▷ The effect of dental biofilm formation on the teeth and gingiva.

▷ Rationale for thorough removal of dental biofilm from the teeth daily, especially before going to sleep.

▷ The type of brush: manual, power, or both, recommended to maintain optimal oral health for a particular patient.

▷ Individualized hands-on instruction using an appropriate manual or power brushing method.

▷ Proper care and maintenance of manual and power brushes.

▷ Indications for and use of a tongue cleaner.

References

1. Hirschfeld I. *The Toothbrush: Its Use and Abuse.* Brooklyn, NY: Dental Items of Interest; 1939:1–27.

2. McCauley HB. Toothbrushes, toothbrush materials and design. *J Am Dent Assoc.* 1946;33:283–293.

3. Weinberger BW. *An Introduction to the History of Dentistry.* St. Louis, MO: Mosby; 1948:140–144.

4. American Academy of Periodontology. Committee report: the tooth brush and methods of cleaning the teeth. *Dent Items Int.* 1920;42:193.

5. Alexander JF. Toothbrushes and toothbrushing. In: Menaker L, ed. *The Biologic Basis of Dental Caries.* Hagerstown, MD: Harper & Row; 1980:482–496.

6. Koecker L. *Principles of Dental Surgery.* Baltimore, MD: American Society of Dental Surgeons; 1842, Chapter III: *exhibiting a new method of treating the diseases of the teeth and gums*:155–156.

7. American Dental Association, Council on Dental Therapeutics. *Accepted Dental Therapeutics.* 40th ed. Chicago, IL: American Dental Association; 1984:386–387.

8. Checchi L, Minguzzi S, Franchi M, et al. Toothbrush filaments end-rounding: stereomicroscope analysis. *J Clin Periodontol.* 2001;28(4):360–371.

9. Breitenmoser J, Mörmann W, Mühlemann HR. Damaging effects of toothbrush bristle end form on gingiva. *J Periodontol.* 1979;50(4):212–216.

10. Silverstone LM, Featherstone MJ. A scanning electron microscope study of the end rounding of bristles in eight toothbrush types. *Quintessence Int.* 1988;19(2):3–23.

11. Stiller S, Bosma MLP, Shi X, et al. Interproximal access efficacy of three manual toothbrushes with extended, x-angled or flat multitufted bristles. *Int J Dent Hyg.* 2010;8(3):244–248.

12. Bass CC. An effective method of personal oral hygiene. *J La State Med Soc.* 1954;106(3):57–73.

13. Hard D. Oral prophylaxis. In: Bunting RW, ed. *Oral Hygiene.* 3rd ed. Philadelphia, PA: Lea & Febiger; 1957:280–283.

14. Stillman PR. A philosophy of the treatment of periodontal disease. *Dent Digest.* 1932;38(9):314.

15. Hirschfeld I. *The Toothbrush: Its Use and Abuse.* Brooklyn, NY: Dental Items of Interest; 1939:380.

16. Charters WJ. Home care of the mouth. I. Proper home care of the mouth. *J Periodontol.* 1948;19:136–139.

17. Charters WJ. Eliminating mouth infections with the toothbrush and other stimulating instruments. *Dent Digest.* 1932;38:130.

18. Miller SC. *Textbook of Periodontia.* 3rd ed. Philadelphia, PA: The Blakiston Co; 1950:327–328.

19. Hirschfeld I. *The Toothbrush: Its Use and Abuse.* Brooklyn, NY: Dental Items of Interest; 1939:369–371.

20. Smith TS. Anatomic and physiologic conditions governing the use of the toothbrush. *J Am Dent Assoc.* 1940;27:874–878.

21. Bell DG. Home care of the mouth. III. Teaching home care to the patient. *J Periodontal Res.* 1948;19(4):140–143.

22. Fones AC. *Mouth Hygiene.* 4th ed. Philadelphia, PA: Lea & Febiger; 1934:299–306.

23. Leonard HJ. Conservative treatment of periodontoclasia. *J Am Dent Assoc.* 1939;26:1308–1315.

24. American Dental Association, Council on Scientific Affairs. *ADA Acceptance Program Guidelines for Toothbrushes.* Chicago, IL: American Dental Association. [about 10 screens]. http://www.ada.org/~/media/ADA/Science%20and%20 Research/Files/guide_toothbrushes.ashx. Updated April 2012. Accessed November 30, 2014.

25. McKendrick AJW, Barbenel LM, McHugh WD. A two-year comparison of hand and electric toothbrushes. *J Periodontal Res.* 1968;3(3):224–231.

26. Frandsen A. Mechanical oral hygiene practices: state-of-the-science review. In: Löe H, Kleinman DV, eds. *Dental Plaque Control Measures and Oral Hygiene Practices.* Oxford: IRL Press; 1986:93–116.

27. Forrest JL, Miller SA. Manual versus powered toothbrushes: a summary of the Cochrane Oral Health Group's Systematic Review, Part II. *J Dent Hyg.* 2004;78:349–354.

28. Heanue M, Deacon SA, Deery C, et al. Manual versus powered toothbrushing for oral health. *Aust Dent J.* 2005;50(2):123–124.

29. Ho HP, Niederman R. Effectiveness of the Sonicare sonic toothbrush on reduction of plaque, gingivitis, probing pocket depth, and subgingival bacteria in adolescent orthodontic clients. *J Clin Dent.* 1997;8(1): Spec No 5–19.

30. Warren PR, Ray TS, Cugini M, et al. A practice-based study of a power toothbrush: assessment of effectiveness and acceptance. *J Am Dent Assoc.* 2000;131(3):389–394.

31. Danser MM, Timmerman MF, Ijzerman Y, et al. A comparison of electric toothbrushes in their potential to cause gingival abrasion of oral soft tissues. *Am J Dent.* 1998;11:S35–S39.

32. Sharma NC, Galustians HJ, Qaqish J, et al. The effect of two power toothbrushes on calculus and stain formation. *Am J Dent.* 2002;15(2):71–76.

33. van der Weijden GA, Timmerman MF, Reijerse E, et al. Toothbrushing force in relation to plaque removal. *J Clin Periodontol.* 1996;23(8):724–729.

34. Heasman P, Wilson Z, Macgregor I, et al. Comparative study of electric and manual toothbrushes in patients with fixed orthodontic appliances. *Am J Orthod Dentofacial Orthop.* 1998;114(1):45–49.

35. Boyd RL, McLey L, Zahradnik R. Clinical and laboratory evaluation of powered electric toothbrushes: in vivo determination of average force for use of manual and powered toothbrushes. *J Clin Dent.* 1997;8 (Special Issue):72–75.

36. van der Weijden GA, van der Velden U. Fluctuation of the microbiota of the tongue in humans. *J Clin Periodontol.* 1991;18:26–29.

37. Niemi ML, Ainamo J, Etemadzadeh H. The effect of toothbrush grip on gingival abrasion and plaque removal during toothbrushing. *J Clin Periodontol.* 1987;14:19–21.

38. Niemi M, Sandholm L, Ainamo J. Frequency of gingival lesions after standardized brushing as related to stiffness of toothbrush and abrasiveness of dentifrice. *J Clin Periodontol.* 1984;11(4):254–261.

39. Kinane DF, Riggio MP, Walker KF, et al. Bacteraemia following periodontal procedures. *J Clin Periodontol.* 2005;32(7):708–713.

40. Forner L, Larsen T, Kilian M, et al. Incidence of bacteremia after chewing, toothbrushing and scaling in individuals with periodontal inflammation. *J Clin Periodontol.* 2006;33(6):401–407.

41. Hartzell JD, Torres D, Kim P, et al. Incidence of bacteremia after routine tooth brushing. *Am J Med Sci.* 2005;329(4):178–180.

42. Glass RT. The infected toothbrush, the infected denture, and transmission of disease: a review. *Compend Contin Educ Dent.* 1992;13(7):592–598.

43. Müller HP, Lange DE, Müller RF. Actinobacillus actinomycetemcomitans contamination of toothbrushes from patients harbouring the organism. *J Clin Periodontol.* 1989;16(6):388–390.

 ENHANCE YOUR UNDERSTANDING

the**Point®** **DIGITAL CONNECTIONS**
(see the inside front cover for access information)
- **Audio glossary**
- **Quiz bank**

 SUPPORT FOR LEARNING
(available separately; visit lww.com)
- ***Active Learning Workbook for Clinical Practice of the Dental Hygienist, 12th Edition***

prepU **INDIVIDUALIZED REVIEW**
(available separately; visit lww.com)
- **Adaptive quizzing with *prepU for Wilkins' Clinical Practice of the Dental Hygienist***

29

Oral Infection Control: Interdental Care

Esther M. Wilkins, BS, RDH, DMD and Deborah M. Lyle, RDH, BS, MS

CHAPTER OUTLINE

LEARNING OBJECTIVES

After studying this chapter, the student will be able to:

1. Review the anatomy of the interdental area and explain why toothbrushing alone cannot remove biofilm adequately for prevention of periodontal infection.

2. Describe types of dental floss and outline steps for use of floss for biofilm removal from proximal tooth surfaces.

3. Develop a list of the types and purposes of various floss aids and provide a rationale for the choice of the best ones to meet a specific patient's needs.

4. Compare types of interdental brushes and explain why they may be more effective than floss for some patients.

5. Demonstrate and recommend other devices for biofilm removal including toothpick in holder, wooden interdental cleaner, interdental rubber tip, and water irrigation.

▶ Toothbrushing cannot accomplish biofilm removal for the proximal tooth surfaces and adjacent gingiva to the same degree that it does for the facial, lingual, and palatal aspects. Interdental biofilm control, therefore, is essential to complete the patient's oral self-care program.

▶ Objectives and procedures for removal of dental biofilm from proximal tooth surfaces are included in this chapter.

▶ Key words are defined in Box 29-1.

▶ When the preventive treatment plan is outlined for an individual, assessment is made of the oral condition, the problem areas, and the overall prognosis for improvement or maintenance of gingival health.

  • Measures for interdental biofilm control are selected to complement biofilm control by toothbrushing.

THE INTERDENTAL AREA

▶ The three types of gingival embrasures are illustrated in Figure 29-1.

▶ In health, the interdental gingiva fills the interproximal area and under the contact of the adjacent teeth in a Type I embrasure.

▶ When the interdental papilla is missing or reduced in height, which is common as a result of periodontal infection, the shape of the interdental gingiva changes, and open Type II or Type III embrasures may be seen.

▶ Figure 29-2 shows a Type II embrasure from the proximal surface with the col and from the facial surface.

I. Anatomy of the Interdental Area

A review of the gingival and dental anatomy of the interdental area can give meaning to and clarify the role and purpose of the various devices available for interdental care.

A. Posterior Teeth

▶ Between adjacent posterior teeth are two papillae, one facial and one lingual or palatal.

▶ The papillae are connected by a col, a depressed concave area that follows the shape of the apical border of the contact area (Figure 29-2).

 BOX 29-1 | KEY WORDS: Interdental Care

Col: the depression in the gingival tissue under a contact area between the lingual (palatal) papilla and the facial papilla.

Embrasure: V-shaped spillway space next to the contact area of adjacent teeth, narrowest at the contact and widening toward the facial, lingual (palatal), and occlusal contacts.

Floss cleft: a cleft in the gingival margin usually at a mesial or distal line angle of a tooth where dental floss was repeatedly applied incorrectly. The lining of the cleft can be completely lined with epithelium.

Floss cut: unintentional incision at the gingival margin due to incorrect positioning and placement of dental floss.

Hydrotherapy: the use of forced intermittent or steady stream of water for a cleansing or therapeutic purpose.

Interproximal space: the triangular region bounded by the proximal surfaces of contacting teeth and the alveolar bone between the teeth, which forms the base of the triangle; the space is normally filled with the interdental papilla; also called the interdental area.

Irrigant: substance used for irrigation.

Irrigation: flushing of a specific area or site with a stream of fluid; application of a continuous or pulsated stream of fluid to a part of the body for a cleansing or therapeutic purpose.

  Supragingival irrigation: the point of delivery of the irrigation is at, or coronal to, the free gingival margin.

  Marginal irrigation: the point of delivery of the irrigation is angled at, or placed apically to, the gingival margin.

  Subgingival irrigation: the point of the delivery of the irrigation is placed in the sulcus or pocket and may reach the base of the pocket depending on its probing depth.

Keratinized epithelium: outer, protective surface of stratified squamous epithelium; covers the masticatory mucosa; interdental col area is not normally keratinized.

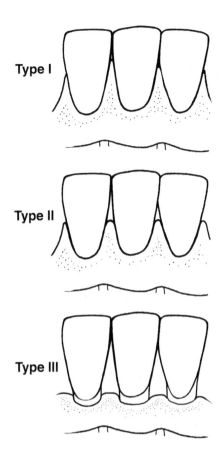

FIGURE 29-1 **Types of Gingival Embrasures.** Type I, interdental papilla fills the gingival embrasure. Type II, with slight-to-moderate recession of the interdental papilla. Type III, with extensive recession or complete loss of the interdental papilla.

B. Anterior Teeth

▶ Between anterior teeth in contact is a single papilla with a pyramidal shape.

▶ Tip of the papilla may form a small col under the contact area (Figure 29-2).

C. Epithelium

▶ The epithelium covering a col is usually thin and not keratinized.

▶ Col epithelium is protected and is less resistant to infection than keratinized surfaces.

▶ Inflammation in the papilla leads to enlargement; with increased inflammatory cells and edema, the col becomes deeper.

▶ The col area is inaccessible for ordinary toothbrushing; microorganisms are harbored in the concave center.

▶ Most gingival disease starts in the col area.

▶ The incidence of gingivitis is greatest in the interdental tissues.[1]

II. Proximal Tooth Surfaces

▶ With bacterial infection and loss of gingival attachment, the interdental papillae are reduced in height.

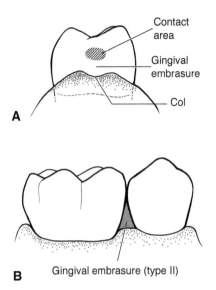

FIGURE 29-2 **Type II Gingival Embrasure. A:** Embrasure shown from the proximal surface with the col. **B:** Facial view, with gingival embrasure shown in blue.

▶ Proximal tooth surfaces become exposed.

▶ Dental biofilm can accumulate.

▶ Irregularities of tooth position, such as rotation or overlapping, and deviations related to malocclusion or tooth loss may be present.

▶ Easy access for removal of bacterial deposits by the individual is prevented.

▶ Root surface morphology of the proximal surfaces is typical for each tooth type.

▶ Concavities and grooves are predisposed to bacterial accumulations.[2,3]

▶ With advanced periodontitis, furcation areas of maxillary first premolars and molars open onto the proximal surfaces.

PLANNING INTERDENTAL CARE

I. Patient Assessment

A. History of Personal Oral Care

▶ Type of toothbrush, dental floss, and other interdental devices currently used.

▶ Frequency and time spent.

▶ Estimate of the patient's apparent priorities on personal oral self-care.

B. Dental and Gingival Anatomy

▶ Position of teeth.

▶ Types and shapes of embrasures: variation throughout the dentition.

▶ Probing depths: classification of the periodontal condition.

▶ Prostheses present: special interdental care required for fixed and removable prostheses.

▶ Areas where toothbrush cannot reach.

C. Extent and Location of Dental Biofilm

▶ Preparation of a "plaque score" (in section on Oral Hygiene Status in Chapter 23) to show the patient the extent of biofilm needing removal on a daily basis.

▶ Use of a disclosing agent to show specific sites where biofilms accumulate.

▶ Evidence of the patient's ability to care for difficult-to-access areas.

D. Personal Factors

▶ Disability that limits ability to carry out needed personal oral hygiene.

▶ Knowledge about and appreciation for interdental oral care.

II. Dental Hygiene Care Plan

A. Objectives

▶ Utilize motivational interviewing (Chapter 26) to select appropriate interdental aids to help the patient reach optimum oral cleanliness and health.

▶ Educate the patient on the oral care aids selected.

▶ Motivate the patient to accept responsibility for daily personal care.

B. Initial Care Plan

▶ At first, the simplest procedures are selected for the patient's convenience and ease of learning based on the patient's current knowledge, preferences, and oral self-care habits.

▶ Minimum frequency: thoroughly twice daily.

▶ Keep the daily oral self-care regimen at a realistic level with respect to the time the patient is able or willing to spend.

▶ As the values the patient places on oral health increase over time, and as the preventive maintenance program becomes a priority in the patient's lifelong self-care health goals, a more refined program can be introduced.

SELECTIVE INTERDENTAL BIOFILM REMOVAL

I. Relation to Toothbrushing

▶ Vibratory and sulcular toothbrushing, such as that performed with the Charters, Stillman, and Bass methods, can be successful to some degree in removing dental biofilm near the line angles of the facial and lingual or palatal embrasures.

▶ Brush in vertical position is effective for additional access around line angles onto the proximal surfaces (Figure 28-12 in Chapter 28).

II. Selection of Interdental Aids

▶ Dependent on oral health, disease status, and the risk for future recurrence.

▶ A patient working to control or arrest disease may need more frequent oral self-care than a patient practicing prevention.

▶ More than a toothbrush is needed for complete biofilm removal from exposed proximal tooth surfaces.

▶ With the judicious selection and use of the various methods for interdental care, disease control can be accomplished by the motivated patient.

DENTAL FLOSS AND TAPE

▶ The effective use of dental floss contributes to gingival health by removing dental biofilm[4–7] and reducing interproximal bleeding.[8]

▶ Dental floss is most effective when interdental papillae are present and there has not been loss of attachment with root surface exposure.[9]

▶ As recession occurs, dental floss may still be used, but greater time, effort, and dexterity are required and complete removal of dental biofilm from the exposed concavities in proximal tooth surfaces may be difficult and require choice of an alternative interdental aid.

I. Types of Floss

▶ Research has shown no difference in the effectiveness of waxed or unwaxed floss for biofilm removal.[4,6,10–12]

▶ Biofilm removal depends on how floss is applied. For optimal patient compliance, the patient may use a preferred type.[4,13]

A. Materials

▷ *Silk*: Historically, floss was made of silk fibers loosely twisted together to form a strand and waxed for proximal surface cleaning.

▷ *Nylon*: Nylon multifilaments, waxed or unwaxed, have been widely used in circular (floss) or flat (tape) form for biofilm removal from proximal tooth surfaces.

▷ *Polytetrafluoroethylene (PTFE)*: Monofilament PTFE is used for proximal tooth surface biofilm removal.

B. Features of Waxed Floss

▶ Smooth surface provided by the wax coating helps the floss slide through the contact area.

▶ Ease in sliding the floss between the teeth may minimize tissue trauma.

▶ Wax gives strength and durability during application to minimize breakage.

C. Features of Unwaxed Floss

▶ Thinner floss may be helpful when contact areas are tight; however, forcing the floss through may break the floss.

▶ Pressure against a tooth surface spreads the nylon fibers and gives a wider surface for biofilm removal.

- Sharper thin edge requires special attention to prevent injury to the gingival tissue when guiding floss through a tight contact area or when moving floss on the tooth surface in an apical direction.

- Squeaking sound effect when floss moves over a clean tooth surface may provide a motivation for patient thoroughness.

- Unwaxed floss, which can fray when rubbed over an irregular tooth surface, rough surface of a restoration, or calculus deposit, might cause the patient to become aggravated and discouraged, thereby resulting in lost motivation to floss regularly.

- Floss that is tightly wound around fingers tends to cut, hurt, and cause discomfort. This problem is as likely with wide dental tape or with waxed floss or tape.

D. Features of PTFE

- Monofilament type resists breakage or shredding when passed over irregular tooth surface, restoration, or calculus deposit.

- Reduces the force required to pass the floss through the contact which may improve patient compliance with regular flossing and reduce tissue injury or trauma.[14]

E. Enhancements

- Color and flavor have been added to dental floss.

- Therapeutic agents that have been added include fluoride and whitening agents. Limited research has been published relative to their effectiveness.

II. Procedure

- When dental floss is applied with firm pressure to a flat or convex proximal tooth surface, biofilm can be removed.

- Older biofilm is tenacious and may require several strokes for removal.

- When floss is placed over a concave surface, contact is not possible (Figure 29-3A), and supplementary devices are needed to remove a bacterial deposit completely.

A. When to Floss

For most patients, the best results can be obtained by using dental floss before toothbrushing. The following reasons may apply:

- When proximal tooth surfaces are flossed first and biofilm is removed, the fluoride from a dentifrice used while brushing reaches the proximal surfaces for prevention of dental caries.

- When brushing is accomplished first, flossing may not be carried out.
  - The mouth feels clean; the need for flossing may not be appreciated.
  - Time may be short and flossing may be postponed.

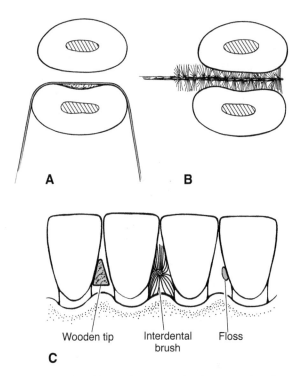

FIGURE 29-3 **Interdental Care. A:** Floss positioned on the mesial surface of a maxillary first premolar shows the inability of the floss to remove dental biofilm on a concave proximal tooth surface. **B:** The use of an interdental brush in the same interproximal area to show how the proximal surfaces can be cleaned free of dental biofilm. **C:** Comparison of the access of a wooden tip, an interdental brush, and a piece of dental floss to an open interdental area.

B. Floss Preparation

- Figure 29-4 outlines the flossing steps described in detail here in this section.

- Hold a 12- to 15-inch length of floss with the thumb and index finger of each hand; grasp firmly with only half inch of floss between the fingertips. The ends of the floss may be tucked into the palm and held by the ring and little finger, or the floss may be wrapped around the middle fingers (Figure 29-4A–C).

- A circle of floss may be made by tying the ends together; the circle may be rotated as the floss is used (Figure 29-5).[15]

C. Application

- *Maxillary teeth:* Direct the floss upward by holding the floss over two thumbs or a thumb and an index finger as shown in Figure 29-4A and B. Rest a side of a finger on teeth of the opposite side of the maxillary arch to provide balance and a fulcrum.

- *Mandibular teeth:* Direct the floss down by holding the two index fingers on top of the strand. One index finger holds the floss on the lingual aspect and the other on the facial aspect (Figure 29-4C). The side of the finger on the lingual side is held on the teeth of the opposite side of the mouth to serve as a fulcrum or rest.

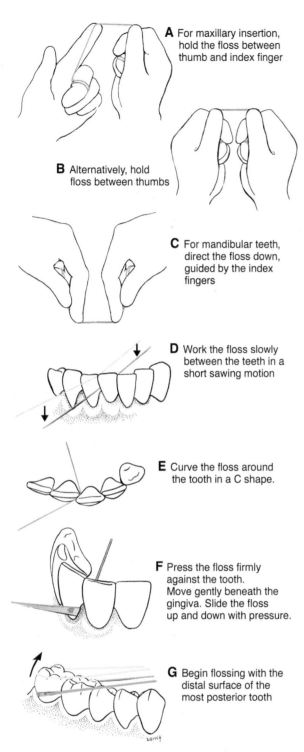

A For maxillary insertion, hold the floss between thumb and index finger

B Alternatively, hold floss between thumbs

C For mandibular teeth, direct the floss down, guided by the index fingers

D Work the floss slowly between the teeth in a short sawing motion

E Curve the floss around the tooth in a C shape.

F Press the floss firmly against the tooth. Move gently beneath the gingiva. Slide the floss up and down with pressure.

G Begin flossing with the distal surface of the most posterior tooth

Figure 29-4 **Use of Dental Floss.** For maxillary insertion, hold the floss between the thumb and index finger **A:** or between thumbs **B:** Grasp the floss firmly. Allow only 1/2-inch length between fingers. **C:** For the mandibular teeth, direct the floss down, guided by the index fingers. **D:** Work the floss slowly between the teeth in a short sawing motion. Avoid snapping through the contact area. **E:** Curve the floss around the tooth in a C-shape. Hold the floss toward the mesial for cleaning the distal surfaces and toward the distal for cleaning the mesial surfaces. **F:** Press the floss firmly against the tooth. Move gently beneath the gingiva until tissue resistance is felt. Slide the floss horizontally and vertically with pressure to remove biofilm. **G:** Begin flossing with the distal surface of the most posterior tooth, and work systematically around the arch.

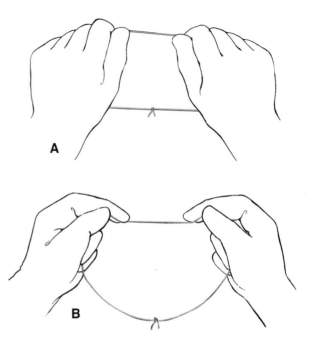

A

B

FIGURE 29-5 **Circle of Floss.** The ends of the floss are tied together for convenient holding. A child may be able to manage floss better with this technique. **A:** Floss held for maxillary teeth. **B:** Floss held for mandibular teeth.

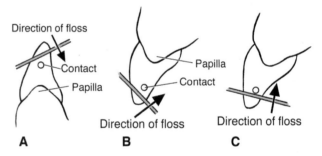

Direction of floss

Contact

Papilla

Papilla

Contact

Direction of floss

Direction of floss

A   **B**   **C**

FIGURE 29-6 **Insertion of Floss.** Hold floss in a diagonal or oblique position over the teeth where the floss will be inserted. Arrows indicate the direction of movement of the floss. **A:** Floss held for mandibular insertion. **B:** Floss held for maxillary insertion. **C:** Floss held incorrectly. When floss is held horizontally, the possibility for damage to the papilla is greater.

D. Insertion

▷ Hold floss firmly in a diagonal or oblique position (Figure 29-6).

▷ Guide the floss past each contact area with a gentle back and forth or sawing motion (Figure 29-4D).

▷ Control floss to prevent snapping through the contact area into the gingival tissue.

E. Cleaning Stroke

▷ Clean adjacent teeth separately; for the distal aspect, curve the floss mesially, and for the mesial aspect, curve the floss distally, around the tooth (Figure 29-4E and F).

▷ Pass the floss below the gingival margin, curve to adapt the floss around the tooth, press, and slide up and down over the tooth surface. Repeat.

► Loop the floss over the distal surfaces of the most posterior teeth in each quadrant and the teeth next to edentulous areas (Figure 29-4G). Hold firmly against the tooth and move the floss in an up-and-down motion.

F. Additional Suggestions

► Slide the floss to a new, unused portion for succeeding proximal tooth surfaces.

► Floss may be doubled to provide a wider rubbing surface.

► When a dentifrice is used with the floss, dental tape may be better than floss in retaining the dentifrice against the tooth.

III. Precautions

A. Pressure in Col Area

► The col area is not keratinized and is vulnerable to bacterial invasion.

► Biofilm control of the area is of great importance because most gingival and periodontal infection begins in the col area.

► Too great a pressure with floss one or more times daily, particularly very fine floss that tends to cut more easily than thicker floss, can be destructive to the attachment.

► Excess pressure of the floss against the attachment is particularly significant in children in whom teeth are in the process of eruption and the junctional epithelium is less firmly attached.

B. Prevention of Floss Cuts and Floss Clefts

► *Location*: Floss cuts or clefts occur primarily on facial and lingual or palatal surfaces directly beside or in the middle of an interdental papilla. They appear as straight-line cuts from the gingival margin and may result in a floss cleft (Figure 18-13B in Chapter 18).[16]

► *Causes*
- Using a piece of floss that is too long between the fingers when held for insertion.
- Snapping the floss through the contact area.
- Not curving the floss about the teeth; holding floss straight across the papilla.
- Not using a rest to prevent undue pressure.

TUFTED DENTAL FLOSS

I. Description

Tufted dental floss is also called a floss/yarn combination. Regular dental floss is alternated with a thickened tufted portion. Two variations are available commercially.

► *Single, precut lengths*

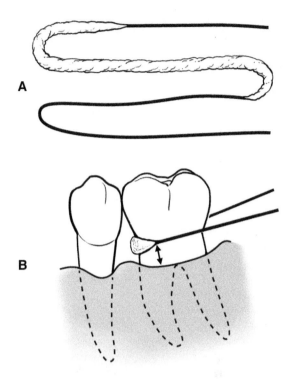

FIGURE 29-7 Tufted Dental Floss. The floss/yarn combination may be "Super Floss" **(A)** in a precut length with a tufted portion and a 3-inch stiffened end for insertion under a fixed prosthesis, **(B)** shows how the tufted part of the floss might be used interproximally to remove biofilm.

- Available in a 2-foot length composed of a 5-inch tufted portion adjacent to a 3-inch stiffened end for inserting under a fixed appliance or orthodontic attachment (Figure 29-7A).
- Example: Super Floss®.[17]

II. Indications for Use

► Biofilm removal from tooth surfaces adjacent to wide embrasures where interdental papillae have been lost.

► Biofilm removal from mesial and distal abutments and under pontic of a fixed partial denture, implant, or orthodontic appliance. The stiff end of Super Floss® is inserted like a floss threader (see Figure 32-3).

III. Procedure

A. Individual Surface of Tooth or Implant

Curve floss and/or tufted portion around the tooth or implant in a "C" to remove dental biofilm. Move floss vertically and horizontally (Figure 29-7B).

B. Fixed Partial Denture

Thread tufted floss over pontic and apply to distal surface of the mesial abutment and mesial surface of the distal abutment (Figure 32-3 in Chapter 32).

AIDS FOR FLOSSING

I. Floss Holder

A floss holder can be helpful for a person with a disability or for a parent or caregiver serving a child or patient. A floss holder is shown in Figure 57-5 for use by a disabled person.

II. Floss Threader

A floss threader is used for biofilm and debris removal around orthodontic appliances or under fixed partial dentures as shown in Figures 32-2 and 32-3 in Chapter 32.

III. Knitting Yarn

▶ *Indications for use*
  - For tooth surfaces adjacent to wide proximal spaces.
  - For isolated teeth, teeth separated by a diastema, and distal surfaces of most posterior teeth.
  - For mesial and distal abutments of fixed partial dentures and under pontics, use a floss threader.

▶ *Procedure*
  - Select about 8–10 inches of 3- or 4-ply smooth synthetic yarn.
  - Fold yarn double. Loop through about 8 inches of dental floss; tie floss with one overhand knot.
  - Insert floss through the contact area. Draw the yarn into the embrasure (Figure 29-8).
  - Clean adjacent teeth separately with a facial-lingual, back-and-forth stroke. Hold the ends of the yarn distally and then around mesially.
  - For specific areas where a papilla may be high or access is not otherwise sufficient for the wide yarn, use the dental floss end of the combination.
  - Apply dentifrice and rub surface with the yarn back and forth, up and down.
  - For closed contacts, use a floss threader (see Figure 32-2 in Chapter 32).

IV. Gauze Strip

▶ *Uses*
  - For proximal surfaces of widely spaced teeth.
  - For surfaces of teeth next to edentulous areas.
  - For outer mesial and distal surfaces of abutment teeth of a fixed partial denture.
  - For areas under posterior cantilevered section of a fixed appliance, such as the distal portion of a denture supported by implants.

▶ *Procedure*
  - Cut 1-inch gauze bandage into a 6- to 8-inch length, and fold in thirds or down the center.
  - Position the fold of the gauze on the cervical area next to the gingival crest and work back and forth several times; hold ends in a distal direction to clean

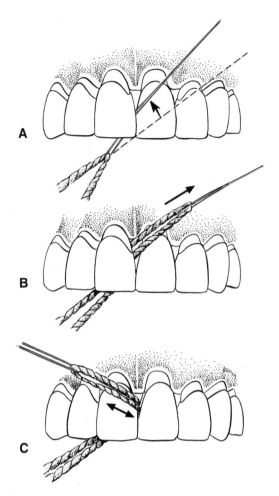

FIGURE 29-8 Knitting Yarn. A: Yarn is looped through dental floss, and the floss is drawn through the contact area in the usual manner, shown by the arrow. **B:** Yarn is drawn through the embrasure. **C:** Yarn is positioned against the surface of the tooth for biofilm removal. When tooth contact is missing and space permits, the yarn is used without floss.

a mesial surface, and in a mesial direction to clean a distal surface (Figure 29-9).

INTERDENTAL BRUSHES

I. Types

A. Small Insert Brushes with Reusable Handle

▶ Soft nylon filaments are twisted into a fine stainless steel wire for insertion into a handle with an angulated shank (Figure 29-10A). Select brush with plastic-coated wire.

▶ The small tapered or cylindrical brush heads are of varying sizes approximately 12–15 mm (1/2 inch) in length, with a diameter of 3–5 mm (1/8–1/4 inch).

B. Brush with Plastic Handle

▶ Soft nylon filaments are twisted into a fine stainless steel wire.

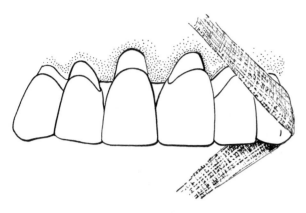

FIGURE 29-9 Gauze Strip. A 6- or 8-inch length of 1-inch bandage is folded in thirds and placed around a tooth adjacent to an edentulous area, a tooth with interdental spacing, or the distal surface of the most posterior tooth. A shoe-shine stroke is used to clean the dental biofilm from the surface.

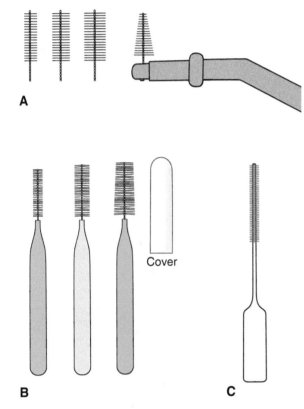

FIGURE 29-10 Single-tuft and Interdental Brushes. A: Insert brushes for a reusable handle with an angulated shank. **B:** Reusable interdental brush with filaments twisted onto a fine wire that ends in a handle and cover. **C:** Disposable interdental brush with handle.

- The wire is continuous with the handle, which is approximately 35–45 mm (1½–1¾ inches) in length (Figure 29-10A).
- Travel brushes are also available (Figure 29-10B) and may be more convenient for patients.
- The very short, soft filaments form a narrow brush approximately 30–35 mm (1¼–1½ inches) in length and 5–8 mm (1/4–5/16 inches) in diameter (Figure 29-10A and B).

C. Soft-picks[18]

- Similar to an interdental brush, but do not have a wire or bristles. The soft-pick has small elastomeric fingers that are perpendicular to a plastic core (Figure 29-10C).
- The soft-pick is effective at biofilm removal and reducing gingival inflammation.

II. Indications for Use

When sufficient space is available for the insertion of an interdental brush without excess force, the following applications are indicated:

A. For Removal of Dental Biofilm and Debris

- Proximal tooth surfaces adjacent to open embrasures, orthodontic appliances, fixed prostheses, dental implants, periodontal splints, and space maintainers, and other areas that are hard to reach with a regular toothbrush.
- Concave proximal surfaces where dental floss and other interdental aids cannot reach (Figure 29-3A). Floss will not access a concave surface, whereas the interproximal brush can reach and cleanse (Figure 29-3B).[1,19]
  - In patients with open embrasures and moderate to severe attachment loss, the interdental brush is more effective than floss.[19]
- Exposed Class IV furcations (Figure 19-9 in Chapter 19).

B. For Application of Chemotherapeutic Agents

- Fluoride dentifrice, gel, and/or mouthrinse for prevention of dental caries, particularly root surface caries, and for surfaces adjacent to any prosthesis.
- Antibacterial agents for control of dental biofilm and the prevention of gingivitis.
- Desensitizing agents.

III. Procedure

- Select brush of appropriate diameter.
- Moisten the brush and insert at an angle in keeping with gingival form; brush in and out.
- For wide embrasures, it will be important to remember to apply pressure against the proximal root surfaces to remove the biofilm thoroughly.
  - Insert the interdental brush as shown in Figure 29-3B and C.
  - Apply pressure toward the mesial proximal surface to remove biofilm.
  - Then apply pressure toward the distal proximal surface and remove the surface biofilm.

IV. Care of Brushes

- Clean brush during use to remove debris and biofilm by holding under actively running water.

FIGURE 29-11 **Single-tuft Brush with Bent Shank.** Adaptation of brush with angulated handle permits easier access to lingual and palatal aspects of the natural teeth, as well as to orthodontic appliances, prostheses, and implant abutments.

▷ Clean thoroughly after use and dry in open air.

▷ Discard before the filaments become deformed or loosened.

SINGLE-TUFT BRUSH (END-TUFT, UNITUFT)

I. Description

The single tuft, or group of small tufts, may be 3–6 mm in diameter and may be flat or tapered (Figure 28-9). The handle may be straight or contra angled.

II. Indications for Use

▷ *For open interproximal areas*

▷ *For fixed dental prostheses*

• The single-tuft brush may be adaptable around and under a fixed partial denture, pontic, orthodontic appliance, precision attachment, or implant abutment.

▷ *For difficult-to-reach areas*

• The lingual surfaces of the mandibular molars, abutment teeth, the distal surfaces of the most posterior teeth, and teeth that are crowded are examples of areas where an end-tuft brush may be of value.

• The shank may be bent for easy adaptation (Figure 29-11).

III. Procedure

▷ Direct the tip of the tuft into the interproximal area and along the gingival margin; go around the distal surfaces from lingual and facial of the most distal teeth in all four quadrants.

▷ Combine a rotating motion with intermittent pressure especially in the interproximal areas to reach as much of the proximal surfaces as possible.

▷ Use a sulcular brushing stroke.

INTERDENTAL TIP

I. Composition and Design

Conical or pyramidal flexible rubber tip is attached to the end of the handle of a toothbrush or is on a special plastic handle. The soft, pliable rubber tip is preferred because it can be adapted to the interdental area and below the gingival margin without causing damage to the epithelial lining.

II. Indications for Use

▷ For cleaning debris from the interdental area and for removal of biofilm by rubbing the exposed tooth surfaces.

▷ For biofilm removal at and just below the gingival margin.

III. Procedure

▷ Trace along the gingival margin with the tip positioned just beneath the margin (1–2 mm). The adaptation is similar to the toothpick in holder (Figure 29-12).

▷ For additional cleaning of the proximal surfaces of the teeth, rub the tip against the teeth as it is moved in and out of an embrasure and under a contact area. Position tip with the gingival form; take care not to flatten the interdental tissue.

▷ Rinse the tip as indicated during use to remove debris, and wash thoroughly at the finish.

TOOTHPICK IN HOLDER[20]

I. Description

A round toothpick is inserted into a plastic handle with contra-angled ends for adaptation to the tooth surface at

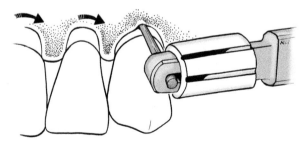

FIGURE 29-12 **Toothpick in Holder for Dental Biofilm at Gingival Margin.** The tip is placed at or just below the gingival margin. Trace the margin around each tooth.

the gingival margin for biofilm removal. The device also is called a Perio-Aid®.

II. Indications for Use

A. Patient with Periodontitis

For biofilm removal at and just under the gingival margin, for interdental cleaning, particularly for concave proximal tooth surfaces, and for exposed furcation area.

B. Orthodontic Patient

For biofilm removal at gingival margin above appliances.

III. Procedure

A. Prepare Instrument

▶ Insert round tapered toothpick into the end of the holder. One type of holder has angulated ends for use in various positions.

▶ Twist the toothpick firmly into place. Break off the long end cleanly so that sharp edges do not scratch the inner cheek or the tongue during use.

B. Application

▶ Apply toothpick at the gingival margin. Apply just under the gingival margin at a slant, with moderate pressure: trace the gingival margin around each tooth to remove biofilm.

▶ To remove biofilm just below the gingival margin, apply the end at less than 45°, maintain the tip on the tooth surface, and follow around the sulcus or pocket (Figure 29-12).

▶ Use a tip that has become soft and slightly frayed from use as a small cleaning "brush" to rub on tooth surfaces where biofilm has collected.

▶ For hypersensitive spots, usually at the cervical third of a tooth, the patient can use the tip daily to massage dentifrice for desensitization on the sensitive area.

▶ When a contact is inadequate and the patient indicates that floss or toothpicks are required to relieve pressure from impacted food, dental attention may be needed. The area is charted or otherwise brought to the attention of the dentist.

WOODEN INTERDENTAL CLEANER

I. Description

The wooden cleaner is a 2-inch-long device made of basswood or birch wood. It is triangular in cross section, as shown in Figure 29-13.

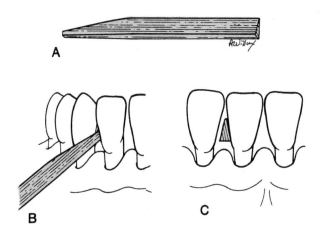

FIGURE 29-13 Wooden Interdental Cleaner. A: The 2-inch wooden triangular cleaner. **B:** Application on the proximal surface of a tooth with a Type III embrasure. The base of the triangle is on the gingival side. **C:** The side of the triangle is rubbed in and out against the proximal surface to remove dental biofilm.

II. Indications for Use

▶ *Application*
  • For cleaning proximal tooth surfaces where the tooth surfaces are exposed and interdental gingiva are missing. Space must be adequate otherwise the gingival tissue can be traumatized.[21]

▶ *Advantages*[21]
  • Ease of use.
  • Transport easily and can be used throughout the day.

▶ *Limitation*
  • As with most interdental devices, the wooden cleaner is advised only for the patient who follows instructions carefully.
  • The wooden interdental cleaner cannot access exposed root concavities and irregularities to adequately remove dental biofilm.
  • Difficult to use in posterior areas and from the lingual aspect of the teeth.[21]
  • A fresh cleaner is advised for each arch or quadrant because the wood may become splayed.

III. Procedure

A. Fulcrum (Rest)

▶ First teach the patient to use a rest by placing the hand on the cheek or chin or by placing a finger on the gingiva convenient to the place where the tip will be applied. This precaution helps prevent insertion of the wedge with too much pressure.

B. Preparation

▶ Soften the wood by placing the pointed end in the mouth and moistening with saliva.

C. Directions

▶ Hold the base of the triangular wedge toward the gingival border of the interdental area and insert with the tip pointed slightly toward the occlusal or incisal surfaces to follow the contour of the embrasure (Figure 29-13B and C). Do not hold the wedge horizontally because the interdental tissue can be flattened.

▶ When the surface feels rough, check for calculus, and remove by scaling.

▶ Clean the tooth surfaces by moving the wedge in and out while applying a burnishing stroke with moderate pressure first to one side of the embrasure and then to the other, about four strokes each.

▶ Discard the cleaner as soon as the first signs of splaying are evident.

ORAL IRRIGATION

I. Description

▶ Irrigation is the targeted application of a pulsated or steady stream of water or other irrigant for preventive or therapeutic purposes.
  • The purpose of irrigation is to reduce the bacteria and inflammatory mediators that lead to the initiation or progression of periodontal infections.
  • For the patient, irrigation can be a part of routine self-care.

▶ Mechanical devices, including toothbrushes and interdental aids, can accomplish dental biofilm removal supragingivally and slightly below the gingival margin for the motivated patient.
  • Toothbrushes penetrate less than 1 mm into the gingival sulcus.[22]

▶ Benefits from removing loosely connected biofilm with the use of an oral irrigator include:
  • Reduction of gingivitis and bleeding.[23,24]
  • Reduction or alteration of subgingival dental biofilm.[25]
  • Subgingival access to pathogenic microorganisms.[26,27]
  • Subgingival delivery of antimicrobial agents.

▶ Supragingival and marginal irrigation are effective for removing loosely attached dental biofilm and reducing gingivitis.

▶ When an antimicrobial agent is used in the irrigator, reduction of the supragingival and subgingival biofilm and of gingivitis is enhanced.[25]

II. Penetration into Pocket: Subgingival Access

▶ The standard jet tip placed supragingivally can penetrate below the gingival margin 44%–71% of the pocket depth.[26]

▶ Specialized tips used for marginal or subgingival delivery have shown penetration between 41% and 90%

depending on tip use, technique, and presence of calculus.[27,28]

III. Power-Driven Device

▶ Generates an intermittent or pulsating jet of fluid with an adjustable dial for regulation of pressure and flow.

▶ Delivers irrigant through a handheld interchangeable tip that rotates 360° for application at or below the gingival margin.

▶ Maintains steady flow or pulsations of irrigant from a reservoir.

DELIVERY METHODS

▶ When a standard delivery tip is directed perpendicular to the long axis of the tooth, two zones of hydrokinetic activity are created.[29]
  • *Zone 1*: impact zone, where the irrigant makes initial contact.
  • *Zone 2*: flushing zone, where the irrigant is deflected from the tooth surface subgingivally.

▶ A pulsating stream has been shown to be superior to a steady stream, a fact to consider when recommending products.

▶ Patient-applied irrigation is divided into three categories based on tip placement and design:
  • Supragingival irrigation
  • Marginal irrigation
  • Subgingival irrigation.

I. Standard Jet Tip

A. Delivery Tips

▶ Monojet (single stream) (Figure 29-14A)

▶ Fractionated microjet (Figure 29-14B)

▶ Pulsating and nonpulsating.

B. Procedure

▶ Described in Box 29-2.

▶ Easy to do for most patients.

C. Special Instructions

▶ Always read and follow manufacturer's instructions regarding use of an irrigator.

▶ Irrigation imparts a clean feeling to the mouth.

▶ It is used as part of a comprehensive oral care regimen.

II. Specialized Tips

A. Delivery Tips

▶ For application at or below the gingival margin for targeted delivery of water or antimicrobial agents.

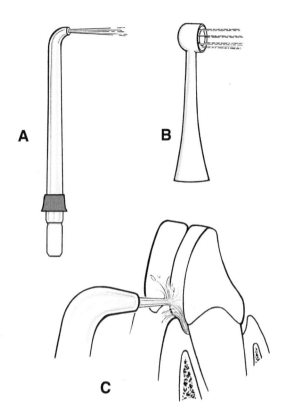

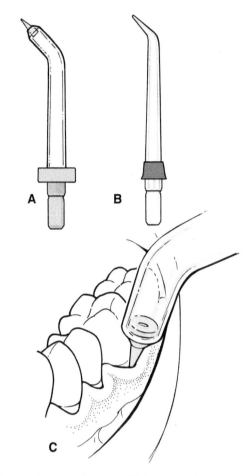

FIGURE 29-14 **Supragingival Irrigation Demonstrating Delivery of Irrigant. A:** Monojet tip (single stream). **B:** Fractionated microjet tip (multiple streams). **C:** Monojet delivery tip showing impact and flushing of subgingival area.

FIGURE 29-15 **Patient-applied Marginal Irrigation. A** and **B:** Special tips for use by the patient. **C:** Soft rubber tip designed to be placed 2 mm below gingival margin.

BOX 29-2

How to Irrigate

▷ Lean over the sink to allow the irrigant to flow from the oral cavity.

▷ Direct the jet tip toward the interdental area until almost touching the tooth surface.

▷ Hold tip at a right angle (90°) to the long axis of the tooth.

▷ This is generally referred to as supragingival irrigation (Figure 29-14C).

▷ Increase pressure slightly over time depending on gingival inflammation and comfort.

▷ Follow a definite pattern around the teeth: maxillary arch first, then the mandibular, facial, palatal, and lingual.

 Types
  • Soft rubber tip designed to be placed 2 mm below the gingival margin (Figure 29-15A).
  • Tapered plastic tip designed to be placed at the gingival margin (Figure 29-15B).

B. Procedure

▷ Identify appropriate areas for use (e.g., specific pocket, furcation, or implant).

▶ Set unit pressure on lowest setting or follow the manufacturer's instructions.

▶ Direct the tip at or below the gingival margin according to the manufacturer's directions. The use of a soft rubber tip or a tapered plastic tip is generally referred to as marginal irrigation (Figure 29-15C).

▶ Activate flow of solution for a few seconds into designated area; stop flow and move to next designated area.

▶ When using a metal or plastic cannula, care must be given to ensure the patient can place the tip subgingivally and deliver the agent accurately and safely. Proper use of a cannula tip is considered subgingival irrigation.

APPLICATIONS FOR PRACTICE

Regular use of daily personal oral irrigation is beneficial.[30] Use a patient-centered approach to evaluate each patient's needs individually to determine which techniques, products, or devices are appropriate.

I. Advantages of Patient-Applied Daily Irrigation

A. Reduction of Gingivitis

▶ The absence of bleeding is the best clinical measurement to predict minimal risk of periodontal breakdown.

▶ Irrigation results in a reduction of bleeding even with water as the irrigant.[30]

B. Problem Areas

▶ Areas that are difficult to access with traditional mechanical methods:

- Open interdental areas
- Malpositioned teeth
- Exposed furcas
- Periodontal pockets
- Postperiodontal surgery problem areas.

C. Special Needs Areas

▶ Prosthetic replacements and fixed partial dentures.

▶ Orthodontic appliances.

▶ Intermaxillary fixation appliances for orthognathic surgery and fractured jaw.

▶ Complex restorations and other extensive rehabilitation.

▶ Implant maintenance with soft rubber specialized tip.

▶ Immunocompromised individuals who have an exaggerated inflammatory response.

▶ Ineffective interdental technique due to physical ability or lack of compliance.

II. Special Considerations

A. Premedication Requirement

A patient who requires antibiotic premedication for dental and dental hygiene treatment is evaluated before introducing the use of an oral irrigator or other mechanical device.

B. Consultation

Contact with the patient's physician is needed when a question arises about the use of adjunctive oral hygiene aids that can create a bacteremia.

BOX 29-3

Example Documentation: Recommendations for Daily Interdental Care

S –A 46-year-old female patient presents for routine 3-month continuing care appointment. Patient states, "I do floss regularly, and have even tried using the 'fuzzy floss' that you gave me last time, but it almost seems as though the floss doesn't do a good job. Is there another way to clean that area?"

O–Generalized recession and extensive loss of interdental papilla on the upper right quadrant. Observed patient flossing that area and found that she uses good flossing technique.

A–Interdental brush may be a better choice than tufted floss for more thorough cleaning of the wide embrasure spaces in that area of her mouth.

P–Showed her examples of several types of interdental brushes and let her choose two she thought she might be most comfortable using. Provided instructions for use of a small interdental brush with a tapered group of filaments as well as an interdental brush handle with replaceable inserts. Provided additional samples of two sizes of interdental inserts (one with medium-sized filaments and one cone- or "Christmas tree"-shaped) to try out and see which works best for her.

Signed _____, RDH
Date _____

EVERYDAY ETHICS

Jane, at the clinic for a routine continuing care appointment, is excited about information she has just read on the Internet about a new device for interdental biofilm removal. She begins to ask Glenna, the dental hygienist, detailed questions about the product such as whether it really works, where it can be purchased, and how much it costs. Glenna is unfamiliar with the aid but doesn't want to be embarrassed in front of the patient so she tells Jane the product doesn't work and spends an extra 5 minutes at the end of the appointment going over manual flossing techniques.

Questions for Consideration

1. Which of the dental hygiene core values (Table II-1, Section II Introduction) have application in this scenario? Also consider the ethical duty for lifelong learning.

2. From the patient's perspective, what is the role of the dental hygienist in this situation? Consider the roles of dental hygiene in Chapter 1.

3. Is it unethical to mislead the patient about a product when the value is unknown or the dental hygienist prefers the benefits of another (perhaps rival) product? Why or why not?

DOCUMENTATION

Documentation for a patient's interdental care progress notes need to include a minimum of the following:

▶ Initially the complete health history including need or not for premedication to prevent bacteremia; extra- and intraoral examination, radiographs; and study casts if used for help in patient instruction.

▶ Information for special needs concerning halitosis (with tests prescribed or given); xerostomia recommendations for oral care.

▶ Notes on all personal oral care demonstrations and products recommended for use.

▶ A sample documentation may be reviewed in Box 29-3.

Factors To Teach The Patient

▷ By demonstration with disclosing agent, how the toothbrush doesn't clean the interdental area thoroughly.

▷ About dental biofilm and how it collects on the proximal tooth surfaces when left undisturbed.

▷ How vulnerable the interdental area is to gingival infection.

▷ How to use each recommended interdental aid to clean the proximal tooth surfaces.

▷ To ask the dental hygienist and the dentist about new products they see advertised and whether the product meets the patient's individual oral self-care needs.

References

1. Smukler H, Nager MC, Tolmie PC. Interproximal tooth morphology and its effect on plaque removal. *Quintessence Int.* 1989;20(4):249–255.

2. Gher ME, Vernino AR. Root morphology—clinical significance in pathogenesis and treatment of periodontal disease. *J Am Dent Assoc.* 1980;101(4):627–633.

3. Fox SC, Bosworth BL. A morphological survey of proximal root concavities: a consideration in periodontal therapy. *J Am Dent Assoc.* 1987;114(6):811–814.

4. Ciancio SG, Shibly O, Farber GA. Clinical evaluation of the effect of two types of dental floss on plaque and gingival health. *Clin Prev Dent.* 1992;14(3):14–18.

5. Abelson DC, Barton JE, Maietti GM, et al. Evaluation of interproximal cleaning by two types of dental floss. *Clin Prev Dent.* 1981;3(4):19–21.

6. Lobene RR, Soparkar PM, Newman MB. Use of dental floss: effect on plaque and gingivitis. *Clin Prev Dent.* 1982;4(1):5–8.

7. Hanes PJ, O'Dell NL, Baker MR, et al. The effect of tensile strength on the clinical effectiveness and patient acceptance of dental floss. *J Clin Periodontol.* 1992;19(1):30–34.

8. Graves RC, Disney JA, Stamm JW. Comparative effectiveness of flossing and brushing in reducing interproximal bleeding. *J Periodontol.* 1989;60(5):243–247.

9. American Academy of Periodontology. *Proceedings of the World Workshop in Clinical Periodontics.* Chicago, IL: American Academy of Periodontology; 1989:II/11–II/15.

10. Hill HC, Levi PA, Glickman I. The effects of waxed and unwaxed dental floss on interdental plaque accumulation and interdental gingival health. *J Periodontol.* 1973;44(7):411–413.

11. Lamberts DM, Wunderlich RC, Caffesse RG. The effect of waxed and unwaxed dental floss on gingival health, Part I: plaque removal and gingival response. *J Periodontol.* 1982;53(6):393–396.

12. Wunderlich RC, Lamberts DM, Caffesse RG. The effect of waxed and unwaxed dental floss on gingival health, Part II: crevicular fluid flow and gingival bleeding. *J Periodontol.* 1982;53(6):397–400.

13. Beaumont RH. Patient preference for waxed or unwaxed dental floss. *J Periodontol.* 1990;61(2):123–125.

14. Dörfer CE, Wündrich D, Staehle HJ, et al. Gliding capacity of different dental flosses. *J Periodontol.* 2001;72(5):672–678.

15. Masters DH. Oral hygiene procedure for the periodontal patient. *Dent Clin North Am.* 1969;13(1):3–17.

16. Hallmon WW, Waldrop TC, Houston GD, et al. Flossing clefts. Clinical and histologic observations. *J Periodontol.* 1986;57(8):501–504.

17. Super-Floss®. Oral-B Laboratories, Inc., 600 Clipper Drive, Belmont, CA 94002-4199.

18. Yost KG, Mallatt ME, Liebman J. Interproximal gingivitis and plaque reduction by four interdental products. *J Clin Dent.* 2006;17(3):79–83.

19. Poklepovic T, Worthington HV, Johnson TM, et al. Interdental brushing for the prevention and control of periodontal diseases and dental caries in adults. *Cochrane Database Syst Rev.* 2013;12:CD009857.

20. Lewis MW, Holder-Ballard C, Selders RJ Jr, et al. Comparison of the use of a toothpick holder to dental floss in improvement of gingival health in humans. *J Periodontol.* 2004;75(4):551–556.

21. Hoenderdos NL, Slot DE, Paraskevas S, et al. The efficacy of woodsticks on plaque and gingival inflammation: a systematic review. *Int J Dent Hyg.* 2008;6(4):280–289.

22. Waerhaug J. Effect of toothbrushing on subgingival plaque formation. *J Periodontol.* 1981;52(1):30–34.

23. Barnes CM, Russell CM, Reinhardt RA, et al. Comparison of irrigation to floss as an adjunct to tooth brushing: effect on bleeding, gingivitis and supragingival plaque. *J Clin Dent.* 2005;16(3):71–77.

24. Flemmig TF, Newman MG, Doherty FM, et al. Supragingival irrigation with 0.06% chlorhexidine in naturally occurring gingivitis. I. 6 month clinical observations. *J Periodontol.* 1990;61(2):112–117.

25. Newman MG, Flemmig TF, Nachnani S, et al. Irrigation with 0.06% chlorhexidine in naturally occurring gingivitis. II. 6 months microbiological observations. *J Periodontol.* 1990;61(7):427–433.

26. Eakle WS, Ford C, Boyd RL. Depth of penetration in periodontal pockets with oral irrigation. *J Clin Periodontol.* 1986;13(1):39–44.

27. Braun RE, Ciancio SG. Subgingival delivery by an oral irrigation device. *J Periodontol.* 1992;63(5):469–472.

28. Boyd RL, Hollander BN, Eakle WS. Comparison of a subgingivally placed cannula oral irrigator tip with a supragingivally placed standard irrigator tip. *J Clin Periodontol.* 1992;19(5):340–344.

29. Lugassy AA, Lautenschlager EP, Katrana D. Characterization of water spray devices. *J Dent Res.* 1971;50(2):466–473.

30. Husseini A, Slot DE, Van der Weijden GA. The efficacy of oral irrigation in addition to a toothbrush on plaque and the clinical parameters of periodontal inflammation: a systematic review. *Int J Dent Hyg.* 2008;6(4):304–314.

 ENHANCE YOUR UNDERSTANDING

the**Point®** **DIGITAL CONNECTIONS**
(see the inside front cover for access information)
- **Audio glossary**
- **Quiz bank**

 SUPPORT FOR LEARNING
(available separately; visit lww.com)
- *Active Learning Workbook for Clinical Practice of the Dental Hygienist, 12th Edition*

prep**U** **INDIVIDUALIZED REVIEW**
(available separately; visit lww.com)
- **Adaptive quizzing with *prepU for Wilkins' Clinical Practice of the Dental Hygienist***

36

Fluorides

Durinda J. Mattana, RDH, BSDH, MS and Erin E. Relich, RDH, BSDH, MSA

CHAPTER OUTLINE

After studying this chapter, the student will be able to:

1. Describe the mechanisms of action of fluoride in the prevention of dental caries.

2. Explain the role of community water fluoridation on the decline of dental caries incidence in a community.

3. Recommend appropriate over-the-counter (OTC) and professionally applied fluoride therapies based on each patient's caries risk assessment.

4. Compare use of fluoride home products (OTC and prescription).

5. Incorporate fluoride into individualized prevention plans for patients of various ages and risk levels.

The use of fluorides provides the most effective method for dental caries prevention and control. Fluoride is necessary for optimum oral health at all ages and is made available at the tooth surface by two general means:

▶ *Systemically*, by way of the circulation to developing teeth (preeruptive exposure).

▶ *Topically*, directly to the exposed surfaces of teeth erupted into the oral cavity[1] (posteruptive exposure).

▶ Maximum caries inhibiting effect occurs when there is systemic exposure before tooth eruption and frequent topical fluoride exposure throughout life.[2]

▶ Key words associated with fluoride and fluoride therapy are defined in Box 36-1.

FLUORIDE METABOLISM[1,3]

I. Fluoride Intake

▶ Sources
- Drinking water that contains fluoride naturally or has been fluoridated
- Prescribed dietary supplements
- Foods, in small amounts
- Foods and beverages prepared at home or processed commercially using water that contains fluoride
- Varying small amounts ingested from dentifrices, mouthrinses, supplements, and other fluoride products used by the individual.

II. Absorption

A. Gastrointestinal Tract

▶ Fluoride is rapidly absorbed as hydrogen fluoride through passive diffusion in the stomach:
- Rate and amount of absorption depend on the solubility of the fluoride compound and gastric acidity.
- Most is absorbed within 60 minutes.

▶ Fluoride that is not absorbed in the stomach will be absorbed by the small intestine.

▶ There is less absorption when the fluoride is taken with milk and other food.

B. Blood Stream

▶ Plasma carries the fluoride for its distribution throughout the body and to the kidneys for elimination.

▶ Maximum blood levels are reached within 30 minutes of intake.

▶ Normal plasma levels are low and rise and fall according to intake.

III. Distribution and Retention

▶ Fluoride is distributed by the plasma to *all* tissues and organs. There is a strong affinity for mineralized tissues.

▶ Approximately 99% of fluoride in the body is located in the mineralized tissues.

▶ Concentrations of fluoride are highest at the surfaces next to the tissue fluid supplying the fluoride.

▶ The fluoride ion (F) is stored as an integral part of the crystal lattice of teeth and bones.
- Amount stored varies with the intake, the time of exposure, and the age and stage of the development of the individual.
- The teeth store small amounts, with highest levels on the tooth surface.

▶ Fluoride that accumulates in bone can be mobilized slowly from the skeleton due to the constant resorption and remodeling of bone.

▶ Once tooth enamel is fully matured, the fluoride deposited during development can be altered by cavitated dental caries, erosion, or mechanical abrasion.[1]

IV. Excretion

▶ Most fluoride is excreted through the kidneys in the urine, with a small amount excreted by the sweat glands and the feces.

▶ There is limited transfer from plasma to breast milk for excretion by that route.[1]

FLUORIDE AND TOOTH DEVELOPMENT

▶ Fluoride is a nutrient essential to the formation of sound teeth and bones, as are calcium, phosphorus, and other elements obtained from food and water.

BOX 36-1 KEY WORDS AND ABBREVIATIONS: Fluorides

Abrasive system: cleaning or polishing substances used in dentifrice; best when compatible with fluoride compounds and other ingredients, and does not alter the tooth structure unfavorably.

Acidogenic: producing acid or acidity.

AAPD: American Association of Pediatric Dentistry.

ADA: American Dental Association.

ADACSA: American Dental Association Council on Scientific Affairs.

APF: acidulated phosphate fluoride.

AWWA: American Water Works Association.

Apatite: a group of minerals of the general formula $Ca_{10}(PO_4)X_2$ wherein the X might include hydroxyl (OH), carbonate (CO), fluoride (F), or oxygen (O); crystalline mineral component of hard tissues (bones and teeth).

Cariogenic challenge: exposure of a tooth surface to an acid attack; acid is from the action of dental biofilm and cariogenic food ingested.

Cariostatic: exerting an inhibitory action on the progress of dental caries.

CDC: Centers for Disease Control and Prevention.

Defluoridation: lowering the amount of fluoride in fluoridated water to an optimum level for the prevention of dental caries and dental fluorosis.

Demineralization: breakdown of the tooth structure with a loss of mineral content, primarily calcium and phosphorus.

Dilution: the reduction in the absolute measurable benefits of the effectiveness of an intervention.

DMFT/dmft: decayed, missing, and filled teeth (permanent and primary dentition, respectively).

Efficacy: with reference to a product: an efficacious product produces a statistically and clinically significant benefit under ideal testing conditions in carefully controlled clinical trials.

Enamel hypocalcification: defect of enamel maturation caused by hereditary or systemic irregularities.

FDA: Food and Drug Administration.

Fluorapatite: the form of hydroxyapatite in which fluoride ions have replaced some of the hydroxyl ions; with fluoride, the apatite is less soluble and therefore more resistant to the acids formed from carbohydrate intake.

Fluorhydroxyapatite: apatite formed when low concentrations of fluoride react with tooth mineral; at higher concentrations, calcium fluoride is formed.

Fluoride: a salt of hydrofluoric acid; the ionized form of fluorine that occurs in many tissues and is stored primarily in bones and teeth.

Fluorosis: form of enamel hypomineralization due to excessive ingestion of fluoride during the development and mineralization of the teeth; depending on the length of exposure and the concentration of the fluoride, the fluorosed area may appear as a small white spot or as severe brown staining with pitting.

Gel: semi-solid or solid phase of a colloidal solution.

Glycolysis: process by which sugar is metabolized by bacteria to produce acid.

Hydroxyapatite: $Ca_{10}(PO_4)_6(OH)_2$; the form of apatite that is the principal mineral component of teeth, bones, and calculus.

Hypocalcification: deficient calcification.

Halo or diffusion effect: occurs when foods and beverages processed in a fluoridated community are imported and consumed in a nonfluoridated community.

Maturation: stage or process of becoming mature or attaining maximal development; with respect to tooth development, maturation results from the continuous dynamic exchange of ions into the surface of the enamel from pellicle, dental biofilm, and oral fluids.

NaF: neutral sodium fluoride.

O.T.C.: over the counter.

Prevented fraction: the proportion of disease occurrence in a population that is averted due to an intervention.

ppm: parts per million; measure used to designate the amount of fluoride used for optimum level in fluoridated water, dentifrice, and other fluoride-containing preparations (1 ppm is equivalent to 1 mg/L).

Remineralization: restoration of mineral elements in a tooth surface; enhanced by the presence of fluoride; remineralized lesions are more resistant to initiation of dental caries than is normal tooth structure.

Rx: prescription.

SnF_2: stannous fluoride.

Subsurface lesion: demineralized area below the surface of the enamel created by acid that has passed through micropores between enamel rods; subject to remineralization by action of fluoride.

Thixotropic: type of gel that sets in a gel-like state but becomes fluid under stress; the fluid form permits the solution to flow into interdental areas.

USPHS: United States Public Health Services.

USDHHS: United States Department of Health and Human Services.

"White spot": term used to describe a small area on the surface of enamel that contrasts in appearance with the rest of the surface and may be visible only when the tooth is dried; two types of white spots can be differentiated: an area of demineralization and an area of fluorosis (also referred to as an "enamel opacity").

▶ A comprehensive review of the histology of tooth development and mineralization is recommended to supplement the information included here.[4,5]

I. Preeruptive: Mineralization Stage

▶ Fluoride is deposited during the formation of the enamel, starting at the dentinoenamel junction, after the enamel matrix has been laid down by the ameloblasts.

- Figure 36-1A shows the distribution of fluoride in all parts of the teeth during mineralization.
- The hydroxyapatite crystalline structure becomes *fluorapatite*, which is a less soluble apatite crystal.[2]
- Pre-eruptive fluoride may contribute to shallower occlusal grooves, and reduce the risk of fissure caries.[2]

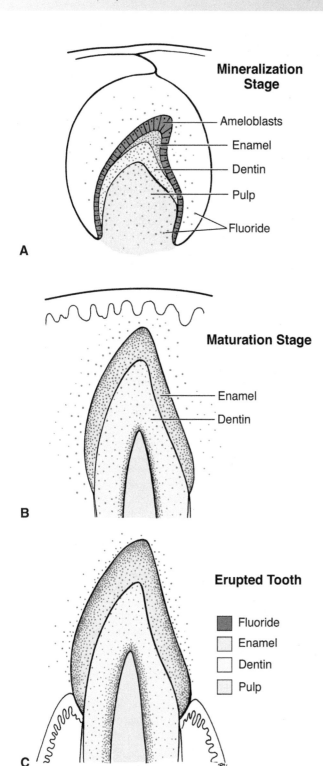

A

B

C

FIGURE 36-1 **Systemic Fluoride.** Green dots represent fluoride ions in the tissues and distributed throughout the tooth. **A:** Developing tooth during mineralization shows fluoride from water and other systemic sources deposited in the enamel and dentin. **B:** Maturation stage before eruption, when fluoride is taken up from tissue fluids around the crown. **C:** Erupted tooth continues to take up fluoride on the surface from external sources. Note concentrated fluoride deposition on the enamel surface and on the pulpal surface of the dentin.

▶ Table 50-4, in Chapter 50, lists the weeks in utero when the hard tissue formation begins for the primary teeth.

▶ The first permanent molars begin to mineralize at birth as listed in Table 16-1, in Chapter 16.

▶ Effect of excess fluoride (fluorosis)[6,7]

- Dental fluorosis is a form of hypomineralization that results from systemic ingestion of an excess amount of fluoride during tooth development.
- During mineralization the enamel is highly receptive to free fluoride ions.
- The normal activity of the ameloblasts may be inhibited, and the defective enamel matrix that can form results in discontinuity of crystal growth.

▶ Dental fluorosis can appear clinically in varying degrees from white flecks or striations to cosmetically objectionable stained pitting as listed in Tables 23-2 and 23-3, in Chapter 23.

II. Preeruptive: Maturation Stage

▶ After mineralization is complete and before eruption, fluoride deposition continues in the surface of the enamel.

- Figure 36-1B shows fluoride around the crown during maturation.
- Fluoride is taken up from the nutrient tissue fluids surrounding the tooth crown.

III. Posteruptive

▶ After eruption and throughout the life span of the teeth, the concentration of fluoride on the outermost surface of the enamel is dependent on:

- Daily topical sources of fluoride to prevent demineralization and encourage remineralization for prevention of dental caries.
- Sources for daily topical fluoride include fluoridated drinking water, dentifrices, mouthrinses, and other fluoride preparations used by the patient.
- The fluoride on the outermost surface is available to inhibit demineralization and enhance remineralization as needed on a daily basis.
- Figure 36-2 depicts the areas on the tooth that acquire fluoride after eruption.
  - The continuous daily presence of fluoride provided for the tooth surfaces can inhibit the initiation and progression of dental caries.
  - Uptake is most rapid on the enamel surface during the first years after eruption.
  - Repeated daily intake of drinking water with fluoride provides a topical source as it washes over the teeth throughout life.

TOOTH SURFACE FLUORIDE

Fluoride concentration is greatest on the surface next to the source of fluoride.

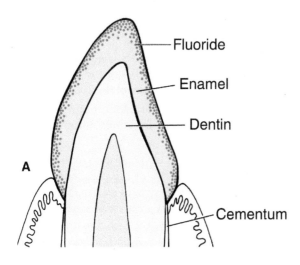

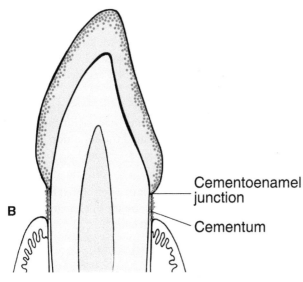

FIGURE 36-2 **Fluoride Acquisition after Eruption. A:** Fluoride represented by green dots on the enamel surface is taken up from external sources, including dentifrice, rinse, topical application, and fluoridated drinking water passing over the teeth. **B:** Gingival recession exposes the cementum to external sources of fluoride for the prevention of root caries and the alleviation of sensitivity.

▶ For the enamel of the erupted tooth, highest concentration is at the outer surface exposed to the oral cavity.

▶ For the dentin, the highest concentration is at the pulpal surface.

▶ Periodontal attachment loss (gingival recession) can often cause the root surface and cementum to become exposed to the oral cavity and external fluoride sources.

I. Fluoride in Enamel

A. Uptake

▶ Uptake of fluoride depends on the level of fluoride in the oral environment and the length of time of exposure.

▶ Hypomineralized enamel absorbs fluoride in greater quantities than sound enamel; it incorporates into

the hydroxyapatite crystalline structure to become fluorapatite.[6]

▶ Demineralized enamel that has been remineralized in the presence of fluoride will have a greater concentration of fluoride than sound enamel.

B. Fluoride in the Enamel Surface

▶ Fluoride is a natural constituent of enamel.

▶ The intact outer surface has the highest concentration that falls sharply toward the interior of the tooth.[8]

II. Fluoride in Dentin[9]

▶ The fluoride level may be greater in dentin than in enamel.

▶ A higher concentration is at the pulpal or inner surface, where exchanges take place.

▶ Newly formed dentin absorbs fluoride rapidly.

III. Fluoride in Cementum[9]

▶ The level of fluoride in cementum is high and increases with exposure.

• With recession of the clinical attachment level, the root surface is exposed to the fluids of the oral cavity.

• Figure 36-2B shows fluoride acquisition to exposed cementum.

• Fluoride is then available to the cementum from the saliva and all the sources used by the patient, including drinking water, dentifrice, and mouthrinse.

DEMINERALIZATION–REMINERALIZATION[8]

Figure 36-3 illustrates the comparative levels of fluoride that may be found in the tooth surface and the sublevel lesion in early dental caries.

I. Fluoride in Biofilm and Saliva

▶ Saliva and biofilm are reservoirs for fluoride; saliva carries minerals available for remineralization when needed.

▶ Fluoride helps to inhibit demineralization when it is present at the crystal surface during an acid challenge.

▶ Fluoride enhances remineralization forming a condensed layer on the crystal surface, which attracts calcium and phosphate ions.

▶ High concentrations of fluoride can interfere with the growth and metabolism of bacteria.

▶ Dental biofilm may contain 5–50 ppm fluoride. The content varies greatly and is constantly changing.

▶ Fluoride may be acquired directly from fluoridated water, dentifrice, and other topical sources and brought by the saliva or by an exchange of fluoride in the biofilm to the demineralizing tooth surface under the biofilm.

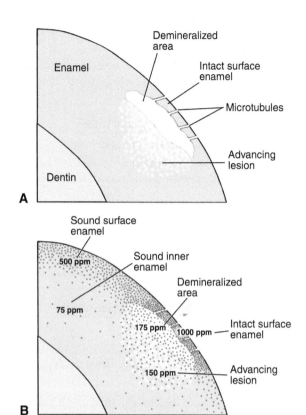

FIGURE 36-3 Examples of Enamel Fluoride Content. A: Early stage of dental caries with an intact surface enamel and subsurface demineralized area. **B:** A demineralized area readily takes up available fluoride. As shown, the fluoride content (1,000 ppm) of the relatively intact surface over a subsurface demineralized white spot is higher than that of the sound surface enamel (500 ppm). The body of the advancing lesion has a higher fluoride content (150 ppm) than does the sound inner enamel (75 ppm). (Source: Melberg JR, Ripa LW, Leske GS. *Fluoride in Preventive Dentistry: Theory and Clinical Applications.* Chicago, IL: Quintessence; 1983:31.)

II. Summary of Fluoride Action

Having fluoride available topically to the tooth posteruptively is key to its effectiveness.

► Frequent exposure to fluoride, such as from fluoridated water, dentifrice, and mouthrinse, is recommended.

► There are three basic topical effects of fluoride to prevent dental caries.[8]
  • Inhibit demineralization.
  • Enhance remineralization of incipient lesions.
  • Inhibit bacterial activity by inhibiting *enolase*, an enzyme needed by bacteria to metabolize carbohydrates.

FLUORIDATION

► *Fluoridation* is the adjustment of the natural fluoride ion content in a municipal water supply to the optimum physiologic concentration that will maximize caries prevention and limit enamel fluorosis.[10]

► Fluoridation has been established as the most efficient, effective, reliable, and inexpensive means for improving and maintaining oral health for all who use it.

► Fluoridation was named by the U.S. Centers for Disease Control and Prevention (CDC) as one of the 10 most significant public health measures of the 20th century.[10]

► The estimated annual cost per person per year is low, with lower cost per person for communities of more than 20,000 people.[11]

► In 2010, 66.2% of the total US population received fluoridated water, whereas 73.9% of the population served by public (municipal) water systems received fluoridated water. These percentages vary greatly from state to state.[12]

I. Historical Aspects[13]

A. Mottled Enamel and Dental Caries

► Dr. Frederick S. McKay
  • Early in the 20th century, Dr. McKay began his extensive studies to find the cause of "brown stain," which later was called mottled enamel and now is known as *dental fluorosis*.
  • He observed that people in Colorado Springs, Colorado, with mottled enamel had significantly less dental caries.[14] He associated the condition with the drinking water, but tests were inconclusive.

► H.V. Churchill

In 1931, H.V. Churchill, a chemist, pinpointed fluorine as the specific element related to the tooth changes that Dr. McKay had been observing clinically.[15]

B. Background for Fluoridation

► Dr. H. Trendley Dean
  • Epidemiologic studies of the 1930s, sponsored by the US Public Health Service (USPHS) and directed by Dr. Dean, led to the conclusion that the level of fluoride in the water optimum for dental caries prevention averages 1 ppm in moderate climates.
  • Clinically objectionable dental fluorosis is associated with levels well over 2 ppm.[16]
  • From this knowledge and the fact many healthy people had lived long lives in communities where the fluoride content of the water was much greater than 1 ppm, the concept of adding fluoride to the water developed.
  • It was still necessary to show the benefits from controlled fluoridation could parallel those of natural fluoride.

C. Fluoridation—1945

► The first communities were fluoridated in 1945.

► Research in the communities began before fluoridation was started to obtain baseline information.

D. Control Cities

► Aurora, Illinois, where the natural fluoride level is optimum (1.2 ppm), was used to compare the benefits of

BOX 36-2

First Fluoridation Research Cities

RESEARCH CITY	CONTROL CITY
Grand Rapids, Michigan (January 1945)	Muskegon, Michigan
Newburgh, New York (May 1945)	Kingston, New York
Brantford, Ontario (June 1945)	Sarnia, Ontario
Evanston, Illinois (February 1947)	Oak Park, Illinois

natural fluoride in the water supply with those of fluoridation, as well as with a fluoride-free city, Rockford, Illinois.

▶ Original cities with fluoridation and their control cities in the research are shown in Box 36-2.

▶ The research conducted in those cities, as well as throughout the world, has documented the influence of fluoride on oral health.

II. Water Supply Adjustment

A. Fluoride Level

▶ Since 1962, the USPHS recommended the optimal fluoride concentration of 0.7 ppm (for warmer climates) to 1.2 ppm (for colder climates) to prevent dental caries and minimize fluorosis.[17]

• The range in fluoride concentration was based on the assumption that people in warmer climates drink more water and therefore receive more fluoride.

▶ In 2015, the US Department of Health and Human Services (USDHHS) updated the recommendation for the optimal concentration of water fluoridation to 0.7 ppm for all communities.

• The decision is based on the fact that Americans have access to many more sources of fluoride today than they did when water fluoridation was introduced in the United States.[18]

• The change still provides an effective level of fluoride to reduce the incidence of dental caries while minimizing the rate of fluorosis.

B. Chemicals Used

▶ All fluoride chemicals must conform to the appropriate American Water Works Association (AWWA) standards to ensure that the drinking water will be safe.[17]

▶ Sources

• Compounds from which the fluoride ion is derived are naturally occurring and are mined in various parts of the world.

• Examples of common sources are fluorspar, cryolite, and apatite.

▶ Criteria for acceptance of a fluoride compound for fluoridation include:

• Solubility to permit regular use in a water plant.

• Relatively inexpensive.

• Readily available to prevent interruptions in maintaining the proper fluoride level.

▶ Compounds used:

• Dry compounds: sodium fluoride (NaF) and sodium silicofluoride.

• Liquid solution: hydrofluorosilicic acid.

EFFECTS AND BENEFITS OF FLUORIDATION

Fluoridated water is a systemic source of fluoride for developing teeth and a topical source of fluoride on the surfaces of erupted teeth throughout life.[19]

I. Appearance of Teeth

▶ Teeth exposed to an optimum or slightly higher level of fluoride appear white, shining, opaque, and without blemishes.

• When the level is slightly more than optimum, teeth may exhibit mild enamel fluorosis seen as white areas in bands or flecks. Without close scrutiny, such spots blend with the overall appearance.

▶ The majority of fluorosis today is mild and not considered an esthetic problem.[10,20]

II. Dental Caries: Permanent Teeth

A. Overall Benefits

▶ Maximum benefit is seen with continuous use of fluoridated water from birth.

▶ Estimates have shown the reduction in caries due to water fluoridation alone (factoring out other sources of topical fluoride) among adults of all ages is 27%.[19]

▶ The effects are similar to communities with optimum levels of natural fluoride in the water.

▶ Many more individuals are completely caries-free when fluoride is in the water.

B. Distribution

▶ Anterior teeth, particularly maxillary, receive more protection from fluoride than do posterior teeth.[16]

• Anterior teeth are contacted by the drinking water as it passes into the mouth.

C. Progression

▶ Not only are the numbers of carious lesions reduced, but the caries rate is slowed.

▶ Caries progression is also reduced in the surfaces that receive fluoride for the first time after eruption.[21]

III. Root Caries

▶ Root caries experience in lifelong residents of a naturally fluoridated community is in direct proportion to the fluoride concentration in the water compared with the experience of residents of a fluoride-free community.[22]

▶ The incidence of root caries is approximately 50% less for lifelong residents of a fluoridated community.[23]

IV. Dental Caries: Primary Teeth

▶ With fluoridation from birth, the caries incidence is reduced up to 40% in the primary teeth.[10]

▶ The introduction of fluoridation into a community significantly increases the proportion of caries-free children and reduces the decayed, missing, and filled teeth (dmft/DMFT) scores when compared to areas that are nonfluoridated over the same time period.[20]

▶ For example, children aged 6–9 years in Newburgh, New York, had five times as many caries-free primary teeth present as did the children of Kingston, where fluoride was not present in the community drinking water.[24]

V. Tooth Loss

▶ Tooth loss due to dental caries is much greater in both primary and permanent teeth without fluoride[24] because of increased dental caries, which progresses more rapidly.

VI. Adults

▶ When a person resides in a community with fluoride in the drinking water throughout life, benefits continue.

▶ In Colorado Springs, adults aged 20–44 years who had used water with natural fluoride showed 60% less caries experience than did adults in fluoride-deficient Boulder, Colorado. In Boulder, adults also had three to four times as many permanent teeth extracted.[25]

▶ In a survey of adults in Rockford, Illinois (no fluoride), there were about seven times as many edentulous persons as there were in a comparable group in Aurora, Illinois (natural fluoride).[26]

VII. Periodontal Health

▶ Indirect favorable effects of fluoride on periodontal health can be shown.
  • Fluoride works to decrease dental caries. The presence of carious lesions favors biofilm retention

which can lead to periodontal infection, particularly adjacent to the gingival margin.

▶ With the use of fluorides, particularly water fluoridation, fewer teeth are lost because of dental caries at younger ages. Periodontal disease prevention and control is to be emphasized in communities with fluoride in the drinking water.

PARTIAL DEFLUORIDATION

▶ Water with an excess of natural fluoride does not meet the requirements of the USPHS.

▶ Several hundred communities in the United States had water supplies that naturally contained more than twice the optimal level of fluoride.

▶ Defluoridation can be accomplished by one of several chemical systems.[27] The efficacy of the methods has been shown.

▶ Examples: The water supply in Britton, South Dakota, has been reduced from almost 7 to 1.5 ppm since 1948, and in Bartlett, Texas, from 8 to 1.8 ppm since 1952. Examinations have shown a significant reduction in the incidence of objectionable fluorosis in children born since defluoridation.[27,28]

SCHOOL FLUORIDATION

▶ To bring the benefits of fluoridation to children living in rural areas without the possibility for community fluoridation, adding fluoride to a school water supply has been an alternative.

▶ Because of the intermittent use of the school water (only 5 days each week during the 9-month school year), the amount of fluoride added was increased over the usual 1 ppm.

▶ Example: 12 years of fluoride at 5 ppm in the school drinking water of Elk Lake, Pennsylvania.
  • Children who had attended that school regularly had 39% fewer decayed, missing, and filled teeth than did those in the control group.
  • The greatest benefits were found on proximal tooth surfaces.[29]

▶ Example: In the schools of Seagrove, North Carolina, after 12 years with the fluoride level at 6.3 ppm, the children experienced a 47.5% decrease in DMF surfaces compared with those in the control group.[29]

▶ Such systems have significance in the long history of efforts for fluoridation for all people in the United States.

▶ School fluoridation has been phased out in several states, and the current extent of this practice is unknown. Operations and maintenance of small fluoridation systems are problematic.[10]

DISCONTINUED FLUORIDATION

▶ When fluoride is removed from a community water supply that had dental caries control by fluoridation, the effects can be clearly shown.

▶ Example: In Antigo, Wisconsin, the action of antifluoridationists in 1960 brought about the discontinuance of fluoridation, which had been installed in 1949.

• Examinations in the years following 1960 revealed the marked drop in the number of children who were caries-free and the steep increases in caries rates.

• From 1960 to 1966, the number of caries-free children in the second grade decreased by 67%.[30]

• Fluoridation was reinstated in 1966 by popular demand.

FLUORIDES IN FOODS

I. Foods[31]

▶ Certain foods contain fluoride, but not enough to constitute a significant part of the day's need for caries prevention.

▶ Examples: meat, eggs, vegetables, cereals, and fruit have small but measurable amounts, whereas tea and fish have larger amounts.

▶ Foods cooked in fluoridated water retain fluoride from the cooking water.

II. Salt[32–34]

▶ Fluoridated salt has not been promoted in the United States, but is widely used in Germany, France, and Switzerland where 30%–80% of the domestic marketed salt is fluoridated.

▶ Another 30 countries or more use fluoridated salt worldwide for its effectiveness as a community health program.

▶ Fluoridated salt results in a reduced incidence of dental caries, but there is insufficient evidence for its overall effectiveness.

▶ Fluoridated salts currently available supply about one-third to one-half of the amount of fluoride ingested daily from 1 ppm fluoridated water.

▶ Fluoridated salt is recommended by the World Health Organization as an alternative to fluoridated water to target underprivileged groups.

III. Halo/Diffusion Effect

▶ Foods and beverages that are commercially processed (cooked or reconstituted) in optimally fluoridated cities can be distributed and consumed in nonfluoridated communities.

▶ The halo or diffusion effect can result in increased fluoride intake by individuals living in nonfluoridated communities, providing them some protection against dental caries.[31]

IV. Bottled Water

▶ Bottled water usually does not contain optimal fluoride unless it has a label indicating that it is fluoridated.

▶ Patients need to be advised to fill their drinking water bottles from a fluoridated water supply.

V. Water Filters[35]

▶ Reverse osmosis and water distillation systems remove fluoride from the water, but water softeners do not.

▶ Carbon filters (for the end of a faucet or in pitchers) vary in their removal of fluoride.

▶ Carbon filters with activated alumina remove fluoride.

▶ Patients need to be warned that water filters may remove fluoride from the drinking water and need to be checked with the manufacturer before purchase.

VI. Infant Formula[36–38]

▶ There has been an increase in breast feeding in the United States, but infant formula remains a major source of nutrition for many infants.

▶ Ready-to-feed formulas do not need to be reconstituted, but water is added to powdered and liquid concentrate formulas.

▶ Breast milk may contain 0.02 ppm fluoride and all types of infant formula themselves contain a low amount of fluoride (0.11–0.57 ppm).[37]

▶ The level of fluoride in the water supply used to reconstitute powdered or liquid concentrate formulas determines the total fluoride intake.

▶ The American Dental Association (ADA) recommends continuing to use optimally fluoridated water to reconstitute infant formula while being aware of the possible risk of mild enamel fluorosis in the primary teeth.[38]

DIETARY FLUORIDE SUPPLEMENTS[10,39,40]

▶ Prescribed dietary supplements were introduced in the late 1940s and are intended to compensate for fluoride-deficient drinking water.

▶ The current supplementation dosage schedule developed by the ADA and the American Association of Pediatric Dentistry (AAPD) and revised in 1994 includes children aged 6 months through 16 years.

• Table 36-1 contains the daily dosage amounts based on the age of the child and the amount of fluoride in the primary water supply.

TABLE 36-1	Fluoride Supplements Dose Schedule (Mg NaF/d)[a]		
	WATER FLUORIDE ION CONCENTRATION (PPM)		
AGE OF CHILD (Y)	**LESS THAN 0.3**	**BETWEEN 0.3 AND 0.6**	**GREATER THAN 0.6**
Birth–6 mo	0	0	0
6 mo–3 y	0.25 mg	0	0
3–6 y	0.50 mg	0.25 mg	0
6–16 y	1.0 mg	0.50 mg	0

[a]About 2.2 mg of sodium fluoride provides 1 mg of fluoride ion.
Source: American Dental Association and the American Academy of Pediatrics.

▶ Clinical recommendations from the American Dental Association Council on Scientific Affairs (ADACSA) include the use of fluoride supplements for children:
  • At high risk of developing dental caries
  • Those whose primary source of drinking water is deficient in fluoride.[41]

I. Assess Possible Need

▶ Review the patient's history to be certain the child is not receiving other fluoride in such preparations as vitamin–fluoride supplements.

▶ Determine the fluoride level of all sources of drinking water is below 0.6 ppm.

▶ Refer to the list of fluoridated communities available from state or local health departments.

▶ Request water analysis when the fluoride level has not been determined, for example, in private well water.

▶ Determine the child's risk for dental caries is high or moderately high before considering the use of fluoride supplements.[39]

▶ Reassess the caries risk at frequent intervals as the status may be affected by the child's development, personal and family situations, and behavioral factors such as changes in oral hygiene practices.[33,41]

II. Available Forms of Supplements

▶ NaF supplements are available as tablets, lozenges, and drops in 0.25, 0.50, and 1.0 mg dosages.

▶ Prescribed on an individual patient basis for daily use at home.

A. Tablets and Lozenges

▶ Tablets are chewed thoroughly, swished/rinsed around in the oral cavity, and forced between the teeth before swallowing.

▶ Lozenges are dissolved for one to 2 minutes in the mouth to provide both preeruptive and posteruptive benefits.[41]

▶ Best taken at bedtime after teeth are brushed.
  • Avoid drinking, eating, or rinsing before going to sleep to gain maximum benefit.

B. Drops

▶ A liquid concentrate with directions that specify the number of drops for the prescription dose daily.

▶ Primary use for child 6 months to 3 years, and patient of any age unable to use other forms that require chewing and swallowing.

III. Prescription Guidelines

▶ No more than 264 mg NaF (120 mg fluoride ion) to be dispensed per household at one time.

▶ Take supplements with juice or water.
  • Avoid taking with dairy products because fluoride can combine with calcium and be poorly absorbed.

▶ Storage
  • Keep products out of reach of children.
  • Keep tablets in the original container, away from heat and direct light, and away from damp places such as a bathroom or kitchen sink area.

▶ Missed dose
  • Take as soon as remembered.
  • If near next dose time, skip that dose and go to next regular time.

IV. Benefits and Limitations

▶ Prenatal use by pregnant women
  • Administration of prenatal dietary fluoride supplements is not recommended.
  • Some evidence has shown that fluoride crosses the placenta during the fifth and sixth months of pregnancy and may enter the prenatal deciduous enamel.[42]
  • Overall, there is weak evidence to support the use of fluoride supplements to prevent dental caries in primary teeth.

▶ Daily fluoride supplements offer caries preventive benefits in permanent teeth. School-aged children who chewed, swished, and swallowed 1 mg fluoride tablets daily on school days had significantly lower caries experience than children who did not use fluoride supplements.

▶ The use of fluoride supplements in children over 6 years of age shows a 24% decrease in DMF tooth surfaces in permanent teeth compared to no fluoride supplements.[43]

▶ Consider the child's age, caries risk, and all sources of fluoride exposure before recommending the use of fluoride supplements.[33,41]

PROFESSIONAL TOPICAL FLUORIDE APPLICATIONS

Topical fluorides are an essential part of a total preventive program for patients of all ages.

▶ Fluoridated water and fluoride toothpaste are the primary sources of topical fluoride for patients of all ages and levels of caries risk.

▶ Additional topical fluoride sources may be professionally applied and/or self-applied by the patient, primarily for those at an elevated caries risk.

I. Historical Perspectives

▶ Professionally applied fluoride has been instrumental in the reduction of dental caries in the United States and other industrialized countries since the early 1940s.

▶ Dr. Basil G. Bibby conducted the initial topical NaF study using Brockton, Massachusetts schoolchildren.[44]

▶ More than one-third fewer new carious lesions resulted from a 0.1% aqueous solution applied at 4-month intervals for 2 years applied by a dental hygienist.

▶ The research led to extensive studies by Dr. John W. Knutson and others sponsored by the USPHS.

- The aim was to determine the most effective concentration of NaF, the minimum time required for application, and procedural details.[45,46]
- Their results provided the basis for the applications currently used and described in the following sections of this chapter.
- Professionally applied fluorides are available as gels or foams delivered in trays, or varnish that is applied with a soft brush on the teeth.

II. Indications

▶ The professional application of a high-concentration fluoride preventive agent is based on caries risk assessment for the individual patient.

▶ See Table 27-1 in Chapter 27 for the criteria to determine low, moderate, and high caries risk.

▶ Indications for a professional fluoride application are outlined in Box 36-3.[47]

III. Compounds

▶ Table 36-2 provides a summary of the available professional fluoride applications.

- 2.0% NaF as gel or foam delivered in trays.

BOX 36-3

Indications for Professional Topical Fluoride Application[47]

▷ Patients at an elevated (moderate or high) risk of developing caries

See Table 27-1 in Chapter 27 for the criteria to determine low, moderate, and high caries risk.

▷ **5% NaF varnish** at least every 3–6 months (for all ages and adult root caries)

Or

▷ **1.23% APF gel** 4-minute trays at least every 3–6 months (for 6 years and older and adult root caries)

▷ Patients at a low risk of developing caries may not benefit from additional topical fluoride other than OTC-fluoridated toothpaste and fluoridated water daily.

Source: American Dental Association Council on Scientific Affairs. Topical fluoride for caries prevention: executive summary of updated clinical recommendations and supporting systematic review. *J Am Dent Assoc.* 2013;144(11):1279–1291.

- 1.23% acidulated phosphate fluoride (APF) as a gel or foam delivered in trays.
- 5% NaF as a varnish brushed on the teeth.

▶ *2.0% NaF gel*

- NaF, also called "neutral sodium fluoride" due to its neutral pH of 7.0, contains 9,050 ppm fluoride ion.
- Clinical trials demonstrating the efficacy of neutral NaF are based on a series of four or five applications on a weekly basis.[48]
- Quarterly or semiannual applications are most common in clinical practice.

▶ *2.0% NaF foam*

- There is limited clinical evidence to demonstrate foam's effectiveness in caries prevention.

▶ *1.23% APF gel*

- Contains 12,300 ppm fluoride ion.
- A 4-minute tray application is recommended at least every 3–6 months per year for individuals 6 years of age and older at an elevated risk for dental caries.[47]
- Widely used because of its storage stability, acceptable taste, and tissue compatibility.
- Low pH of 3.5 enhances fluoride uptake, which is greatest during the first 4 minutes.[49]
- APF may etch porcelain and composite restorative materials, so it is not indicated for patients with porcelain, composite restorations, and sealants.[50]
- The hydrofluoride component of APF can dissolve the filler particles of the composite resin restorations.
- Macroinorganic filler particles of composite materials demonstrate noticeable etched patterns generated by APF, whereas many of the more recently available microfilled composites/resins are not as sensitive to the APF.[50]

TABE 36-2	Professionally Applied Topical Fluorides			
AGENT	**FORM**	**CONCENTRATION**	**APPLICATION MODE/FREQUENCY**	**NOTES**
NaF neutral or 7 pH	2% Gel or foam[a]	9,050 ppm 0.90% F ion	Tray (4 min)/no currently recommended interval	Do not overfill: see Figure 36-5
Acidulated phosphate 3.5 pH	1.23% Gel or foam[a]	12,300 ppm 1.23% F ion	Tray (4 min)/at least every 3–6 mo[47]	Do not overfill: see Figure 36-5
NaF neutral or 7 pH	5% Varnish	22,600 ppm 2.6% F ion	Apply thin layer with a soft brush (1–2 min)/at least every 3–6 mo[47]	Sets up to a hard film

[a]There is limited published clinical evidence supporting the effectiveness of foam.[47]

- The prevented fraction of dental caries ranged from 18% to 41% with the use of APF or NaF gels.[51]

▶ *1.23% APF foam*

- There is limited clinical evidence to show the effectiveness of foam in caries prevention.

▶ *5% NaF varnish*

- Fluoride varnishes were developed during the late 1960s and early 1970s to prolong contact time of the fluoride with the tooth surface.[52]
- Varnishes are safe and effective, fast and easy to apply, and patient acceptance is good.
- The use of fluoride varnish 2–4 times per year is associated with a 43% decrease in DMFT surfaces in permanent teeth and 37% in primary teeth.[53]
- Varnish has a higher concentration of fluoride than gel or foam (22,600 ppm fluoride ion), but an overall less amount of fluoride is used per application (<7 mg varnish versus 30 mg of gel for a child).
- Varnish sets quickly and remains on the teeth for a number of hours releasing fluoride into the pits and fissures, proximal surfaces, and cervical areas of the tooth where it is needed the most.[54]
- Application is recommended at least every 3–4 months per year for individuals at an elevated risk for dental caries.[47]
- Varnish is effective in reversing active pit and fissure enamel lesions in the primary dentition[55] and remineralizing enamel lesions regardless of whether the varnish is applied over or around the demineralizng lesion.[56]
- Varnish is also effective in reducing demineralization (white areas) around orthodontic brackets.[57]
- Varnish is the fluoride application of choice for those with dentin hypersensitivity; see Chapter 44.

- Varnish is the only professional topical fluoride to be used for children under the age of 6 years.
- Varnish received approval from the United States FDA in 1994 for use as a cavity liner and for treatment of hypersensitive teeth.
- Its use in the United States as a caries preventive agent is considered off-label, but has become a standard of care in practice.[54]

CLINICAL PROCEDURES: PROFESSIONAL TOPICAL FLUORIDE

I. Objectives

▶ *Prevention of dental caries*

- Identify special problems, including areas adjacent to restorations, orthodontic appliances, xerostomia, and other risk factors.
- Box 36-3 contains indications for the application of a professional fluoride.
- Examples: Active or secondary caries, exposed root surfaces, current orthodontic treatment, low or no fluoride exposure, or compromised salivary flow.

▶ *Remineralization of demineralized areas*

- Demineralized white areas on the cervical third, especially under dental biofilm.

▶ *Desensitization*

- Fluoride aids in blocking dentinal tubules, as explained in Chapter 44.

▶ Varnish covers and protects a sensitive area, and fluoride is slowly released for uptake.

II. Preparation of the Teeth for Topical Application

▶ *General preparation for tray and varnish applications*

- Instruct patients about all methods of caries prevention and how they work together.

- Most patients will receive the professional topical application following their routine continuing care appointment with complete dental hygiene procedures of personal oral hygiene care instruction, scaling, and stain removal.
- When the fluoride application is to be applied at a time other than following scaling and debridement, rubber cup polishing is not routinely necessary because fluoride will penetrate biofilm and provide the same benefits with or without prior polishing.[47,58]
- Calculus and stain removal are completed first.
- After calculus removal, apply principles of selective polishing for stain removal.

- Select an appropriate cleaning or polishing agent that will not harm the tooth surface or the restorative material present.
- A fluoride-containing polishing paste is not effective as a fluoride application.[59]
- Preparation and procedure for gel or foam tray application is included in Table 36-3; preparation and procedure for varnish application is described in Table 36-4.

III. Patient and/or Parent Counseling

▶ Help patients understand the purposes and benefits as well as the limitations of topical applications.

TABLE 36-3	**Procedure for Topical Gel or Foam Professional Tray**
Patient	■ Determine need based on caries risk assessment (not to be used for children under age 6 y)
	■ Choose the type of fluoride (APF or NaF and gel or foam); data support use of APF Gel
	■ Seat upright
	■ Explain procedure including length: 4 min
	■ Instruct not to swallow
	■ Tilt head forward slightly
Tray coverage	■ Choose appropriate size for full coverage
	■ Complete dentition must be covered, including anterior and posterior vertical coverage, distal dam depth, and close fit to teeth
	■ Check for coverage of areas of recession (if unable to cover exposed root surfaces use varnish application)
	■ Proper and improper tray coverage is shown in Figure 36-4
Place gel or foam	■ Use minimum amount of gel or foam in the trays, as shown in Figure 36-5
	■ Fill tray 1/3 full with gel; completely fill, but do not overfill with foam
Dry the teeth	■ Place a saliva ejector in the mouth during the drying procedure
	■ Dry the teeth before insertion of trays starting with the maxillary teeth; facial, occlusal, and palatal surfaces and then the mandibular teeth; lingual, occlusal, and facial surfaces
Insert trays	■ Place both filled trays in mouth
	■ A two-step procedure (one tray at a time) may be required; if so, patient may not rinse but must expectorate after the removal of each tray to prevent swallowing
Isolation	■ Use a saliva ejector with maximum efficiency suction
Attention	■ Do not leave patient unattended
Timing	■ Use a timer; do not estimate (4 min)
	■ Procedure will take 8 min when a two-step procedure is used
Completion	■ Tilt head forward for removal of tray
	■ Request patient to expectorate for several minutes; do not allow swallowing
	■ Wipe excess gel or foam from teeth with gauze sponge
	■ Use high-power suction to draw out saliva and gel
	■ Instruct patient that nothing is to be placed in the mouth for 30 min; do not rinse, eat, drink, or brush teeth

TABLE 36-4	Procedure for Varnish Application (5% NaF)
Patient	■ Determine need based on caries risk assessment (only professional fluoride recommended for children under age 6 y)
	■ Explain procedure
	■ Seat supine
	■ For the infant and toddler the parent and clinician can sit knee to knee with the child held across the knees (Figure 49-4)
	■ Instruct not to swallow during the procedure
Prepare product	■ Dispense from a tube or open a single-dose packet
	■ Have applicator brush available
Dry teeth	■ Varnish sets up in the presence of saliva, but it is recommended to remove excess saliva by wiping the teeth with a gauze square
Apply varnish	■ Dip applicator brush in varnish and mix well
	■ Systematically brush a thin layer over all tooth surfaces
	■ For prevention of early childhood caries in the infant, toddler, or very young child, apply to the maxillary anterior teeth first and then proceed to other areas of the dentition if patient is cooperative
	■ For all other patients, use a systematic approach. Begin with mandibular teeth; facial, occlusal, and lingual surfaces and then the maxillary teeth; palatal, occlusal, and facial surfaces
	■ Provide full coverage to all areas of the teeth including areas of recession and the cervical third of facial, lingual, and palatal surfaces and occlusal surfaces
	■ Application time is approximately 1–3 min
Completion	■ Instruct patient that the teeth will feel like they have a coating or film, but this is not visible if clear product has been used
	■ Ask the patient to avoid hard foods, drinking hot or alcoholic beverages, brushing, and flossing the teeth until the next day or at least 4–6 hr after application
	■ It is advisable to drink through a straw for the first few hours after application

▶ Fluoride is one part of the total prevention program that includes daily biofilm control and limitation of cariogenic foods.

IV. Tray Technique: Gel or Foam

▶ *Tray application appointment preparation*
- Schedule the appointment to end at least 30 minutes before the patient's eating time.
- Prepare the patient for any discomfort, for example, the 4-minute timing when tray application is to be used.
- Explain the need not to swallow but to expectorate immediately after the tray is removed.

▶ *Tray selection and preparation*
- Figure 36-4 shows tray selection for coverage of all exposed root surfaces.
- Design of trays: maxillary and mandibular trays may be hinged together or separated, are of a natural rounded arch shape to hold the gel and prevent ingestion, and are available in various sizes and brands.

- Figure 36-5 shows the amount of gel to be placed in each tray.
- Most gels are thixotropic to offer better physical and handling characteristics for use in trays.
- Procedures for a professional gel or foam tray fluoride application are listed in Table 36-3.

V. Varnish Technique[54]

▶ *Varnish application appointment sequence:*
- Schedule the appointment when the patient can refrain from consuming hard foods and hot liquids.
- Avoid toothbrushing and flossing for 4–6 hours after the application or until the next morning.

▶ Dispense varnish: If dispensed from a tube (rather than a single-dose packet), discard any clear varnish because the ingredients have separated and will contain only a fraction of the intended amount of fluoride.[60]

▶ Unit-dosed 5% NaF varnish is available in premeasured wells or individual packets of different dosages with an applicator brush to mix the varnish and then apply.

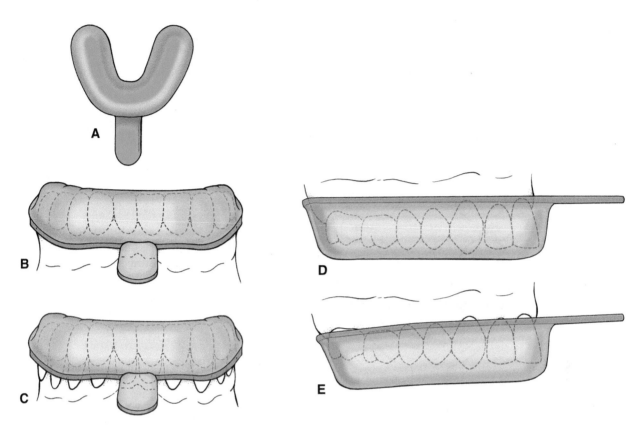

FIGURE 36-4 Tray Selection. A: Mandibular tray held for try-in. **B:** Tray over teeth is deep enough to cover the entire exposed enamel above the gingiva. **C:** In the patient with recession and areas of root surfaces exposed, the tray may not be deep enough to cover the root surfaces where fluoride is needed for prevention of root caries or hypersensitivity. A custom-made tray is needed. **D:** Tray adequately covers the distal surface of the most posterior tooth. **E:** If the tray does not cover the distal surface of the most posterior tooth or the cervical third of canine and central incisor adequately, the tray may need to be repositioned to cover the distal surface, or a larger stock or custom tray is needed.

▷ Unit dosages are generally 0.25, 0.4, or 0.5 mL for the primary, mixed, and permanent dentitions, respectively, and are available in different flavors and colors (yellow, white, and clear).

▷ Procedures for a professional varnish fluoride application are listed in Table 36-4.

VI. After Application

▷ *Tray application*

- Instruct patients not to rinse, eat, drink, brush, or floss until at least 30 minutes after gel or foam applications.
- Rinsing immediately after a tray application has been shown to significantly lessen the benefits.[61]

▷ *Varnish application*

- Instruct patients to avoid hot drinks and alcoholic beverages, eating hard foods, and brushing or flossing the teeth until the next morning to allow fluoride uptake to continue undisturbed.
- Varnish is removed by the patient using toothbrushing and flossing the next day.

SELF-APPLIED FLUORIDES

▷ Self-applied fluorides (prescription (Rx) and OTC products) are available as dentifrices, mouthrinses, and gels.

▷ Concentrations of 1,500 ppm fluoride or less can be sold OTC.[39] Some products containing less than 1,500 ppm of fluoride are available only by Rx.

▷ May be applied by toothbrushing, rinsing, or trays that are custom made or disposable.

I. Indications

▷ Patient needs are determined as part of total care planning.

▷ Indications for use of tray, rinsing, and/or toothbrushing depend on the individual patient prevention needs and caries risk assessment.

▷ Certain patients need multiple procedures combined with professional applications at the regular continuing care appointments. Special indications are suggested as each method is described in the following sections.

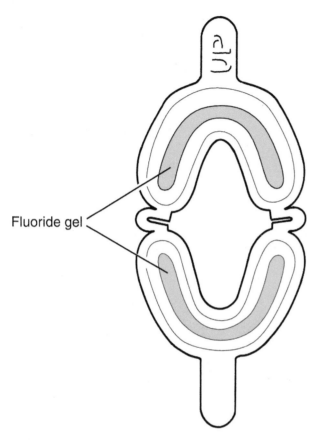

Fluoride gel

FIGURE 36-5 **Measured Gel in Tray.** No more than 2 mL of gel is placed in each tray for children, and no more than 5 mL is placed in each tray for adults. This amount fills each tray size one-third full.

II. Methods

The three methods for self-application are by tray, rinsing, and toothbrushing.

▶ *Tray*
  • Custom-made or disposable tray: The tray is selected to fit the individual mouth and completely cover the teeth being treated.
  • Figure 36-4 shows adequate and inadequate tray coverage on the teeth.
  • Instruction is provided not to overfill the tray.
▶ *Rinsing*
  • The patient swishes for 1 minute with a measured amount of a fluoride rinse and expectorates.
  • Certain patients will need to learn how to rinse properly to force the solution between the teeth. Box 30-4, in Chapter 30, lists steps for teaching how to rinse.
▶ *Toothbrushing*
  • A fluoride-containing dentifrice is used for regular brushing after breakfast and before going to bed without further eating.
  • Brush-on gel is used after regular brushing to provide additional benefits.
  • Use an interdental brush to apply fluoride to proximal surfaces or open furcations.

TRAY TECHNIQUE: HOME APPLICATION

▶ The original gel tray studies using custom-fitted polyvinyl mouthpieces compared the use of 1.1% APF with plain NaF gel.
▶ The gel was applied daily over a 2-year period by schoolchildren aged 11–14 years during the school years. Dental caries incidence was reduced up to 80%.[62]

I. Indications for Use

▶ Rampant enamel or root caries in persons of any age to prevent additional new carious lesions and promote remineralization around existing lesions.
▶ Xerostomia from any cause, particularly loss of salivary gland function.
▶ Exposure to radiation therapy.
▶ Root surface hypersensitivity.

II. Gels Used (Available by Prescription)

▶ *Concentrations*[39]
  • 1.1% NaF; 5,000 ppm fluoride.
  • 1.1% APF; 5,000 ppm fluoride.
▶ *Precautions*[39]
  • Dispense small quantities.
  • Maximum adult dose is 16 drops per day (4–8 drops on the inner surface of each custom-made tray).
  • Use neutral sodium preparations on porcelain, composites, titanium, or sealants.
  • Patients with mucositis may experience irritation with the APF due to the high acidity.
▶ *Patient instructions*
  • Use the gel tray once each day, preferably just before going to bed without further eating and after tooth brushing and flossing.
  • Box 36-4 outlines the procedures for the patient to follow for a home tray application.
  • A printed copy of the instructions is given to the patient.

FLUORIDE MOUTHRINSES

▶ Mouthrinsing is a practical and effective means for self-application of fluoride for individuals at moderate or high caries risk.
▶ Do not use for patients age 6 or younger, or for patients unable to rinse for a physical or other reason.[63]
▶ Rinsing can be part of an individual care plan or can be included in a group program conducted during school attendance.

BOX 36-4

Instructions for Home Tray Application

1. One daily application just before bedtime; do not eat or drink until morning. If applied at other time of day, do not eat or drink for at least 30 minutes.
2. Brush and floss before applying tray to remove biofilm and food debris.
3. Use prepared custom-made polyvinyl trays. Disposable trays can be used if the appropriate fit can be obtained.
4. Distribute no more than 4–8 drops or a thin ribbon of the gel on the inner surface of each tray. Each drop is equivalent to 0.1 mL.
5. Expectorate to minimize saliva in the mouth.
6. Apply one tray at a time. Hold head upright.
7. Apply the mandibular tray first; close gently to hold the tray in place.
8. Time by a clock for 4 minutes. Do not swallow.
9. Expectorate several times when the tray is removed to prevent swallowing gel, and prepare the mouth for the other tray.
10. Apply the maxillary tray and follow steps 7–9 as for the mandibular tray.
11. After tray removal, do not eat, drink, or brush teeth for at least 30 minutes.
12. After both trays are removed, rinse the trays under running water and brush them clean.
13. Keep in open air for drying.

I. Indications

▶ Mouthrinsing with a fluoride preparation may be an additional benefit for the following:
- Young persons during the high-risk preteen and adolescent years.
- Patients with areas of demineralization.
- Patients with root exposure following recession and periodontal therapy.
- Participants in a school health group program for children older than 6 years.
- Patients with moderate to rampant caries risk who live in a fluoridated or nonfluoridated community.
- Patients whose oral health care is complicated by biofilm-retentive appliances, including orthodontics, partial dentures, or space maintainers.
- Patients with xerostomia from any cause, including head and neck radiation and saliva-depressing drug therapy
- Patients with hypersensitivity of exposed root surfaces.

II. Limitations

▶ Children under 6 years of age and those of any age who cannot rinse because of oral and/or facial musculature problems or other disability.

▶ Alcohol content:
- Use of alcohol-based mouthrinses are not recommended; aqueous solutions are available.
- Alcohol content of commercial preparations is not advisable for children, especially adolescents.
- Alcohol-containing preparations are never to be recommended for a recovering alcoholic person; however, a history of former alcoholism would not necessarily be known to the clinician.

▶ Compliance is greater with a daily rinse than with a weekly rinse when practiced on an individual basis at home.

III. Preparations[39]

▶ Oral rinses are categorized as low-potency/high-frequency rinses or high-potency/low-frequency rinses.

▶ Most low-potency rinses may be purchased directly OTC, whereas most high potency rinses are provided by Rx.

▶ Table 36-5 contains the compounds, concentration, and recommended frequency of use for currently available self-applied fluoride rinses.

▶ Low potency/high frequency (available OTC)
- *Preparations*
  - 0.05% NaF; 230 ppm
  - 0.044% NaF or APF; 200 ppm. (available by Rx or OTC depending on the brand)
  - 0.0221% NaF; 100 ppm.
- *Specifications*
  - No more than 264 mg NaF (120 mg of fluoride) can be dispensed at one time.
  - A 500-mL bottle of 0.05% NaF rinse contains 100 mg of fluoride.
  - Bottle is required to have a child-proof cap.

TABLE 36-5	Patient-Applied Fluoride Mouthrinses (age 6 y and older)	
TYPE/PERCENTAGE (RX OR OTC)	CONCENTRATION IN PPM	FREQUENCY OF USE (10 ML OR 2 TEASPOONS SWISHED FOR 1 MIN)
0.2% NaF (Rx)	905	Once daily or once weekly
0.044% NaF and APF (Rx and OTC)	200	Once daily
0.05% NaF (OTC)	230	Once daily
0.0221% NaF (OTC)	100	Twice daily

- Rinses are not to be used by children under 6 years of age or by children or adults with a disability involving oral and/or facial musculature.
- Young children do not have sufficient control to expectorate and they tend to swallow quickly.
- The rinse is to be fully expectorated without swallowing.
- *Procedure for use*
  - Low-potency rinses are used once or twice daily with 2 teaspoonfuls (10 mL) after brushing and before retiring. Follow manufacturer's ADA-approved specifications.
  - The adult and pediatric maximum dose is 10 mL of solution.
  - Swish between teeth with lips tightly closed for 60 seconds; spit out.
  - See directions for rinsing in Box 30-4, in Chapter 30.
  - Have the patient practice rinsing at the dental chair.
  - Instruct patient: Do not eat or drink for 30 minutes after rinsing.
- *High potency/low frequency (available by Rx)*
  - *Preparation*
    - 0.20% NaF; 905 ppm
    - Originally recommended as a weekly rinse, but can be used up to once per day.[47]
  - *Procedure for use*: the same as for high-frequency/low-potency rinses.

The prevented fraction of dental caries ranges from 30% to 59%, with the use of 0.2% fluoride rinse on various rinsing schedules.[51]

IV. Benefits

- Benefits from fluoride mouthrinsing have been documented many times since the original research using various percentages of various fluoride preparations.[64,65]
- Frequent rinsing with low concentrations of fluoride has the following effects:
  - A 26%–29% average reduction in dental caries incidence.[66]

- Greater benefit for smooth surfaces, but some benefit to pits and fissures.
- Greatest benefit to newly erupted teeth.
- The program needs to be continued through the teenage years to benefit the second and third permanent molars.
- Added benefits for a community with fluoridation.[66]
- Effective in preventing and reversing root caries.[67]
- Primary teeth present in school-aged children benefit by as much as a 42.5% average reduction in dental caries incidence.[68]

BRUSH-ON GEL

▶ Brush-on gel has been used as an adjunct to the daily application of fluoride in a dentifrice and as a supplement to periodic professional applications.

▶ Regular use has been shown to help control demineralization about orthodontic appliances.[69]

▶ Provides protection against postirradiation caries in conjunction with other fluoride applications.[70]

I. Preparations

Table 36-6 contains the type, concentration, and daily usage guidelines for currently available self-applied fluoride gels.

▶ *1.1% NaF (Neutral pH) or 1.1% APF (3.5 pH); 5,000 ppm*
  - Available as a gel to be used separate from toothbrushing.

▶ 1.1% neutral NaF is also available as a dentifrice with an abrasive system added.
  - The rationale for the dentifrice product is to increase compliance with one step (brushing only) rather than brushing, followed by application of the high-concentration gel with a toothbrush.
  - Requires a prescription.

▶ *Stannous fluoride (SnF$_2$) 0.4% in glycerin base (1,000 ppm)*

▶ Available as a gel to be used separate from toothbrushing.

▶ Available OTC.

TABLE 36-6	Patient-Applied Fluoride Gels: Brush-on or Use in Custom Trays (age 6 y or older)	
TYPE/PERCENTAGE (RX OR OTC)	**CONCENTRATION IN PPM**	**DAILY USAGE GUIDELINES**
1.1% NaF gel or paste (Rx)	5,000	Brush-on teeth, twice per day or 4–8 drops on inner surface of custom tray or brush-on teeth
1.1% APF (Rx)	5,000	Brush-on teeth, preferably at night or 4–8 drops on inner surface of custom tray
0.4% SnF (OTC)	1,000	Brush-on teeth, preferably at night

II. Procedure

▶ Teeth are cleaned first with thorough brushing and flossing before gel application with a separate toothbrush.

▶ Use once a day or more as recommended, preferably at night after toothbrushing and flossing.

▶ Place about 2 mg of the gel over the brush head and spread over all teeth.

▶ Brush 1 minute, then swish to force the fluid between the teeth several times before expectorating.

▶ Do not rinse.

FLUORIDE DENTIFRICES

I. Development

▶ Historically tried with various compounds, including stannous fluoride, NaF, sodium monofluorophosphate, and amine fluoride.

▶ Early research objectives: to find compatible fluoride, abrasive systems, and formulations containing available fluoride for uptake by the tooth surface.

▶ In 1960 the first fluoride dentifrice gained approval by the ADA, Council on Dental Therapeutics: 0.4% stannous fluoride.[71]

II. Indications

▶ *Dental caries prevention*

• Fluoride dentifrice approved by the ADA is an integral part of a complete preventive program and is a basic caries prevention intervention for all patients.[71]

• All patients regardless of their caries risk

• Toothbrushing that covers all the teeth on all sides at least twice per day with a fluoride toothpaste is the foundation for all patients' fluoride regimen.

• Patients with moderate to rampant dental caries are advised to brush three or four times each day with a fluoride-containing dentifrice and to chew xylitol gum after a meal when they cannot brush.

• Expectorate, but do not rinse after toothbrushing, to give the fluoride a longer time to be effective.

III. Preparations

Fluoride dentifrices are available as gels or pastes. Amine fluorides are used in other countries, but not available in the United States.

▶ *Current fluoride constituents*[72]

• NaF 0.24% (1,100 ppm).

• Sodium monofluorophosphate (Na_2PO_3 F) 0.76% (1,000 ppm).

• Stannous fluoride (SnF_2) 0.45% (1,000 ppm).

▶ *Guidelines for acceptance*

The requirements for acceptance of a fluoride-containing toothpaste by the ADA are described in Chapter 30. The Seal of Acceptance is illustrated in Figure 30-1.

IV. Patient Instruction: Recommended Procedures

Advise the patient in the selection of a fluoride dentifrice, the need for frequent use, the method for application to all the tooth surfaces, and the importance of using a fluoride dentifrice to promote oral health.

▶ Select an ADA accepted fluoride-containing dentifrice.

▶ Place recommended amount of dentifrice on the toothbrush.

▶ *Children (age less than 3 years)*: Twice daily brushing (morning and night) with no more than a "smear" or the size of a grain of rice of fluoride dentifrice spread along the brushing plane.[73,74] Figure 50-8, in Chapter 50, illustrates a small smear.

• Daily oral care begins with the eruption of the first primary tooth.

• At this time, the oral hygiene of parents and family with attention to daily biofilm removal by toothbrushing can make a significant impact on the small child's oral health.

▶ The paste is then spread over all the teeth before starting to brush so that all teeth benefit and large amounts of paste are not available for swallowing.

▶ *Older child (ages 3–6 years)*: Twice daily brushing (morning and night) with fluoride toothpaste the size of a small pea.

• Demonstrate spreading this amount over the ends of the filaments, and explain that the child is not to swallow excess amounts of dentifrice.[73,74]

▶ *Adults*: Use 1/2 inch fluoride dentifrice twice daily.

▶ Spread dentifrice over the teeth with a light touch of the brush.

▶ Proceed with correct brushing positions for sulcular removal of dental biofilm (see Chapter 28).

▶ Do not rinse after brushing to keep fluoride in the oral fluids.[73,75]

▶ Keep dentifrice container out of reach of children.

V. Benefits

▶ Twice daily use has greater benefits than once daily use.[63]

▶ Moderate and high caries risk patients and patients who live in a nonfluoridated community benefit from using a dentifrice several times per day to maintain salivary fluoride levels.

▶ The dentifrice is a continuing source of fluoride for the tooth surface in the control of demineralization and the promotion of remineralization.

► The use of a dentifrice with a fluoride concentration of 1,000 ppm and above compared to a dentifrice without fluoride can prevent dental caries up to an average of 23%.[76]

COMBINED FLUORIDE PROGRAM

► All patients, regardless of caries risk, benefit from at least twice daily use of a fluoridated dentifrice and consumption of fluoridated water multiple times during each day.

► Patients at moderate to high caries risk benefit from additional methods of fluoride exposure.

► Additional caries reduction can be expected when another topical fluoride such as a mouthrinse or gel tray is combined with a fluoride dentifrice.[77]

► When self-administered methods are chosen, patient cooperation is a significant factor.

► Age and eruption pattern influence the method selected.

► Newly erupted teeth need frequent fluoride exposure as soon after eruption as possible and continued indefinitely to control demineralization.

► Continuing care appointments are to be scheduled for frequent professional topical applications for those at moderate and high caries risk and for continuing instruction and motivation regarding daily fluoride use for all patients.

► All methods are supplements to the daily use of fluoridated water and a dentifrice with fluoride.

FLUORIDE SAFETY

► Fluoride preparations and fluoridated water have wide margins of safety.

► Fluoride is beneficial in small amounts, but it can be injurious if used without attention to correct dosage and frequency.

► All dental personnel need to be familiar with the following:
  • Recommended approved procedures for use of products containing fluoride.
  • Potential toxic effects of fluoride.
  • How to administer general emergency measures when accidental overdoses occur as listed in Table 8-3 and the section on Internal Poisoning in Table 8-4 in Chapter.

I. Summary of Fluoride Risk Management

► Use professionally and recommend only approved fluoride preparations for patient use.
  • Products may have approval from the Food and Drug Administration (FDA) and the ADA in the United States.

• Read about the programs of the ADACSA and the Seal of Approval of Products in Chapter 30.

► Use only researched, recommended amounts and methods for delivery.

► Know potential toxicity of the various products, and be prepared to administer emergency measures for treating an accidental toxic response.

► Instruct patients in proper care of fluoride products.
  • Dentist prescribes no more than 120 mg of fluoride at one time (no more than 480 of the 0.25 mg tablets or 240 of the 0.5 mg tablets).[39] Do not store large quantities in the home.
  • Request parental supervision of a child's brushing or other fluoride administration. Rinses, for example, are not to be used by children under 6 years of age.
  • Fluoride products have child-proof caps and are to be kept out of reach of small children and other persons, such as the mentally challenged, who may not understand limitations.
  • In school health programs, dispensing of the fluoride product is to be supervised by responsible adults. Containers are to be stored under lock and key when not in active use.

II. Toxicity

► *Acute toxicity* refers to rapid intake of an excess dose over a short time.
  • Acute fluoride poisoning is extremely rare.[78]

► *Chronic toxicity* applies to long-term ingestion of fluoride in amounts that exceed the approved therapeutic levels.

► *Accidental ingestion* of a concentrated fluoride preparation can lead to a toxic reaction.

► *Certainly lethal dose (CLD)*[79]
  • A lethal dose is the amount of a drug likely to cause death if not intercepted by antidotal therapy.
  • *Adult CLD*: About 5–10 g of NaF taken at one time. The fluoride ion equivalent is 32–64 mg of fluoride per kilogram body weight (mg F/kg; Box 36-5).
  • *Child*: Approximately 0.5–1.0 g, variable with size and weight of the child.

► *Safely tolerated dose (STD)*: one-fourth of the CLD
  • *Adult STD*: About 1.25–2.5 g of NaF (8–16 mg F/kg).
  • *Child*: Box 36-5B shows STDs and CLDs for children.
    ◦ Weights given for each selected age are minimal, and calculations for the doses are conservative.
    ◦ As can be noted in Box 36-5B, less than 1 g (1,000 mg) may be fatal for children 12 years old and younger, and 0.5 g (500 mg) exceeds the STD for all ages shown.

BOX 36-5
Lethal and Safe Doses of Fluoride

A. Lethal and Safe doses of Fluoride for A 70-Kg Adult CLD

5–10 g NaF
Or
32–64 mg F/kg
STD = 1/4 CLD
1.25–2.5 g NaF
Or
8–16 mg F/kg

B. CLDS AND STDS of Fluoride for Selected Ages

Age (years)	Weight (lbs/kg)	CLD (mg)	STD (mg)
2	22/10	320	80
4	29/13	422	106
6	37/17	538	135
8	45/20	655	164
10	53/24	771	193
12	64/29	931	233
14	83/38	1,206	301
16	92/42	1,338	334
18	95/43	1,382	346

Reprinted with permission from Heifetz SB, Horowitz HS. The amounts of fluoride in current fluoride therapies: safety considerations for children. *ASDC J Dent Child.* 1984;51(4):257–269.

- For children under 6 years of age, however, 500 mg could be lethal.[79]

III. Signs and Symptoms of Acute Toxic Dose

Symptoms begin within 30 minutes of ingestion and may persist for as long as 24 hours.

▶ *Gastrointestinal tract*

Fluoride in the stomach is acted on by the hydrochloric acid to form hydrofluoric acid, an irritant to the stomach lining. Symptoms include:
- Nausea, vomiting, diarrhea.
- Abdominal pain.
- Increased salivation, thirst.

▶ *Systemic involvements*
- *Blood*: Calcium may be bound by the circulating fluoride, thus causing symptoms of hypocalcemia.
- *Central nervous system*: Hyperreflexia, convulsions, paresthesias.

- *Cardiovascular and respiratory depression*: If not treated, may lead to death in a few hours from cardiac failure or respiratory paralysis.

IV. Emergency Treatment

▶ *Induce vomiting*
- *Mechanical*: Digital stimulation at back of tongue or in throat.
▶ *Second person*
- Call emergency service; transport to hospital.
▶ *Administer fluoride-binding liquid when patient is not vomiting*
- Milk.
- Milk of Magnesia.
- Lime water ($CaOH_2$ solution 0.15%).
▶ *Support respiration and circulation*
▶ *Additional therapy indicated at emergency room*
- Calcium gluconate for muscle tremors or tetany.
- Gastric lavage.
- Cardiac monitoring.
- Endotracheal intubation.
- Blood monitoring (calcium, magnesium, potassium, pH).
- Intravenous feeding to restore blood volume, calcium.

V. Chronic Toxicity

▶ *Skeletal fluorosis*[78]
- Isolated instances of osteosclerosis, an elevation in bone density, can result from chronic toxicity after long-term (10 or more years) ingestion of water with 8–10 ppm fluoride or from inhalation of industrial fumes or dust.
- Skeletal fluorosis in its early stages is characterized by stiff and painful joints and becomes crippling in its later stages.
- It has never been a public health concern in the United States, even in communities that have had high levels of fluoride in the water for generations.
- Is endemic in certain countries such as China and India with high levels of natural fluoride in the water.
- Predisposing factors, dietary deficiencies, and population differences with regard to fluoride metabolism may play a role in its development in addition to exposure.
- Methods for defluoridation have been developed, as described in the section on Defluoridation in this chapter.

▶ *Dental fluorosis*
- Ingestion of naturally occurring excess fluoride in the drinking water and/or fluoride dental products can produce visible fluorosis only when used during the years of development of the crowns of the teeth, namely, from birth until age 16 or 18 years or

when the crowns of the third permanent molars are completed.

- No systemic symptoms result from the fluoride, and the individual has protection against dental caries.
- Scoring system used to describe dental fluorosis is found in Chapter 23, Tables 23-2 and 23-3.

▶ *Mild fluorosis*

1. *Clinical evaluation*
   - Mild and very mild forms, dental fluorosis appears as white opacities in the enamel surface.
   - No esthetic or health problem is involved. Many such white spots are not visible except when scrutinized under a dental light and the surface is dried.
   - All white spots in the enamel are not related to fluoride intake; distinction can be made by reviewing the patient's dental and fluoride-intake history, by noting the location and distribution of

the white spots, and by considering the sequence of tooth development.

2. *Relation to fluoride sources*
   - Mild fluorosis may result from inadvertent ingestion of excess fluoride by young children during topical procedures both self-applied and professional.
   - No problem exists when care is taken to follow basic steps, such as those listed in Tables 36-3 and 36-4 for professional applications.
   - Mouthrinses are not indicated for children less than 6 years of age.
   - Small amounts of dentifrice may be swallowed incidentally at each brushing. A child of 4 years who lives in a nonfluoridated community uses a daily supplement (0.5 mg), and swallows two or three small amounts of dentifrice ingests far less than the STD of 106 mg shown in Box 36-5B.

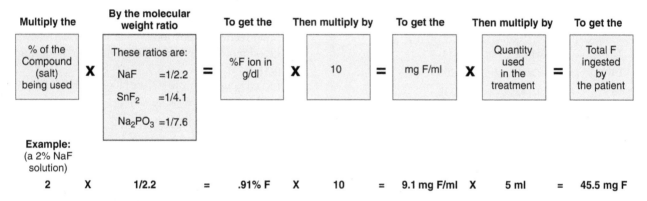

FIGURE 36-6 Fluoride Calculation. Flowchart shows steps in the calculation of the amount of fluoride in a compound used in treatment. The example shows that 5 mL of a 2% solution of NaF contains 45.5 mg F, an amount slightly greater than half of the STD for a 2-year-old child (Box 36-5B). (Source: Heifetz SB, Horowitz HS. The amounts of fluoride in current fluoride therapies: safety considerations for children. *ASDC J Dent Child.* 1984;51(4):257–269.)

 **EVERYDAY ETHICS**

Daniel was a well-behaved and cooperative 4 1/2-year-old boy at an elevated risk for dental caries due to having one carious lesion and living in a nonfluoridated area. At the time for the fluoride treatment, the dental hygienist, Nina, spent a few extra minutes explaining to Daniel how she will brush a coating on his teeth to make them stronger. Although Daniel's parents did not have insurance coverage, the hygienist decided it would be important for him to receive a fluoride application regardless of the fee. Daniel tolerated the procedure well. After the appointment, Nina explained to Daniel's mother the varnish postoperative instructions. Daniel's mother became upset and said, "why did you give my son a fluoride treatment without my permission? My husband just lost his job and I cannot afford this added cost."

Questions for Consideration

1. Because Daniel's mother brought him to the clinic for a scheduled appointment, Nina assumed *implied consent* for Daniel to receive dental hygiene treatment. Was it appropriate for Nina to assume consent for the fluoride application was also implied? Why or why not?

2. Discuss ways in which the legal/ethical concepts of professional liability, scope of practice, standard of care, and informed consent are related to this scenario.

3. Answer the questions in Box 1-10 for resolving ethical issues or dilemmas found in the Ethical Applications section of Chapter 1. Use the answers to determine at least one course of action Nina can take now to resolve the issue. Make sure to consider all individuals who might be affected by the decision.

VI. How to Calculate Amounts of Fluoride[79,80]

Figure 36-6 is a flowchart that shows the steps necessary to determine the amount of fluoride in a fluoride compound. By doing so, one can then calculate the amount ingested by the patient.

▶ Multiply the percentage of fluoride ion in the compound by the molecular weight conversion ratio, as shown in Figure 36-6.

▶ Obtain the ratio by dividing the molecular weight of the compound by the atomic weight of fluoride.

▶ Example: The molecular weight of NaF is 42 (Na = 23, F = 19). When divided by 19, a 1–2.2 ratio results, as used in the example in Figure 36-6.

DOCUMENTATION

A patient receiving a topical fluoride application and/or counseling regarding fluoride needs the following documented in the permanent record:

▶ Caries risk level (document as low, moderate, high, or extreme).

▶ Current use of fluoride toothpaste and exposure to fluoridated water.

▶ Type, concentration, mode of delivery, and postoperative instructions if a professional fluoride application is provided.

▶ Type, amount, and instructions for the use of any Rx or OTC patient-applied fluoride products recommended.

▶ A sample documentation using the SOAP format is provided in Box 36-6.

BOX 36-6
Example Documentation: Professional Fluoride Application and Prescribing Home Fluoride

S –A 26-year-old male patient presents for a periodic oral examination, radiographs, and dental prophylaxis. Patient states that he drinks high-sucrose beverages on a frequent, daily basis. He also states that he uses toothpaste with fluoride twice daily and consumes fluoridated water.

O –Patient presents with medication induced xerostomia. Two proximal cavitated lesions were discovered on bitewing X-rays.

A –Patient was classified as being high risk for caries after conducting a caries risk assessment analysis.

P –Applied 5% NaF varnish to the entire dentition and provided postoperative instructions. Prescribed 1.1% NaF gel (2 refills) to apply with a separate toothbrush at night. Discussed the need for an additional varnish application in three months to help prevent the future onset of dental caries.

Signed: _____, RDH

Date: _____

Factors To Teach The Patient

I. Personal Use of Fluorides
▷ Purposes, action, and expected benefits relative to the specific forms of fluoride treatment the patient will receive based upon individual caries risk.
▷ Specific instructions concerning self-applied techniques that will be performed at home.

II. Need for Parental Supervision
▷ Supervise daily care of child's teeth and mouth with the recommended amount of fluoridated toothpaste to prevent excess ingestion of fluoride.
▷ Keep fluoride products out of reach of small children.

III. Determine Need for Fluoride Supplements
▷ Must determine child is at high caries risk and consumes fluoride-deficient drinking water.
▷ Where to send private water source sample for fluoride analysis.

IV. Fluorides Are Part of the Total Preventive Program
▷ Emphasize fluoride toothpaste and fluoridated water as the cornerstone for prevention of dental caries.
▷ Regular professional supervision and care.

V. Fluoridation
▷ How drinking fluoridated water helps people of all ages.
▷ How to access the CDCP Community Water Fluoridation website to obtain reliable information about fluoridation in the United States.

VI. Bottled Drinking Water/Water Filters
▷ When bottled water does not have a label indicating that it is fluoridated, recommend filling a water bottle from a fluoridated water supply.
▷ Check with the water filter manufacturer to be certain the fluoride will not be removed through filtration.
▷ Distillation and reverse osmosis systems remove fluoride from drinking water, but water softeners do not.

VII. Infant Formula
▷ Educate parents that powdered or liquid concentrate infant formula and the water used to reconstitute this formula may contain fluoride.

References

1. Ellwood R, Fejerskov O, Cury JA, et al. Chapter 18: Fluorides in caries control. In: Fejerskov O, Kidd E, eds. *Dental Caries The Disease and its Clinical Management.* 2nd ed. Oxford: Blackwell Munksgaard; 2008:293–294.

2. Newbrun E. Systemic benefits of fluoride and fluoridation. *J Public Health Dent.* 2004;64 (Suppl S1):35–39.

3. Ekstrand J. Chapter 4: Fluoride metabolism. In: Fejerskov O, Ekstrand J, Burt BA, eds. *Fluoride in Dentistry.* 2nd ed. Copenhagen: Munksgaard; 1996:55–67.

4. Bath-Balough M, Fehrenbach M. *Dental Embryology, Histology, and Anatomy.* 2nd ed. St. Louis, MO: Saunders; 2006: 179–189.

5. Melfi RC, Alley KE. *Permar's Oral Embryology and Microscopic Anatomy.* 10th ed. Philadelphia, PA: Lippincott Williams & Wilkins; 2000:43–87.

6. Levy S. An update on fluorides and fluorosis. *J Can Dent Assoc.* 2003;69(5):286–291.

7. Aoba T, Fejerskov O. Dental fluorosis: chemistry and biology. *Crit Rev Oral Bio Med.* 2002;13(2):155–170.

8. Featherstone JD. The science and practice of caries prevention. *J Am Dent Assoc.* 2000;131(7):887–899.

9. Yoon SH, Brudevold F, Gardner DE, et al. Distribution of fluoride in teeth from areas with different levels of fluoride in the water supply. *J Dent Res.* 1960;39:845–856.

10. Centers for Disease Control and Prevention. Recommendations for using fluoride to prevent and control dental caries in the United States. *MMWR Recomm Rep.* 2001;50 (RR-14):1–42.

11. Centers for Disease Control and Prevention. Populations receiving optimally fluoridated public drinking water–United States, 1992–1996. *MWWR Morb Mortal Wkly Rep.* 2008;57(27):737–741.

12. Department of Health and Human Services, Centers for Disease Control and Prevention. *Community Water Fluoridation.* Atlanta, GA: Water Fluoridation Data and Statistics; 2010. [about 4 screens]. http://www.cdc.gov/fluoridation/index.htm. Updated July 13, 2013. Accessed August 25, 2013.

13. Herschfeld JJ. Classics in dental history: Frederick S. McKay and the "Colorado brown stain." *Bull Hist Dent.* 1978;26(2):118–126.

14. McKay FS. The relation of mottled enamel to caries. *J Am Dent Assoc.* 1928;15:1429–1437.

15. Churchill HV. Occurrence of fluorides in some waters of United States. *J Ind Eng Chem.* 1931;23:996–998.

16. Dean HT, Arnold FA Jr, Elvove E. Domestic water and dental caries. V. Additional studies of the relation of fluoride domestic waters to dental caries experience in 4425 white children, aged 12 to 14 years, of 13 cities in 4 states. *Public Health Rep.* 1942;57:1155–1179.

17. Centers for Disease Control and Prevention. Engineering and administrative recommendations for water fluoridation, 1995. *MMWR Recomm Rep.* 1995;44 (RR-13):1–40.

18. Department of Health and Human Services (US). U.S. Public Health Service Recommendation for Fluoride Concentration in Drinking Water for the Prevention of Caries. [Internet] Public Health Reports July/August 2015. [Cited 2015 June 12] 130; 1-14. Available from: http://www.cdc.gov/fluoridation/index.htm

19. Griffin SO, Regnier E, Griffin PM, et al. Effectiveness of fluoride in preventing caries in adults. *J Dent Res.* 2007;86(5):410–415.

20. Yeung CA. A systematic review of the efficacy and safety of fluoridation. *Evid Based Dent.* 2008;9(2):39–43.

21. Dirks OB, Houwink B, Kwant GW. Some special features of the caries preventive effect of water fluoridation. *Arch Oral Biol.* 1961;4:187–192.

22. Burt BA, Ismail AI, Eklund SA. Root caries in an optimally fluoridated and a high-fluoride community. *J Dent Res.* 1986;6(9):1154–1158.

23. Stamm JW, Banting DW, Imrey PB. Adult root caries survey of two similar communities with contrasting natural water fluoride levels. *J Am Dent Assoc.* 1990;120(2):143–149.

24. Ast DB, Fitzgerald B. Effectiveness of water fluoridation. *J Am Dent Assoc.* 1962;65:581–587.

25. Russell AL, Elvove E. Domestic water and dental caries. VII. A study of the fluoride-dental caries relationship in an adult population. *Public Health Rep.* 1951;66(43):1389–1401.

26. Englander HR, Wallace DA. Effects of naturally fluoridated water on dental caries in adults: Aurora-Rockford, Illinois, Study III. *Public Health Rep.* 1962;77(10):887–893.

27. Horowitz HS, Maier FJ, Law FE. Partial defluoridation of a community water supply and dental fluorosis. *Public Health Rep.* 1967;82(11):965–972.

28. Horowitz HS, Heifetz SB. The effect of partial defluoridation of a water supply on dental fluorosis—final results in Bartlett, Texas, after 17 Years. *Am J Public Health.* 1972;62(6):767–769.

29. Horowitz HS. Effectiveness of school water fluoridation and dietary fluoride supplements in school-aged children. *J Public Health Dent.* 1989;49(5 Spec No):290–296.

30. Lemke CW, Doherty JM, Arra MC. Controlled fluoridation: the dental effects of discontinuation in Antigo, Wisconsin. *J Am Dent Assoc.* 1979;80(4):782–786.

31. Jackson RD, Brizendine EJ, Kelly SA, et al. The fluoride content of foods and beverages from negligibly and optimally fluoridated communities. *Community Dent Oral Epidemiol.* 2002;30(5):382–391.

32. Burt BA, Marthaler TM. Chapter 16: Fluoride tablets, salt fluoridation, and milk fluoridation. In: Fejerskov O, Ekstrand J, Burt BA, eds. *Fluoride in Dentistry.* 2nd ed. Copenhagen: Munksgaard; 1996:291–310.

33. Espelid I. Caries preventive effect of fluoride in milk, salt and tablets: a literature review. *Eur Arch Paediatr Dent.* 2009;10(3):149–156.

34. European Academy of Paediatric Dentistry. Guidelines on the use of fluoride in children: an EAPD policy document. *Eur Arch Paediatr Dent.* 2009;10(3):129–135.

35. American Dental Association. *Fluoridation Facts.* Chicago, IL: American Dental Association; 2005.

36. Hujoel PP, Zina LG, Moimaz SA, et al. Infant formula and enamel fluorosis: a systematic review. *J Am Dent Assoc.* 2009;140(7):841–854.

37. Siew C, Strock S, Ristic H, et al. Assessing the potential risk factor for enamel fluorosis: a preliminary evaluation of fluoride content in infant formulas. *J Am Dent Assoc.* 2009;140(10):1228–1236.

38. Berg J, Gerweck C, Hujoel P, et al. Evidence-based clinical recommendations regarding fluoride intake from reconstituted infant formula and enamel fluorosis. *J Am Dent Assoc.* 2011;142(1):79–87.

39. Burrell KH. Chapter 10: Fluorides. In: Mariotti AJ, Burrell KH, eds. *American Dental Association, Council on Scientific Affairs: ADA/PDR Guide to Dental Therapeutics.* 5th ed. Chicago, IL: American Dental Association and Thomson PDR; 2009:323–337.

40. Ismail AI, Hasson H. Fluoride supplements, dental caries, and fluorosis: a systematic review. *J Am Dent Assoc.* 2008;139(11):1457–1468.

41. Rozier RG, Adair S, Graham F, et al. Evidence-based clinical recommendations on the prescription of dietary

fluoride supplements for caries prevention. *J Am Dent Assoc.* 2010;141(12):1480–1489.

42. Toyama Y, Nakagaki H, Kato S, et al. Fluoride concentrations at and near the neonatal line in human deciduous tooth enamel obtained from a naturally fluoridated and a non-fluoridated area. *Arch Oral Biol.* 2001;46(2):147–153.

43. Tubert-Jeannin S, Auclair C, Amsallem E, et al. Fluoride supplements (tablets, drops, lozenges or chewing gums) for preventing dental caries in children. *Cochrane Database Syst Rev.* 2011;(12):CD007592.

44. Bibby BG. Use of fluorine in the prevention of dental caries. II. The effects of sodium fluoride applications. *J Am Dent Assoc.* 1944;31:317.

45. Knutson JW. Sodium fluoride solutions: technique for application to the teeth. *J Am Dent Assoc.* 1948;36(1):37–39.

46. Galagan DJ, Knutson JW. The effect of topically applied fluorides on dental caries experience; experiments with sodium fluoride and calcium chloride; widely spaced applications; use of different solution concentrations. *Public Health Rep.* 1948;63(38):1215–1221.

47. Weyant RJ, Tracy SL, Anselmo T, et al. Topical fluoride for caries prevention: Executive summary of the updated clinical recommendations and supporting systemic review. *J Am Dent Assoc.* 2013;144(11):1279–1291.

48. Warren DP, Chan JT. Topical fluorides: efficacy, administration, and safety. *Gen Dent.* 1997;45(2):134–140, 142.

49. Ripa LW. An evaluation of the use of professionally (operator applied) topical fluorides. *J Dent Res.* 1990;69 (Spec No):786–796.

50. Soeno K, Matsumura H, Atsuta M, et al. Influence of acidulated fluoride agents and effectiveness of subsequent polishing on composite material surfaces. *Oper Dent.* 2002;27(3):305–310.

51. Poulsen S. Fluoride-containing gels, mouth rinses and varnishes: an update of evidence of efficacy. *Eur Arch Paediatr Dent.* 2009;10(3):157–161.

52. Beltrán-Aguilar ED, Goldstein JW, Lockwood SA. Fluoride varnishes: a review of their clinical use, cariostatic mechanism, efficacy and safety. *J Am Dent Assoc.* 2000;131(5):589–596.

53. Marinho VC, Worthington HV, Walsh T, et al. Fluoride varnishes for preventing dental caries in children and adolescents. *Cochrane Database Syst Rev.* 2013;(7):CD002279.

54. Bawden JW. Fluoride varnish: a useful new tool for public health dentistry. *J Public Health Dent.* 1998;58(4):266–269.

55. Autio-Gold JT, Courts F. Assessing the effect of fluoride varnish on early enamel carious lesions in the primary dentition. *J Amer Dent Assoc.* 2001;132(9):1247–1253.

56. Castellano JB, Donly KJ. Potential remineralization of demineralized enamel after application of fluoride varnish. *Am J Dent.* 2004;17(6):462–464.

57. Demito CF, Vivaldi-Rodrigues G, Ramos AL, et al. The efficacy of fluoride varnish in reducing enamel demineralization adjacent to orthodontic brackets: an in vitro study. *Orthod Craniofac Res.* 2004;7(4):205–210.

58. Ripa LW. Need for prior toothcleaning when performing a professional topical fluoride application: review and recommendations for change. *J Am Dent Assoc.* 1984;109(2):281–285.

59. Vrbic V, Brudevold F, McCann HG. Acquisition of fluoride by enamel from fluoride pumice pastes. *Helv Odontol Acta.* 1967;11(1):21–26.

60. Shen C, Autio-Gold J. Assessing fluoride concentration uniformity and fluoride release from three varnishes. *J Am Dent Assoc.* 2002;133(2):176–182.

61. Stookey GK, Schemehorn BR, Drook CA, et al. The effect of rinsing with water immediately after a professional fluoride gel application on fluoride uptake in demineralized enamel: an in vivo study. *Pediatr Dent.* 1986;8(3):153–157.

62. Englander HR, Keyes PH, Gestwicki M, et al. Clinical anticaries effect of repeated topical sodium fluoride applications by mouthpieces. *J Am Dent Assoc.* 1967;75(3):638–644.

63. Adair SM. Evidence-based use of fluoride in contemporary pediatric dental practice. *Pediatr Dent.* 2006;28(2):133–142.

64. Torell P, Ericsson Y. The potential benefits derived from fluoride mouth rinses. In: Forrester DJ, Schulz EM, eds. *International Workshop on Fluorides and Dental Caries Reductions.* Baltimore, MD: University of Maryland School of Dentistry; 1974:114–176.

65. Birkeland JM, Torell P. Caries-preventive fluoride mouthrinses. *Caries Res.* 1978;12 (Suppl 1):38–51.

66. Driscoll WS, Swango PA, Horowitz AM, et al. Caries-preventive effects of daily and weekly fluoride mouthrinsing in a fluoridated community: final results after 30 months. *J Am Dent Assoc.* 1982;105(6):1010–1013.

67. Heijnsbroek M, Paraskevas S, Vav der Weijden GA. Fluoride interventions for root caries: a review. *Oral Health Prev Dent.* 2007;5(2):145–152.

68. Ripa LW, Leske GS, Varma A. Effect of mouthrinsing with a 0.2 percent neutral NaF solution on the deciduous dentition of first to third grade school children. *Pediatr Dent.* 1984;6(2):93–97.

69. Stratemann MW, Shannon IL. Control of decalcification in orthodontic patients by daily self-administrated application of a water-free 0.4 percent stannous fluoride gel. *Am J Orthod.* 1974;66(3):273–279.

70. Wescott WB, Starcke EN, Shannon IL. Chemical protection against postirradiation dental caries. *Oral Surg Oral Med Oral Pathol.* 1975;40(6):709–719.

71. American Dental Association, Council on Dental Therapeutics. Evaluation of Crest toothpaste. *J Am Dent Assoc.* 1960;61:272.

72. Mariotti MJ, Burrell K. Mouthrinses and dentifrices. In: *American Dental Association, Council on Scientific Affairs: ADA/PDR Guide to Dental Therapeutics.* 5th ed. Chicago, IL: American Dental Association and Thomson PDR; 2009:305–321.

73. American Academy of Pediatric Dentistry Liaison with Other Groups Committee; and American Academy on Pediatric Dentistry Council on Scientific Affairs. Guideline on fluoride therapy. *Pediatr Dent.* 2013;36:171–174.

74. American Dental Association Council on Scientific Affairs. Fluoride toothpaste use for young children. *JADA.* 2014;145(2):190–191.

75. Sjogren K, Melin NH. The influence of rinsing routines on fluoride retention after toothbrushing. *Gerodontology.* 2001;18(1):15–20.

76. Walsh T, Worthington HV, Glenny AM, et al. Fluoride toothpastes of different concentrations for preventing

dental caries in children and adolescents. *Cochrane Database Syst Rev.* 2010;(1):CD007868.

77. Marinho VC. Cochrane reviews of randomized trials of fluoride therapies for preventing dental caries. *Eur Arch Paediatr Dent.* 2009;10(3):183–191.

78. Whitford GM. Acute and chronic fluoride toxicity. *J Dent Res.* 1992;71(5):1249–1254.

79. Heifetz SB, Horowitz HS. The amounts of fluoride in current fluoride therapies: safety considerations for children. *ASDC J Dent Child.* 1984;51(4):257–269.

80. Bayless JM, Tinanoff N. Diagnosis and treatment of acute fluoride toxicity. *J Am Dent Assoc.* 1985;110(2):209–211.

ENHANCE YOUR UNDERSTANDING

thePoint® **DIGITAL CONNECTIONS**
(see the inside front cover for access information)

- **Audio glossary**
- **Quiz bank**

SUPPORT FOR LEARNING
(available separately; visit lww.com)

- *Active Learning Workbook for Clinical Practice of the Dental Hygienist, 12th Edition*

prepU **INDIVIDUALIZED REVIEW**
(available separately; visit lww.com)

- **Adaptive quizzing with *prepU for Wilkins' Clinical Practice of the Dental Hygienist***

37

Sealants

Jill C. Moore, RDH, BSDH, MHA

CHAPTER OUTLINE

LEARNING OBJECTIVES

After studying this chapter, the student will be able to:

1. Describe the development and purposes of dental sealant materials.

2. Explain types of sealant material and list criteria of an ideal dental sealant material.

3. List indications and contraindications for placement of dental sealants.

4. Describe clinical procedures for placement and maintenance of a dental sealant.

5. Explain factors that affect sealant penetration.

6. Identify factors to document a dental sealant placement in the patient record.

INTRODUCTION

A pit and fissure sealant is an organic polymer (resin) that flows into the pit or fissure of a posterior tooth and bonds by mechanical retention to the tooth.

▶ Placement of dental sealants is an evidence-based preventive recommendation that can significantly reduce the incidence of dental caries.[1]

▶ As part of a complete preventive program, pit and fissure sealants are indicated for selected patients.

▶ Topically applied fluorides protect smooth tooth surfaces more than occlusal surfaces; dental sealants reduce the incidence of occlusal dental caries.

▶ Incidence of new pit and fissure caries can be lowered by 86% if the sealant is retained at 1 year, 78.6% at 2 years, and 58.6% at 4 years.[2]

▶ Sealant application is a part of a complete prevention program, not an isolated procedure.

▶ As an isolated procedure, patient (and parent) may the specific role of sealants in prevention.

▶ Other surfaces and other teeth still need other methods of preventive protection.

▶ Box 37-1 provides definitions and terminology related to sealants and their application.

I. Development of Sealants

Sealants were developed by Dr. Michael Buonocore and the group of dental scientists at the Eastman Dental Center in Rochester, New York.

▶ The focus of the early research was on the need to prepare the enamel surface so a dental material would adhere.

▶ They demonstrated that by using an acid-etch process, the enamel could be altered to increase retention.

▶ The research proved to be a major breakthrough, particularly in esthetic and preventive dentistry.[3,4]

II. Purposes of the Sealant

▶ To provide a physical barrier to "seal off" the pit or fissure.

▶ To prevent oral bacteria and their nutrients from collecting within the pit or fissure to create the acid environment necessary for the initiation of dental caries.

▶ To fill the pit or fissure as deep as possible and provide tight smooth margins at the junction with the enamel surface.

▶ When sealant material is worn or cracked away on the surface around the pit or fissure, the sealant in the depth of the micropore can remain and provide continued protection while sealant material is added for repair and to reseal the enamel/sealant junction.

BOX 37-1 KEY WORDS: Pit and Fissure Sealants

Acid etchant: in sealant placement, the enamel surface is prepared by the application of phosphoric acid, which etches the surface to provide mechanical retention for the sealant.

Articulating paper: paper treated with dye or wax used to mark points of contact (occlusion) between the maxillary and mandibular teeth.

Bibulous: absorbent; a flat bibulous pad, placed in the cheek over the opening of Stensen's duct, is used to aid in maintaining a dry field while placing sealants.

Biocompatibility: the ability of things to exist together without harm.

Bis-GMA: bisphenol A–glycidyl methylacrylate; plastic material used for dental sealants.

Bonding (mechanical): physical adherence of one substance to another; the adherence of a sealant to the enamel surface is accomplished by an acid-etching technique that leaves microspaces between the enamel rods; the sealant becomes mechanically locked (bonded) in these microspaces.

Bond strength: expression of the degree of adherence between the tooth surface and the sealant.

Conditioner: a substance added to another substance to increase its usability; in sealant placement, the acid etchant is added to the enamel to prepare it for bonding with the sealant.

Curing: the process is used for polymerization of resin-based sealant and composites so the material hardens by which plastic becomes rigid.

Incipient caries: early or beginning caries, caries not limited to the enamel.

In vitro: under laboratory conditions.

In vivo: within the living body.

Micropores: tiny openings.

Polymer: a compound of high molecular weight formed by a combination of a chain of simpler molecules (monomers).

Polymerization: a reaction in which a high-molecular-weight product is produced by successive additions of a simpler compound.

　Photopolymerization: polymerization with the use of an external light source.

　Autopolymerization: self-curing; a reaction in which a high-molecular-weight product is produced by successive additions of a simpler compound; hardening process of pit and fissure sealants.

Sealant: organic polymer that bonds to an enamel surface by mechanical retention accommodated by projections of the sealant into micropores created in the enamel by etching; the two types of sealants, filled and unfilled, both are composed of Bis-GMA.

　Filled sealant: contains, in addition to Bis-GMA, microparticles of glass, quartz, silica, and other fillers used in composite restorations; fillers make the sealant more resistant to abrasion.

Viscosity: in general, the resistance to flow or alteration of shape by any substance as a result of molecular cohesion.

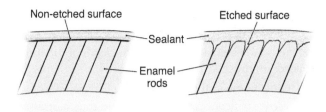

FIGURE 37-1 Enamel–Sealant Interface. Diagram of enamel–sealant interface to compare nonetched with etched surface. Etching produces microscopic porosities in the enamel to increase the area of retention. The unpolymerized resin flows into the porosities and hardens in taglike projections, as shown on the right. (Source: Buonocore MG, Matsui A, Gwinnett AJ. Penetration of resin dental materials into enamel surfaces with reference to bonding. *Arch Oral Biol.* 1968;13(1):61–70.)

III. Purposes of the Acid Etch

▶ To produce irregularities or micropores in the enamel.

▶ To allow the liquid resin to penetrate into the micropores and create a bond or mechanical locking.

▶ Figure 37-1 illustrates the sealant placed on a smooth enamel surface in contrast with placement on an etched surface with retention.

SEALANT MATERIALS

I. Criteria for the Ideal Sealant[3]

▶ Achieve prolonged bonding to enamel.

▶ Be biocompatible with oral tissues.

▶ Offer a simple application procedure.

▶ Be a free-flowing, low-viscosity material capable of entering narrow fissures.

▶ Have low solubility in the oral environment.

II. Classification of Sealant Materials

▶ A majority of sealants in clinical use are made of Bis-GMA (bisphenol A–glycidyl methylacrylate). The techniques of application vary slightly among available products.

A. Classification by Method of Polymerization

▶ *Self-cured or autopolymerized*
  • Preparation: material supplied in two parts. When the two are mixed they quickly polymerize (harden).
  • Advantage: no curing light required.
  • Disadvantages: mixing required; working time limited because polymerization begins when the material is mixed.

▶ *Visible light–cured or photopolymerized*
  • Preparation: material hardens when exposed to a special curing light.

  • Advantages: no mixing required; increased working time due to control over start of polymerization.
  • Disadvantages: extra costs and disinfection time required for curing light, protective shields, and/or glasses.

B. Classification by Filler Content

▶ *Filled*
  • Purpose of filler: To increase bond strength and increase resistance to abrasion and wear.
  • Fillers: Glass and quartz particles give hardness and strength to resist occlusal forces.
  • Effect: Viscosity of the sealant is increased. Flow into the depth of a fissure varies.

▶ *Unfilled*
  • Clear, does not contain particles.
  • Less resistant to abrasion and wear.
  • May not require occlusal adjustment after placement, so provides and advantage for school and community health programs where sealants are placed.

▶ *Fluoride releasing*
  • Purpose: enhance caries resistance.
  • Action: remineralization of incipient caries at base of pit or fissure.

C. Classification by Color

▶ Available: clear, tinted, and opaque.

▶ Purpose: quick identification for evaluation during maintenance assessment.

▶ Effect: clear, tinted, or opaque sealants do not differ in retention.

INDICATIONS FOR SEALANT PLACEMENT

I. Patients with Risk for Dental Caries (Any Age)

▶ Xerostomia: from medications or other reasons.

▶ Patient undergoing orthodontics.

▶ Incipient pit and fissure caries (limited to enamel) with no radiographic evidence of caries on adjacent proximal surface.

▶ Low socioeconomic status.

▶ Diet high in sugars.

▶ Inadequate daily oral health care.

II. Selection of Teeth

▶ Newly erupted: place sealant as soon as tooth is fully erupted.

▶ Occlusal contour: when pit or fissure is deep and irregular as illustrated in Figure 37-2.

▶ Caries history: other teeth restored or have carious lesions.

▶ Figure 37-3 is a flowchart to assist in decision making.

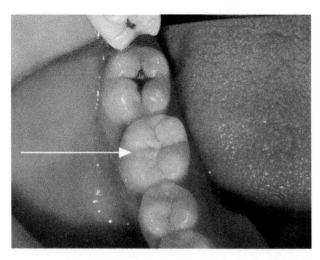

FIGURE 37-2 **Molar Tooth with Pits and Fissures.** Tooth #30 with deep fissures is selected for placing a dental sealant. Note the amalgam filling on tooth #31, which is evidence of previous dental caries experience. (Photograph courtesy of Jill Moore, RDH, BSDH, MHA, Sealant Coordinator, Michigan Department of Health and Human Services.)

III. Contraindications for Sealant Placement

▶ Radiographic evidence of adjacent proximal dental caries.

▶ Pit and fissures are well coalesced and self-cleansing; low caries risk.

▶ Tooth not completely erupted.

▶ Primary tooth near exfoliation.

PENETRATION OF SEALANT

Penetration of sealant material to the depth of the fissure depends on the following:

▶ Configuration of the pit or fissure

▶ Presence of deposits and debris within the pit or fissure

▶ Properties of the sealant itself.

I. Pit and Fissure Anatomy

The shape and depth of pits and fissures vary considerably even within one tooth. Anatomic differences include:

▶ *Wide V-shaped* (Figure 37-4B) or *narrow V-shaped fissures*.

▶ *Long narrow pits* and grooves reach to, or nearly to, the dentinoenamel junction (Figure 37-4C).

▶ *Long constricted fissures with a bulbous terminal portion* (Figure 37-4D) that may take a wavy course, which may not lead directly from the outer surface to the dentinoenamel junction.

II. Contents of a Pit or Fissure

A pit or fissure may contain the following:

▶ Dental biofilm, pellicle, debris

▶ Rarely but possibly intact remnants of tooth development.

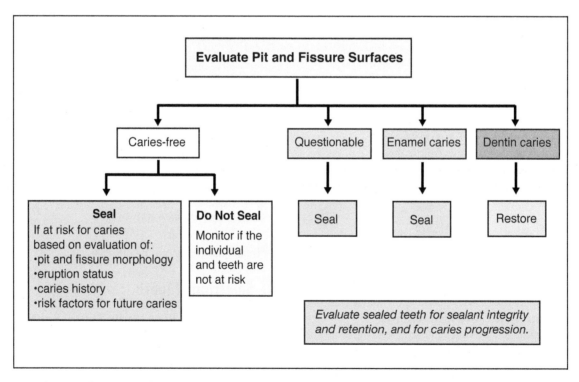

FIGURE 37-3 **Tooth Selection for Sealant Placement.** Flowchart to assist in decision making for placement of sealants. (Adapted from Workshop on guidelines for sealant use: recommendations. The Association of State and Territorial Dental Directors, the New York State Health Department, the Ohio Department of Health and the School of Public Health, University of Albany, State University of New York. *J Public Health Dent.* 1995;55(5 Spec):263–273.)

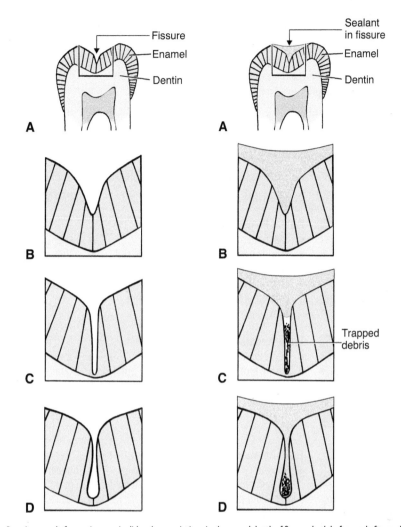

FIGURE 37-4 Occlusal Fissures. Drawings made from microscopic slides show variations in shape and depth of fissures both before and after sealant placement. **A:** Tooth with section enlarged for B, C, and D. **B:** Wide V-shaped fissure shows full sealant penetration. **C:** Long narrow groove that reaches nearly to the dentinoenamel junction. **D:** Long constricted form with a bulbous terminal portion.

III. Effect of Cleaning

▸ The narrow, long fissures are difficult to clean completely.

▸ Cleaning the tooth with pumice prior to dental sealant placement is avoided; if used, complete removal of pumice is necessary.

▸ Retained cleaning material can block the sealant from filling the fissure and can also become mixed with the sealant.

▸ Removal of pumice used for cleaning and thorough washing are necessary for retention of the sealant.

IV. Amount of Penetration

▸ Wide V-shaped and shallow fissures are more apt to be filled by sealant (Figure 37-4B).

▸ Although ideally the sealant penetrates to the bottom of a pit or fissure, such penetration is frequently impossible.

▸ Microscopic examination of pits and fissures after sealant application has shown that the sealant material often does not penetrate to the bottom because residual debris, cleaning agents, and trapped air prevent passage of the material (Figure 37-4C and D).

▸ The bacteria in incipient dental caries at the base of a well-sealed pit or fissure have no access to nutrients required for survival.

CLINICAL PROCEDURES

▸ Treat each quadrant separately while placing sealants on all eligible teeth.

▸ Use four-handed method with an assistant
 • To ensure moisture control.
 • To work efficiently and save time.

▸ Follow manufacturer's directions for each product.

▸ Success of treatment (retention) depends on the precision in each step of the application.

► Retention of sealant depends on maintaining a dry field during etching and sealant placement.
► Step-by-step clinical procedures and equipment/ supplies needed for placement of a dental sealant are illustrated in Table 37-1. Additional details for each step are provided in the following section.

I. Patient Preparation (Table 37-1, Step 1)

► Explain the procedure and steps to be performed.
► Provide patient with ultraviolet (UV) protective safety eyewear for protection from:
   • Chemicals used during etching and sealant placement
   • The UV light from the curing lamp.

Table 37-1	Steps for Placement of a Dental Sealant		
STEP	**ILLUSTRATION**	**DESCRIPTION**	**EQUIPMENT AND SUPPLIES**
Step 1		**Patient Preparation** ■ Seat patient comfortably ■ Provide patient education materials and answer questions ■ Provide UV protective eyewear for protection from chemicals and curing light	■ Patient education materials ■ Safety glasses for patient
Step 2		**Tooth Preparation** ■ Clean the tooth with a toothbrush ■ Ensure tooth is free from debris, external stain, and calculus prior to sealant placement	■ Toothbrush ■ Examination instruments (mirror and explorer)

Step 3		**Tooth Isolation**
		■ Maintain a working field that is not contaminated by saliva during all steps of sealant placement
		■ Options include:
		  • rubber dam (not shown)
		  • cotton rolls on the mandibular arch (top left)
		  • triangular bibulous pad to cover the parotid duct for the maxillary arch (lower left)
		■ Note: Take care to moisten all cotton prior to removal to avoid sticking to dry mucosa
			■ Rubber dam setup (optional)
			■ Cotton rolls and holders (Figure 37-3)
			■ Bibulous pads (lower left)

Step 4		**Acid Etch** ■ Dry entire area for 20–30 seconds with air/water syringe ■ Maintain a dry field ■ Use commercial etchant applicator (shown), brush, or cotton pellet to dispense etchant material ■ Place the acid etch only within the grooves and fissures where the sealant will be placed (shown at lower left) ■ Note: Follow product manufacture directions for application time; usually between 15 and 60 seconds	■ Air/water syringe ■ Acid-etch material and applicator, brush, or cotton pellet

STEP	ILLUSTRATION	DESCRIPTION	EQUIPMENT AND SUPPLIES
Step 5		**Rinse and Air Dry Tooth** ■ Place the high-velocity evacuation over the tooth ■ Rinse the tooth with the air/water syringe. ■ Spray water until surface is free of etch (30–60 seconds) ■ Spray air with air/water syringe until dry ■ Reisolate if necessary	■ High-velocity evacuation system ■ Air/water syringe
Step 6		**Evaluate for Complete Etching** ■ A completely etched tooth will have a chalky-white appearance when dry ■ If surface is not chalky appearing, repeat the acid-etch step	■ Air/water syringe ■ Mouth mirror for retraction and indirect vision
Step 7		**Place Sealant Material** ■ Continue to maintain a dry field ■ Use external fulcrum (fingers resting lightly on patient's chin or cheek) ■ Place the wet sealant material in the prepared pits and fissures ■ Adjust flow so sealant material is deposited only within the grooves, pits, and fissures	■ Sealant material and applicator ■ Slow-speed saliva ejector to help maintain dry field
Step 8		**Cure Sealant** ■ If using light-polymerized sealant material: • Ensure clinician and patient UV protective eye protection • Cover entire tooth with light and cure for 20–30 seconds in accordance with manufacturer instructions ■ If using self-curing sealant material: • Maintain dry field and allow drying time as indicated in manufacturer's instructions	■ UV protective goggles/glasses for patient and clinicians. ■ Curing light ■ Saliva ejector to help maintain dry field
Step 9		**Final/Cured Sealant** ■ Gently check for voids in sealant material with explorer ■ Additional material can be added if the surface has not been contaminated or wet	■ Mirror and explorer ■ Saliva ejector to help maintain dry field ■ Additional sealant material if needed to fill voids
Step 10		**Check Occlusion** ■ Use articulating paper to locate high spots and adjust as needed ■ Unfilled sealant material will wear down via normal attrition ■ Filled sealant material will require occlusal adjustment	■ Articulating paper ■ Holder

(continues)

Table 37-1	Steps for Placement of a Dental Sealant (*continued*)		
STEP	**ILLUSTRATION**	**DESCRIPTION**	**EQUIPMENT AND SUPPLIES**
Step 11		**Follow-up** ■ Provide patient education materials for the patient to take home. ■ Answer patient's questions ■ Re-evaluate sealants at each subsequent maintenance appointment	■ Excellent patient education materials are available for free from the National Institute of Dental and Craniofacial Research website. Available at: https://www.nidcr.nih.gov/orderpublications/

Photographs in Steps 2, 4a, 7, 8, and 10 courtesy of Susan J. Jenkins, RDH, MS, CAGS, Forsyth School of Dental Hygiene, MCPHS University. Additional photographs courtesy of Jill Moore, RDH, BSDH, MHA, Dental Sealant Coordinator, Michigan Department of Health and Human Services.

II. Tooth Preparation (Table 37-1, Step 2)

A. Purposes

▶ Remove deposits and debris.

▶ Permit maximum contact of the etch and the sealant with the enamel surface.

▶ Encourage sealant penetration into the pit or fissure.

B. Methods

▶ Examine tooth surfaces: remove calculus and stain.

▶ For the patient with no stain or calculus, apply toothbrush filaments straight into occlusal pits and fissures. (see Figure 28-14A in Chapter 28).

▶ Suction the pits and fissures with high-velocity evacuator.

▶ Gently use explorer tip to remove debris and bacteria from the pit or fissure and suction again to remove loosened material.

▶ Evaluate need for additional cleaning; the brushing may be sufficient.

III. Tooth Isolation (Table 37-1, Step 3)

A. Purposes of Isolation

▶ Maintaining a dry tooth is the single most important factor in sealant retention.

▶ Keep the tooth clean and dry for optimal action and bonding of the sealant.

▶ Eliminate possible contamination by saliva and moisture from the breath.

▶ Keep the materials from contacting the oral tissues, being swallowed accidentally, or being unpleasant to the patient because of flavor.

B. Rubber Dam Isolation

▶ Rubber dam application is the method of choice because the most complete isolation is obtained. This method is especially helpful when more than one tooth in the same quadrant is to be sealed.

▶ Rubber dam is essential when profuse saliva flow and overactive tongue and oral muscles make retraction and consistent maintenance of a dry, clean field impossible.

▶ When a quadrant has a rubber dam and anesthesia for restoration of other teeth, teeth indicated for sealant can be treated at the same time.

▶ Use anesthesia when application of the clamp cannot be tolerated by the patient.

▶ Rubber dam may not be possible when a tooth that is essential for holding the clamp is not fully erupted.

C. Cotton-Roll Isolation

▶ Patient position: tilt head to allow saliva to pool on the opposite side of the mouth.

▶ Position cotton-roll holder. Figure 37-5 shows the placement of two types of cotton role holders.

▶ Place saliva ejector.

▶ Apply triangular saliva absorber (bibulous pad) over the opening of the parotid duct in the cheek.

▶ Take care to prevent saliva contamination from entering the area to be etched.

D. Additional Isolation Options

▶ Commercially available isolation systems that can be attached to the dental unit offer intraoral quadrant isolation, illumination, and suction.

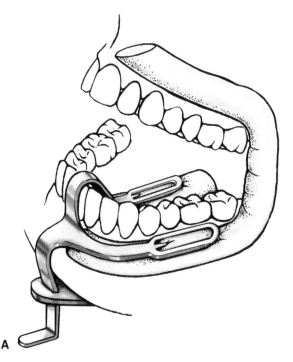
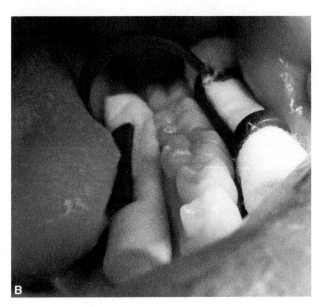

FIGURE 37-5 Tooth Isolation. A: Demonstrates a garmer-type cotton-roll holder, which can be used to treat two quadrants simultaneously. A continuous cotton role extends from the mandibular anterior vestibule to the maxillary anterior vestibule. **B:** Illustrates a disposable plastic cotton-roll holder used to isolate teeth in a mandibular quadrant. (Photograph courtesy of Jill Moore, RDH, BSDH, MHA, Sealant Coordinator, Michigan Department of Health and Human Services.)

IV. Acid Etch (Table 37-1, Step 4)

A. Dry the Tooth

▶ Purposes
  - Prepare the tooth for acid etch.
  - Eliminate moisture and contamination.
▶ Use clean, dry air
  - Clear water from the air/water syringe by releasing the spray into a sink.
  - Test for absence of moisture by blowing on a mouth mirror or other dry surface.
▶ Air dry the tooth for at least 10 seconds.

B. Apply Etchant

▶ Action
  - Creates micropores to increase the surface area and provide retention for the sealant.
  - Removes contamination from enamel surface.
  - Provides antibacterial action.
▶ Etchant solution forms
  - *Phosphoric acid:* 15%–50%, depends on product and manufacturer.
  - *Liquid:* Low viscosity allows good flow into pit or fissure but may be difficult to control.
  - *Gel:* Tinted gel with thick consistency allows increased visibility and control but may be difficult to rinse off the tooth surface.
  - *Semigel:* Tinted, with enough viscosity to allow good visibility, control, and rinsing ease.

▶ Etchant timing varies from 15 to 60 seconds. Follow manufacturer's instructions for each product.
▶ Etchant delivery
  - *Liquid etch:* Use a small brush, sponge, or cotton pellet; continuously pat rather than rub, when applying to keep the surface moist.
  - *Gel and semigel:* Use a syringe, brush, or manufacturer-supplied single-use cannula.

V. Rinse and Air Dry Tooth (Table 37-1, Step 5)

▶ Rinse thoroughly; apply continuous suction to prevent saliva from reaching the etched surface.
▶ Dry for 15–20 seconds; maintain dry isolation ready for sealant application.

VI. Evaluate for Complete Etching (Table 37-1, Step 6)

▶ Dry, and examine the etched surface.
▶ Repeat etching process if the surface does not appear chalky white.

VII. Place Sealant Material (Table 37-1, Step 7)

Follow manufacturer's instructions included in the sealant material package. General instructions include:

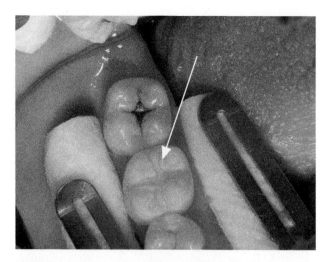

FIGURE 37-6 **Placement of Dental Sealant Material.** Appropriate placement of a dental sealant will completely fill pits and fissures, but not compromise occlusion by overfilling to a high, flat surface. (Photograph courtesy of Jill Moore, RDH, BSDH, MHA, Sealant Coordinator, Michigan Department of Health and Human Services.)

▶ Avoid overmanipulation of sealant materials to prevent producing air bubbles.

▶ Use disposable implement supplied in the sealant material package for application.

▶ Flow minimal amount into all pits and fissures; do not overfill to a high, flat surface.

▶ Figure 37-6 illustrates a correctly filled dental sealant surface.

VIII. Cure Sealant (Table 37-1, Step 8)

▶ If using a light-cured sealant material:
  • Leave liquid sealant material in place for 10 seconds to allow for optimum penetration.
  • Use UV blocking eye protection for both clinician and patient.
  • Apply the curing light for 20–30 seconds in accordance with manufacturer's instructions. Cover entire tooth surface with the light to ensure complete polymerization.

▶ If using an autopolymerized sealant material, consult manufacturer's instructions for curing time.

IX. Evaluate Cured Sealant (Table 37-1, Step 9)

▶ Check for voids gently with explorer: Additional sealant material can be added if surface has not been contaminated or wet.

X. Check Occlusion (Table 37-1, Step 10)

▶ Use articulating paper to locate high spots; adjust as required.

▶ Occlusal wear: unfilled sealants wear down via normal attrition to correct height; filled sealants require occlusal adjustment.

XI. Follow-Up (Table 37-1, Step 11)

▶ Educate the patient.

▶ Administer fluoride treatment.

▶ Re-evaluate at each subsequent appointment.

MAINTENANCE

I. Retention

▶ At each continuing care appointment, or at least every 6 months, each sealant needs to be examined for retention and to identify deficiencies that may have developed.

▶ Properly placed dental sealants can be retained for many years.[1]

II. Factors Affecting Retention

▶ *During placement*: precision of technique with exclusion of moisture and contamination.

▶ *Patient self-care*: Advise patient to avoid biting or chewing on hard surfaces such as a pencil or ice cubes.

▶ *Dental hygiene care*: Avoid using an air-powder polisher on intact existing sealants during maintenance appointments.[5]

III. Replacement

▶ Consult the manufacturer's instructions.

▶ Tooth preparation: same as for original application.

▶ Removal of firmly attached sections of retained sealant is not usually necessary.

▶ Re-etching of the tooth surface prior to replacement of a dental sealant is always essential.

SCHOOL-BASED DENTAL SEALANT PROGRAMS

▶ Delivery of dental sealants in school-based settings is a proven strategy[6,7] that can:
  • Effectively increase the percent of children in communities who receive dental sealants.
  • Reduce risk for decay for high-risk children.

▶ Many such school-based programs provide additional preventive services such as screening, prophylaxis, topical fluoride application, and oral health education.[5]

▶ Programs that provide sealants on sound surfaces and noncavitated lesions are an effective adjunct to preventive care provided in traditional dental care settings.[8]

▶ Figure 37-7 shows a portable dental unit set up in a school library.

FIGURE 37-7 Delivery of dental sealants in a school-based program using portable dental equipment set up in the school library. (Photograph courtesy of Jill Moore, RDH, BSDH, MHA, Sealant Coordinator, Michigan Department of Health and Human Services.)

DOCUMENTATION

Documentation in the record of a patient receiving a sealant contains a minimum of the following:

▶ Reason for selection of certain teeth for sealants; informed consent of patient, parent, or other caregiver.

▶ Type of sealant used, preparation of tooth, manner of isolation, patient cooperation during administration; postinsertion instructions given.

▶ Sample documentation for placement of dental sealants may be reviewed in Box 37-2.

BOX 37-2

Example Documentation: Placement of Dental Sealants

S –A 12 year-old male patient presents for dental sealant placement.

O –Occlusal contour and previous history of dental caries in primary dentition indicate need for sealant placement for 2nd molars; X-rays indicate no dental caries on proximal surfaces of 2nd molars. Tooth #30 partially erupted with operculum.

A –Need to wait until #30 is completely erupted to place sealant.

P –Reviewed sealant education materials with mother and patient. Mother provided consent for placement of the recommended sealants. Sealants placed on #3-O, 14-O, 14-L, 19-O, 19-B pit using right side, then left side isolation. Autopolymerized opaque sealant material used with 15% acid etch applied with manufacturer's directions. Patient tolerated treatment well, no gagging, minimal saliva, easy isolation.

Next steps: Schedule in 1 month to re-examine for sealant placement on #30 and retention check on 3, 14, and 19.

Signed:_____, RDH

Date: _____

EVERYDAY ETHICS

Lillian had always enjoyed doing sealants when she was in dental hygiene school. They had been required to do quite a few, and as students they got to participate in "Sealant Day," a volunteer program carried out by the local dental hygienists every spring.

Now, when she came back from the state dental hygiene meeting, she was all excited about the new interpretation of the practice act by the Dental Board and greeted her employer, Dr. Fine, with the news first thing Monday morning. The Board had voted that the dental hygienist who had been in practice for 2 years full-time (or part-time equivalent) could make the decision whether a pit or fissure needed a sealant. There was a continuing education course and an examination required.

Lillian added: "Remember Jack—that teenager that was here last week? He had some really deep fissures that I was sure would benefit from sealants. Can I go ahead and schedule him? I told him he needed them. He has an appointment with you to have a few cavities filled, but that wouldn't fit in your book until nearly the end of the month. They are giving the exam and CE next week."

Dr. Fine continued quietly to tie on his gown for the first patient, and then he smiled and said, "Well, Lil, let's wait until he comes in for his appointment with me and I'll look at them."

Questions for Consideration

1. Professionally, what action(s) can Lillian take to initiate a system of calibration between her and Dr. Fine to pursue the new practice protocols?

2. What ethical issues may be involved here? How can they be resolved?

3. Which of the core values describe the friendly relationship between Lillian and Dr. Fine? And which core values describe Lillian's wishes to extend the services for Jack's (the patient's) benefit?

Factors To Teach The Patient

▷ Sealants are part of a total preventive program. Sealants are not substitutes for other preventive measures. Limitations of dietary sucrose, use of fluorides, and dental biofilm control are major factors with sealants for prevention of dental caries.

▷ What a sealant is and why such a meticulous application procedure is required.

▷ What can be expected from a sealant; how long it lasts, and how it prevents dental caries.

▷ Need for examination of the sealant at frequent, scheduled maintenance appointments, and need for replacement when missing or chipped.

▷ Avoid biting hard items such as a pencil or ice cubes to increase sealant retention.

References

1. Ahovuo-Saloranta A, Forss H, Walsh T, et al. Sealants for preventing dental decay in the permanent teeth. *Cochrane Database Syst Rev.* 2013;(3):CD001830. doi:10.1002/14651858.CD001830.pub4.

2. Beauchap J, Caufiel PW, Crall JJ, et al. Evidence-based clinical recommendations for the use of pit-and-fissure sealants: a report of the American Dental Association Council on Scientific Affairs. *J Am Dent Assoc.* 2008;139(3):257–268.

3. Handleman SL, Shey Z. Michael Buonocore and the Eastman Dental Center. A historic perspective on sealants. *J Dent Res.* 1996;75(1):529–534.

4. Cueto EI, Buonocore MG. Sealing of pits and fissures with an adhesive resin: its use in caries prevention. *J Am Dent Assoc.* 1967;75(1):121–128.

5. Huennekens SC, Daniel SJ, Bayne SC. Effects of air polishing on the abrasion of occlusal sealants. *Quintessence Int.* 1991;22(7):581–585.

6. Children's Dental Health Project. *Dental Sealants: Proven to Prevent Decay.* Washington, DC: Children's Dental Health Project; 2014:21. https://www.cdhp.org/resources/314-dental-sealants-proven-to-prevent-tooth-decay. Accessed May 16, 2014.

7. PEW Center on the States. *Falling Short: Most States Lag on Dental Sealants.* Washington, DC: The PEW Charitable Trusts; 2013. http://www.pewstates.org/research/reports/falling-short-85899434875. Accessed May 16, 2014.

8. Gooch BF, Griffin SO, Gray SK, et al. Preventing dental caries through school-based sealant programs: updated recommendations and reviews of evidence. *J Am Dent Assoc.* 2009;140(11):1356–1365.

ENHANCE YOUR UNDERSTANDING

the Point® **DIGITAL CONNECTIONS**
(see the inside front cover for access information)

- **Audio glossary**
- **Quiz bank**

SUPPORT FOR LEARNING
(available separately; visit lww.com)

- *Active Learning Workbook for Clinical Practice of the Dental Hygienist, 12th Edition*

prepU **INDIVIDUALIZED REVIEW**
(available separately; visit lww.com)

- **Adaptive quizzing with *prepU for Wilkins' Clinical Practice of the Dental Hygienist***

44

Dentin Hypersensitivity

Terri S.I. Tilliss, RDH, PhD and Janis G. Keating, RDH, MA

CHAPTER OUTLINE

LEARNING OBJECTIVES

After studying this chapter, the student will be able to:

1. Describe stimuli and pain characteristics specific to hypersensitivity, and explain how this relates to differential diagnosis.

2. Describe factors that contribute to dentin exposure and behavioral changes that could decrease hypersensitivity.

3. Explain the steps in the hydrodynamic theory.

4. Describe two mechanisms of desensitization and their associated treatment interventions for managing dentin hypersensitivity.

BOX 44-1 KEY WORDS AND ABBREVIATIONS: Dentin Hypersensitivity

Abfraction: wedge- or V-shaped cervical lesion created by the stresses of lateral or eccentric tooth movements during occlusal function, bruxing, or parafunctional activity resulting in enamel microfractures.

ADA: American Dental Association.

Burnishing: repeated rubbing of a tooth surface with a toothpick or wooden stick.

Dentin hypersensitivity: transient pain arising from exposed dentin, typically in response to a stimulus, which cannot be explained as arising from any other form of dental defect or pathology and subsides quickly when stimulus is removed.

FDA: Food and Drug Administration.

Hydrodynamic theory: currently accepted mechanism for pain impulse transmission to the pulp as a result of fluid movement within the dentinal tubule, which stimulates the nerve endings at the dentinopulpal interface.

Intertubular dentin: dentin located between dentinal tubules.

Intratubular or peritubular dentin: increased deposition of minerals into tubules that become more mineralized with increasing age, resulting in thicker, sclerotic dentin.

Neural depolarization mechanism (sodium/potassium pump): reduction of the resting potential of the nerve membrane so that a nerve impulse is fired. At rest, the inner surface of the nerve fiber is negatively charged and impermeable to sodium ions. A stimulus temporarily alters the membrane, making it permeable so that potassium

leaks out and sodium rushes into the nerve fiber. This mechanism is known as the sodium–potassium pump. The reversal of electrical charge, or **depolarization**, creates the nerve impulse. The process then reverses, and the membrane potential is restored, or **repolarized**.

Osmosis: the passage of fluids and solutions of lesser concentration through a selective membrane to one of greater solute concentration.

OTC: over the counter.

Patent: open, unobstructed; a patent dentinal tubule allows fluid flow to signal pain; many desensitizing agents work by decreasing the patency of the tubule.

Randomized Clinical Trials (RCT): a specific type of scientific experiment that is the gold standard for a clinical trial. RCTs are often used to test the efficacy and/or effectiveness of various types of interventions within a patient population.

Secondary dentin: dentin that is secreted slowly over time after root formation to "wall off" the pulp from fluid flow within dentinal tubules following a stimulus; results in narrower pulp chamber and root canals.

Smear layer: has been referred to as "grinding debris" from instrumentation or other devices applied to the tooth; consists of microcrystalline particles of cementum, dentin, tissue, and cellular debris; serves to plug tubule orifices.

Tertiary/reparative dentin: a type of dentin formed along the pulpal wall or root canal as a protective mechanism in response to trauma or irritation, such as caries or a traumatic cavity preparation.

The dental hygienist is often the first oral health professional to become aware of the presence of hypersensitive teeth when a patient presents for care. Individuals who suffer from hypersensitivity may be uncomfortable during dental hygiene treatment, since exposure to stimuli such as a cold water spray or contact with metal instruments can elicit the pain of hypersensitive teeth.

▶ Patients often report that activities of daily living such as eating or drinking cold foods or beverages cause pain and request information about causes and treatment for their discomfort.

▶ Hypersensitivity is often difficult to diagnose because the presenting symptoms can be confused with other types of dental pain with a different etiology.

▶ Management of hypersensitivity can be a challenge because there are numerous treatment approaches with varying degrees of efficacy.

▶ Knowledge of the predisposing factors that lead to gingival recession and loss of enamel or cementum and dentin can assist patients in preventing conditions that cause or exacerbate dentin hypersensitivity.

▶ Box 44-1 provides definitions for terms related to hypersensitivity.

HYPERSENSITIVITY DEFINED

A definitive characteristic associated with dentin hypersensitivity is pain elicited by a stimulus and alleviated upon its removal. Numerous types of stimuli can lead to pain response in individuals with exposed dentin surfaces.

I. Stimuli That Elicit Pain Reaction

▶ *Tactile*: contact with toothbrush and other oral hygiene devices, eating utensils, dental instruments, and friction from prosthetic devices such as denture clasps.

▶ *Thermal*: temperature change caused by hot and cold foods and beverages, and cold air as it contacts the teeth. Cold is the most common stimulus for pain.

▶ *Evaporative*: dehydration of oral fluids as from high-volume evacuation or application of air to dry teeth during intraoral procedures.

▶ *Osmotic*: alteration of pressure in dentinal tubules through a selective membrane.

▶ *Chemical*: acids in foods and beverages such as citrus fruits, condiments, spices, wine, and carbonated beverages;

acids produced by acidogenic bacteria following carbohydrate exposure; acids from gastric regurgitation.

II. Characteristics of Pain from Hypersensitivity

▶ Sharp, short, or transient pain with rapid onset.

▶ Cessation of pain upon removal of stimulus.

▶ Presents as a chronic condition with acute episodes.

▶ Pain in response to a non-noxious stimulus, one that would not normally cause pain or discomfort.

▶ Discomfort that cannot be ascribed to any other dental defect or pathology.[1]

ETIOLOGY OF DENTIN HYPERSENSITIVITY

A review of tooth anatomy facilitates an understanding of the mechanism of hypersensitivity.

I. Anatomy of Tooth Structures

A. Dentin

▶ The portion of the tooth covered by enamel on the crown and cementum on the root.

▶ Composed of fluid-filled dentinal tubules that narrow and branch as they extend from the pulp to the dentinoenamel junction (Figure 44-1).

▶ Only the portions of the dentinal tubules closest to the pulp are innervated with nerve fiber endings from the pulp chamber.

▶ Tubules are wider and more numerous in sensitive areas.[2]

B. Pulp

▶ Highly innervated with nerve cell fiber endings that extend just beyond the dentinopulpal interface of the dentinal tubules.[3]

▶ Body portions of odontoblasts (dentin-producing cells) located adjacent to the pulp extend their processes from the dentinopulpal junction a short way into each dentinal tubule (Figure 44-1).

C. Nerves

▶ Nerve fiber endings extend just beyond the dentinopulpal junction[4] and wind around the odontoblastic processes as shown in Figure 44-1.

▶ Nerves react via the same neural depolarization mechanism (sodium potassium pump, defined in Box 44-1), which characterizes the response of any nerve to a stimulus.

II. Mechanisms of Dentin Exposure

▶ The sequential events of gingival recession, loss of cementum or enamel, and subsequent dentin exposure, as seen in Figure 44-2, can result in hypersensitivity.

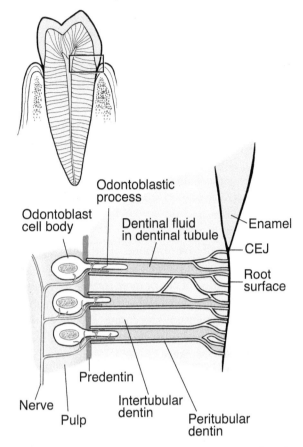

FIGURE 44-1 **Relationship of Dentin Tubules and Pulpal Nerve Endings.** Nerve endings from the pulp wrap themselves around the odontoblasts that extend only a short distance into the tubule. Fluid-filled dentin tubules transmit fluid disturbances through the mechanism known as hydraulic conductance.

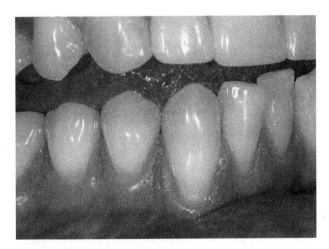

FIGURE 44-2 **Gingival Recession.** Note recession from the mandibular right central incisor to the 2nd premolar. If the thin cemental layer of the exposed root surface is lost, dentin hypersensitivity can develop.

▶ Loss of enamel or cementum can expose dentin gradually or suddenly as in tooth fracture.

▶ As a result of the lower mineral content of cementum and dentin compared with enamel, demineralization occurs more rapidly and at a lower critical pH.

▶ Acute hypersensitivity may occur with sudden dentin exposure since gradual exposure allows for the development of natural desensitization mechanisms such as smear layer or sclerosis. After many years, secondary or reparative dentin may form, which also protects the pulp.

A. Factors Contributing to Gingival Recession and Subsequent Root Exposure

The occurrence of gingival recession has a multifactorial etiology. Potential causes include:

▶ Effects of improper oral self-care:
  • Use of a medium or hard bristle toothbrush.
  • Frequent aggressive use of the toothbrush and/or other oral hygiene devices.

▶ An anatomically narrow zone of attached gingiva is more susceptible to abrasion.

▶ Facial orientation of one or more teeth.

▶ A tight and short labial or buccal frenum attachment that pulls on gingival tissues during oral movement.

▶ Scaling and root debridement procedures that result in gingival tissue shrinkage.

▶ Subgingival instrumentation involving excessive scaling and debridement in shallow sulci.[5]

▶ Tissue alteration due to apical migration of junctional epithelium from periodontal diseases.

▶ Periodontal surgical procedures can alter the architecture of gingival tissues resulting in recession.

▶ Periodontal surgery procedures such as crown lengthening, repositioning of gingival tissues, or tooth extractions can affect gingival coverage of adjacent teeth.

▶ Orthodontic tooth movement may result in loss of periodontal attachment.

▶ Restorative procedures, such as crown preparation, that abrade marginal gingival tissues.

▶ Metal jewelry used in an oral piercing of the lip or tongue that repeatedly traumatizes the adjacent facial or lingual gingival tissue.

B. Factors Contributing to Loss of Enamel and Cementum

▶ Loss of tooth structure rarely develops from a single cause but rather from a combination of contributing factors.

▶ Cementum at the cervical area is thin and easily abrades when exposed.

▶ Enamel and cementum do not meet at the cementoenamel junction (CEJ) in about 10% of teeth, leaving an area of exposed dentin, as shown in Figure 18-10 (Chapter 18).

C. Attrition, Abrasion, and Erosion

▶ Effects of attrition and abrasion are exacerbated when acid erodes the tooth surface or when the tooth is brushed immediately after consumption of acidic foods and beverages.

▶ Hypersensitivity may be a clinical outcome of erosion.[6]

▶ Erosion can occur from dietary acids, such as citrus fruits/juices, wine, and carbonated drinks.[7]

▶ Dietary acid intake results in an immediate drop in oral pH; after normal salivary neutralization, a physiologic pH of 7 re-establishes within minutes.

▶ Frequent acid consumption is a critical factor; holding or "swilling" of acidic agents, holding low pH foods such as citrus fruits against teeth, or continual snacking increases erosion risk.

▶ Gastric acids from conditions such as gastric reflux, morning sickness, or self-induced vomiting (bulimia) repeatedly expose teeth to a highly acidic environment.

D. Abfraction

▶ Abfraction, a wedge-shaped cervical lesion, has a questionable etiology.[8–11]

▶ A cervical lesion caused by lateral/occlusal stresses or tooth flexure from bruxing.

▶ Microscopic portions of the enamel rods chip away from the cervical area of the tooth resulting in loss of tooth structure (Figure 44-3).

▶ Lesion appears as a wedge- or V-shaped cervical notch.

▶ Is a co-factor with abrasion for loss of tooth structure and potential sensitivity.

E. Other Factors

▶ Crown preparation procedures that remove enamel or cementum can expose dentin at the cervical area.

▶ Instrumentation during scaling or root debridement procedures on thinning cementum.

▶ Frequent or improper stain-removal techniques, in which abrasive particles wear away the cementum and dentin.

▶ Root surface carious lesions.

▶ Removal of proximal enamel using a sandpaper disk or strip to create additional space for orthodontic movement of crowded teeth, also known as "enamel stripping."

III. Hydrodynamic Theory

Hydrodynamic theory is a currently accepted explanation for transmission of stimuli from the outer surface of the dentin to the pulp.

▶ Described by Brannstrom in the 1960s,[12] who theorized that a stimulus at the outer aspect of dentin will cause fluid movement within the dentinal tubules.

▶ Fluid movement creates pressure on the nerve endings within the dentinal tubule, which transmits the pain impulse by stimulating the nerves in the pulp.

▶ Credibility for this theory is supported by the greater number of widened dentin tubules seen in hypersensitive teeth compared with nonsensitive teeth.[2] Figure 44-4 depicts open dentinal tubules at the microscopic level. Figure 44-5 depicts partially occluded dentinal tubules.

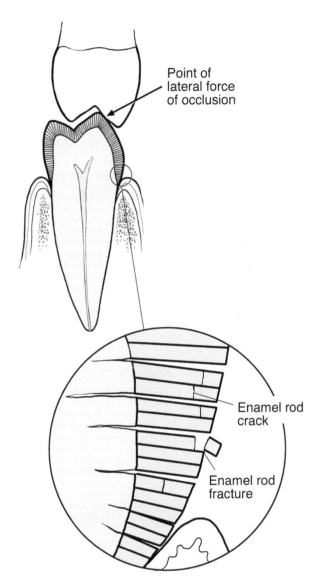

FIGURE 44-3 **Process of Abfraction.** Lateral occlusal forces stress the enamel rods at the cervical area, resulting in enamel rod fracture over time. In an advanced stage, a wedge- or V-shaped cervical lesion is visible. Although minute cracks in the enamel rods may not be clinically evident, the tooth can exhibit hypersensitivity.

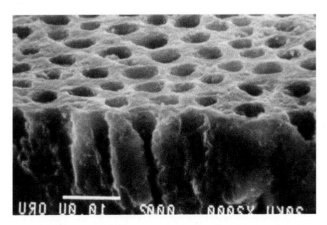

FIGURE 44-4 **Open Dentin Tubules.** Note cross-section and transverse views of tubules. Courtesy of Dr. Sheldon Newman.

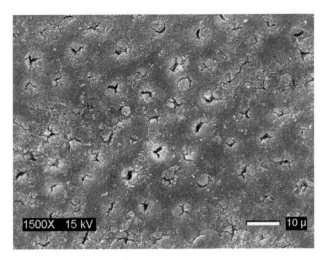

Figure 44-5 **Partially Occluded Dentin Tubules.** These dentin tubules are nearly filled. Courtesy of Anthony Giuseppetti.

NATURAL DESENSITIZATION

▶ Hypersensitivity can decrease naturally over time, even without treatment interventions.

▶ There are several mechanisms by which desensitization can occur naturally over time, including the following:

I. Sclerosis of Dentin

▶ Occurs by mineral deposition within tubules as a result of traumatic stimuli, such as attrition or dental caries.

▶ Creates a thicker, highly mineralized layer of peritubular dentin (deposited within the periphery of the tubules).

▶ Results in a smaller-diameter tubule that is less able to transmit stimuli through the dentinal fluid to the nerve fibers at the dentinopulpal interface.

II. Secondary Dentin

▶ Deposited gradually on the floor and roof of the pulp chamber after teeth are fully developed.

▶ Secreted more slowly than primary dentin formed before tooth eruption; both types of dentin are created by odontoblasts.

▶ Creates a "walling off" effect between the dentinal tubules and the pulp to insulate the pulp from dentin fluid disturbances caused by a stimulus such as dental caries.

▶ With aging, secondary dentin accumulates, resulting in a smaller pulp chamber with fewer nerve endings and less sensitivity.

III. Smear Layer

▶ Consists of organic and inorganic debris that covers the dentinal surface and the tubules.[13]

- Accumulates following scaling and root instrumentation, use of toothpaste (abrasive particles), cutting with a bur, attrition, or abrasion (burnishing with a toothbrush or toothpick, or other device).
- Occludes the dentinal tubule orifices, forming a "smear plug" or a natural "bandage" that blocks stimuli.
- The nature of the smear layer changes constantly since it is subject to effects such as mechanical disruption from ultrasonic debridement, or dissolution from acid exposure.

IV. Calculus

- Provides a protective coating to shield exposed dentin from stimuli.
- Postdebridement sensitivity can occur after removal of heavy calculus deposits; dentinal tubules may become exposed as calculus is removed.

THE PAIN OF DENTIN HYPERSENSITIVITY

Individuals react differently to pain based on factors such as age, gender, situation and context, previous experiences, pain expectations, and other psychological and physiological parameters.

I. Patient Profile

The prevalence of reported hypersensitivity varies due to differences in the stimulus, and whether data are gathered by patient report or standardized clinical examination. Patient accounts may not represent true hypersensitivity since the pain can be confused with other conditions.

A. Prevalence of Hypersensitivity

- A large multipractice cross-sectional survey found a prevalence of dentin hypersensitivity of 12.3%, with an average of 3.5 hypersensitive teeth; the highest prevalence occurred in those 18–44 years of age.[14]
- Higher prevalence has been reported in periodontally involved populations.[15]
- Incidence and severity declines with advancing age, due to the effects of sclerosis and secondary dentin.[16]
- Gingival recession is more prevalent with aging.[17] Dentin hypersensitivity is not more prevalent with aging.
- Hypersensitivity, when measured objectively, occurs more often in women.[14]

B. Teeth Affected

- Hypersensitivity has been reported to occur primarily at the cervical one-third of the facial surfaces of premolars and mandibular anterior teeth,[18] or on premolars and molars.[14]
- Can occur on any tooth exhibiting predisposing factors.

II. Pain Experience

A. Neural Activity

- Stimuli that affect the fluid flow within the dentinal tubules can activate the terminal nerve endings near to or surrounding the dentinal tubules; activation of these nerve fibers elicits the pain response.
- Occurs via the depolarization/neural discharge mechanism that characterizes all nerve activity.
- The sodium–potassium pump depolarizes the nerve as potassium leaves the nerve cell and sodium enters it.

B. Pain Perception

- The degree of pain is not always proportional to the amount of recession, the percentage of tooth structure loss, or to the quality or quantity of stimulus.
- Individuals experience the subjective phenomenon of pain differently. Many diverse variables such as stress, fatigue, and health beliefs can impact pain perception.

C. Impact of Pain

- Hypersensitivity can manifest as acute or chronic pain; acute pain may result in anxiety, whereas chronic pain may contribute to depression.
- Stress may exacerbate the pain response.
- Persistent discomfort from dentin hypersensitivity may affect quality of life.

DIFFERENTIAL DIAGNOSIS

- Etiology of pain can be systemic, pulpal, periapical, restorative, degenerative, or neoplastic.
- A differential diagnosis can rule out other causes of pain before treating for hypersensitivity.
- Skilled interviewing and diagnostics contribute to the differential diagnosis.
- Components to consider in the differential diagnosis of tooth pain are detailed in Table 44-1.

I. Differentiation of Pain

- Hypersensitivity pain elicited by a non-noxious stimulus, such as cold water, can mimic pain elicited by a noxious agent, such as cavitated dental caries.
- The pain of hypersensitivity subsides when the stimulus is removed.
- It is difficult to distinguish between the pain of hypersensitivity and other causes of dental pain when both are in the mild-to-moderate range. Many types of dental pain can be intensified by thermal, sweet, and sour stimuli.
- Chewing pain (occlusal pressure) can be indicative of pulpal pathology.

TABLE 44-1	Differential Diagnosis of Tooth Pain	
CONDITION	SIGNS AND SYMPTOMS	CLINICAL ASSESSMENT
Dentinal hypersensitivity	Thermal, mechanical, evaporative, osmotic, chemical sensitivity Sharp, sudden, transient pain	Clinical examination: gingival recession and loss of tooth structure
Caries extending into dentin	Thermal sensitivity Pain on pressure Pain with sweets	Clinical examination Radiographic examination
Pulpal caries	Thermal sensitivity Severe, intermittent or throbbing pain Pain on chewing	Clinical examination Radiographic examination
Fractured restoration	Thermal sensitivity Pain on pressure	Clinical examination
Fractured tooth	Thermal sensitivity Pain on pressure	Occlusal examination Transillumination
Recently placed restoration	Thermal sensitivity Pain on pressure	Dental history Clinical examination Occlusal examination
Occlusal trauma	Chemical sensitivity Thermal sensitivity Pain on pressure Mobility	Occlusal examination
Pulpitis	Severe, intermittent throbbing pain	Thermal and electric pulp tests Percussion
Sinus infection	"Nondescript" tooth pain Nasal congestion (drainage) Sinus pressure Headache	Clinical examination, including extraoral sinus palpation Radiographic examination
Galvanic pain	Sudden, sharp stabbing pain on tooth to tooth contact	Examination for contact between restoration of dissimilar nonprecious metals
Periodontal ligament inflammation	Pain on chewing Clinical examination, including palpation for apical tenderness	Percussion
Abfraction	"Cratered" areas of enamel or dentin at CEJ in the shape of a wedge- or V-shaped notch	Clinical examination Occlusal examination

▶ Pulpal pain is severe, intermittent, and throbbing. The pain results from deep dental caries, pulpal inflammation, vertical tooth fracture, or infection, and may occur without provocation and persist after stimulus is removed.

II. Data Collection by Interview

▶ Utilize direct, open-ended and non-leading questions.
  • Establish the location, degree of pain, onset/duration, source of stimulus, intensity, and alleviating factors related to the painful response; patients may have difficulty characterizing the pain.
  • Ask trigger questions as suggested in Box 44-2 to elicit detailed information to characterize the pain and assist in the dental hygiene diagnosis.

▶ Establish rapport, combined with effective listening and counseling skills to develop collaborative treatment/management strategies.

▶ Record a thorough dental history, including pain chronology, nature, location, aggravating and alleviating factors, and history of dental treatment/restorations.

Trigger Questions for Data Collection

▷ Which tooth or teeth surfaces is/are sensitive?

▷ On a scale from 1 to 10, with 10 being the most painful, what is your pain intensity?

▷ How long does the pain last?

▷ Which words best describe the pain: sharp, dull, shooting, throbbing, persistent, constant, pressure, burning, intermittent?

▷ Does it hurt when you bite down (pressure)?

▷ On a scale from 1 to 10, with 10 being a major impact, how much does the pain impact your daily life?

▷ Is the pain stimulated by certain foods? Sweet? Sour? Acidic?

▷ Does sensitivity occur with hot or cold food or beverages?

▷ Does discomfort stop immediately upon removal of the painful stimulus, such as cold food or beverage, or does it linger?

▷ Have you whitened your teeth lately?

III. Diagnostic Techniques and Tests

When patients have difficulty describing and localizing their pain, the following diagnostic techniques and tests can aid in differentiating among the numerous causes of tooth pain.

▶ Visual assessment of tooth integrity and surrounding tissues.

▶ Palpation of extra- and intraoral soft tissues.

▶ Evaluation of nasal congestion, drainage, or sinus expressed as tooth pain.

▶ Occlusal examination with use of marking paper to detect a premature contact or hyperfunction following placement of a new restoration.

▶ Radiographic assessment to determine signs of pulpal pathology, vertical tooth fracture, or other irregularities of the teeth or surrounding structures.

▶ Percussion with use of an instrument handle to lightly tap on each tooth. A pain response may indicate pulpitis.

▶ Mobility testing may detect trauma or periodontal pathology.

▶ Pain from biting pressure with use of a bite stick to assess pain indicative of tooth fracture.

▶ Transillumination with a high-intensity focused light to enhance visualization of a cracked tooth; dye may also indicate a fracture line.

▶ Pulpal pathology assessment with thermal or electric pulp tests.

HYPERSENSITIVITY MANAGEMENT

When the differential diagnosis indicates dentinal hypersensitivity, the dental hygiene care plan includes further assessment and patient counseling combined with treatment interventions.

I. Assessment Components

▶ Determine extent and severity of pain.
- Solicit a self-report of symptoms, including the eliciting stimuli.
- Quantify and record the baseline pain intensity using objective measures such as the visual analog scale (VAS) and/or the verbal rating scale (VRS), as described in Box 44-3.

▶ Determine if oral self-care procedures contribute to loss of gingiva or tooth structure.

▶ Use a diet analysis to assess the frequency of acidic food and beverage intake; correlate intake with timing of toothbrushing.

Subjective Pain Assessment Form

Name: _____
Date: _____
Teeth: _____

VAS—Visual Analog Scale

Please place an "X" on the line at a position between the two extremes to represent the level of pain that you experience.

No Discomfort |————————————| Severe Discomfort

VRS—Verbal Rating Scale

Please describe the pain you experience on a scale from 0 to 3:

   0 = No discomfort/pain, but aware of stimulus
   1 = Slight discomfort/pain
   2 = Significant discomfort/pain
   3 = Significant discomfort/pain that lasted more than 10 seconds

▶ Explore parafunctional habits, such as bruxing, that may contribute to abfraction.

II. Educational Considerations

▶ Provide education regarding etiology and contributing factors. Explain the natural mechanisms for resolution of hypersensitivity over time.

▶ Discuss realistic oral self-care measures that the patient is likely to maintain and include technique demonstrations.

▶ Utilize effective communication and motivational interviewing skills to promote compliance and to decrease patient anxiety (see Chapter 26).

III. Treatment Hierarchy

▶ There are two basic treatment goals:
  • Pain relief.
  • Modification or elimination of contributing factors.

▶ Address mild-to-moderate pain with conservative approaches or agents; more severe pain may require an aggressive approach.

▶ Sequence treatment approaches from the most conservative and least invasive measures to more aggressive modalities.

▶ Prognosis of pain resolution is difficult to predict due to variable success with different treatment options among individuals.
  • Historically, a vast array of treatment approaches have been utilized with varying degrees of success; no one best method has been identified due to lack of quality randomized clinical trial (RCT) data, difficulties inherent in dentin hypersensitivity research design, and a significant placebo effect.
  • A trial-and-error approach may be necessary to determine the most effective treatment option.
  • Characteristics of an ideal desensitizing agent are listed in Box 44-4 and can be useful evaluation criteria when selecting a desensitizing agent.

▶ Treatment options that include both oral self-care measures and professional interventions with the same objective of reducing hypersensitivity have a synergistic effect.

IV. Reassessment

▶ Evaluate treatment interventions.
  • Allow sufficient time to elapse (2–4 weeks) to evaluate effectiveness of treatment recommendations; assess and reinforce behavioral changes.
  • Repeat the VAS and/or the VRS to compare changes in pain perceptions from baseline.

▶ If pain persists, a different option may provide relief.

ORAL HYGIENE CARE AND TREATMENT INTERVENTIONS

I. Mechanisms of Desensitization

Desensitization agents and oral self-care measures disrupt the pain transmission as described by the hydrodynamic theory in one of two ways:[19]

▶ Prevent nerve depolarization that interrupts the neural transmission to the pulp. This physiologic process is the mechanism of action for potassium-based products.[20]

▶ Prevent a stimulus from moving the tubule fluid by occlusion of dentin tubule orifices or reduction in tubule lumen diameter.

II. Behavioral Changes

Encourage habits that allow tubules to remain occluded or that occlude patent tubules.

▶ Use a motivational interviewing approach (Chapter 26) to help the patient commit to appropriate oral hygiene self-care and dietary habits before or in conjunction with self-applied or professionally applied desensitizing agents.

▶ Educate the patient that some products may take 2–4 weeks to decrease sensitivity.

A. Dietary Modifications

▶ Have patient analyze acidic food and beverage habits that incite pain from dissolution of the smear layer which covered open dentinal tubules.[21] Examples include citrus fruits and juices, acidic soda/cola beverages, sharp flavors and spices, pickled foods, wines, and ciders.

▶ Counsel patient regarding change in dietary habits.

▶ Help patient determine if brushing is sequenced immediately after consuming acidic foods and beverages. Advise altering sequence to eliminate combined effects of erosion and abrasion, which can accelerate tooth structure loss.[22]

▶ Guide patient toward mouth rinses with a non-acidic formulation.

BOX 44-4

The Ideal Desensitizing Agent

▷ Minimal application time
▷ Easy application procedure
▷ Does not endanger the soft tissues
▷ Inexpensive
▷ Requires few dental appointments
▷ Does not cause pulpal irritation or pain
▷ Rapid and lasting effect
▷ Causes no staining
▷ Consistently effective
▷ Acceptable taste

► Provide professional treatment referrals for patients with eating disorders such as bulimia or systemic conditions such as acid reflux that repeatedly create an acidic oral environment.

► The acidic environment created by bulimia and acid reflux can be neutralized by rinsing with water (particularly fluoridated water) or an alkaline rinse such as bicarbonate of soda in water.

► Counsel patient to eliminate extremes of hot and cold foods and beverages to avoid discomfort.

B. Dental Biofilm Control

► In the presence of dental biofilm, the dentinal tubule orifices increase to three times the original size; with re-establishment of biofilm control measures, there is a 20% decrease in size.[23]

► The presence/amount of dental biofilm on exposed root surfaces does not directly correlate with the degree of dentin sensitivity,[17] suggesting biofilm composition maybe a factor.

C. Toothbrush Type and Technique

► Brush one or two teeth at a time with a soft or ultra-soft toothbrush, rather than using long horizontal strokes over several teeth to prevent further recession and loss of tooth structure.

► Identify brushing sequence and adjust by beginning in least sensitive areas and ending with more sensitive areas. In the initial phases of brushing, toothbrush filaments are stiffer and brushing is more aggressive.

► Explore option of brushing with the nondominant hand, if dexterity permits; nondominant hand exerts less pressure than the dominant hand.

► Help patient investigate current toothbrush grip. Adjust to a modified pen grasp rather than a traditional palm grasp to reduce the amount of pressure applied.

► Explore receptivity to use of a power toothbrush because it removes dental biofilm effectively with less than half the pressure of a manual toothbrush; an individual using a manual toothbrush typically exerts 200–400 g of pressure; 70–150 g of pressure is usually exerted with a power toothbrush.[24] Some power toothbrushes have a self-limiting mechanism to reduce filament action if too much pressure is applied.

► Recommend and demonstrate dental biofilm control measures that are meticulous, yet gentle, and do not contribute to abrasion of hard or soft tissues.

D. Burnishing

A wooden toothpick is repeatedly rubbed over the root surface with moderate pressure. Figure 44-6 shows placement of a toothpick.

► The toothpick may be dipped into fluoride dentifrice or other desensitization agents, although it is the burnishing process that forms a smear layer over dentin, occluding the dentinal tubule orifices.[25]

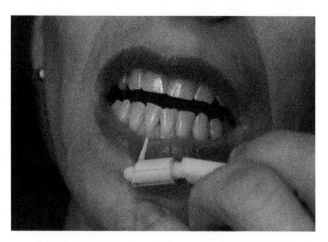

FIGURE 44-6 Burnishing Sensitive Root Surface. A small amount of a fluoride dentifrice or other fluoride agent can be burnished into the sensitive area with a toothpick or wooden point. Moderate pressure with a "rubbing" or circular stroke is applied. A toothpick holder facilitates effective use of a toothpick to burnish an exposed root surface.

► May stimulate the production of secondary or reparative dentin; a very slow process.

E. Eliminate Parafunctional Habits

► Help patient assess bruxing and clenching behaviors and whether additional treatment is indicated.

► Determine need for occlusal adjustments to eliminate abfractive forces.

► Coach patient to monitor occurrence of subconscious parafunctional behaviors and levels of stress. Identify whether stress reduction protocols are needed.

III. Desensitizing Agents

► There are study design challenges when researching desensitization due to subjectivity of the pain response, the strong placebo effect, and the process of natural desensitization.

► Despite widespread professional recommendation and use, there is little in vivo scientific evidence validating the efficacy and mechanisms of action of desensitizing agents.

► Randomized controlled trials (RCTs) are needed to support professional recommendation and treatment. The exception is fluoride, with a substantial body of knowledge validating its usefulness as a desensitizing agent.

► Desensitizing agents can be categorized according to their mechanisms of action, either depolarization of the nerve or occlusion of the dentinal tubule. Potassium salts are the only agents that are theorized to work by depolarization.

A. Potassium Salts

► Formulations containing potassium chloride, potassium nitrate, potassium citrate, or potassium oxalate reduce depolarization of the nerve cell membrane and transmission of the nerve impulse.[22]

► Potassium nitrate dentifrices containing fluoride are widely used[20] and readily available OTC.

B. Fluorides

▶ Precipitate calcium fluoride (CaF_2) crystals within the dentinal tubule to decrease the lumen diameter.[22]

▶ Create a barrier by precipitating CaF_2 at the exposed dentin surface, to block open dental tubules.[26]

- Fluoride varnishes are FDA approved for tooth desensitization and a cavity liner; although they are frequently used "off-label" for dental caries prevention. FDA approval is not required for the off-label use of fluoride varnish.

- Fluoride gels and varnishes are most commonly used and are a successful treatment modalilty.[27,28]

C. Oxalates

▶ Block open dental tubules.[29]

▶ Oxalate salts such as potassium oxalate and ferric oxalate precipitate calcium oxalate crystals to decrease the lumen diameter.[29]

D. Gluteraldehyde

▶ Coagulates proteins and amino acids within the dentinal tubule to decrease the dentinal tubule lumen diameter.[29]

▶ Can be combined with HEMA, a hydrophilic resin, which seals tubules.[29]

▶ Creates calcium crystals within the dentinal tubule to decrease the lumen diameter.[30]

E. Calcium Phosphate Technology

▶ Advocated for use as a caries control agent to reduce demineralization and increase remineralization by releasing calcium and phosphate ions into saliva for deposition of new tooth mineral (hydroxyapatite).[31]

- Calcium phosphates can compromise the bioavailability of fluorides since calcium and fluoride react to form calcium fluoride.[32]

- May be effective for patients with poor salivary flow and consequent deficient calcium phosphate levels.[33]

▶ Agents that support remineralization may lessen dentinal hypersensitivity by occluding dentinal tubule openings.

▶ Most studies in support of calcium phosphate technology are animal, in vitro, or *in situ* models designed to analyze remineralization rather than hypersensitivity.

- One *in vivo* study found a reduction in bleaching-induced sensitivity at days 5 and 14 when amorphous calcium phosphate (ACP) was added to a bleaching gel.[34]

- Additional research related to calcium phosphate technologies is needed.[35]

▶ ACP

- Theorized to plug dentinal tubules with calcium and phosphate *precipitate*; promotes an ACP reservoir within the saliva.

- Enhances fluoride delivery in calcium and phosphate-deficient saliva.[33]

- May remineralize areas of acid erosion and abrasion, and reduce hypersensitivity.[33]

▶ Calcium sodium phosphosilicate (CSP)

- Contains sodium and silica in addition to calcium and phosphorous.

- Delivered in solid bioactive glass particles that react in the presence of saliva and water to release calcium and phosphate ions and create a calcium phosphate layer that crystallizes to hydroxyapatite.

- Reacts with saliva; sodium buffers the acid, and calcium and phosphate saturate saliva to fill demineralized areas with new hydroxyapatite.

- Claims include remineralizing enamel and dentin, positive impact on acid erosion and abrasion, a bactericidal effect, and reduction in hypersensitivity.

- RCT comparing a CSP and a potassium nitrate toothpaste found, using a VAS, that CSP paste was significantly better at reducing dentin hypersensitivity.[36]

▶ Casein phosphopeptide–amorphous calcium phosphate (CPP-ACP)

- CPP is a milk-derived protein that stabilizes ACP and allows it to be released during acidic challenges.

- Researchers are exploring benefits such as remineralization of acid erosion, caries inhibition and reduction of dentinal hypersensitivity.

▶ Tricalcium phosphate (TCP)

- Developed in an effort to create a calcium material that can coexist with fluoride to provide greater efficacy than fluoride alone.[33] Additional components are added to β-TCP to "functionalize" it. Increased remineralization has been demonstrated in vitro[37]; in vivo evidence is needed.

F. Arginine and Calcium Carbonate Technology

▶ Desensitization approach that occludes the dentinal tubules utilizing arginine, a naturally occurring amino acid, bicarbonate (pH buffer), and calcium carbonate.

▶ Marketed as a prophylaxis paste to be applied before instrumentation, using a slow-speed handpiece with a rubber cup and moderate pressure.

▶ Randomized controlled trials that adhere to clinical research standards are still necessary.

IV. Self-Applied Measures

A. Dentifrices

▶ In many OTC sensitivity-reducing dentifrices, 5% potassium nitrate, sodium fluoride, or stannous fluoride separately or in combination are the active desensitizing agents. Studies have suggested that some of the desensitizing effects of dentifrices may be due to the blocking action of the abrasive particles.[22]

▶ Tartar control dentifrices may contribute to increased tooth sensitivity for some individuals, although the mechanism is unclear.

▶ Dentifrices are available containing highly concentrated fluoride (5,000 ppm fluoride) combined with an abrasive to facilitate extrinsic stain control are available by prescription. This formulation is also available with the addition of potassium nitrate.

B. Gels

▶ Gels containing 5,000 ppm fluoride are a prescription product brushed on for generalized hypersensitivity or burnished into localized areas of sensitivity.

▶ Contain no abrasive agents for biofilm and stain control.

▶ Can be self-applied with custom or commercially available fluoride or whitening trays.

C. Mouthrinses

▶ Mouthrinse containing 0.63% stannous fluoride mouthrinse can be prescribed for daily use to treat hypersensitivity.

▶ Short-term use (2–4 weeks) will limit staining concerns.

V. Professionally Applied Measures

A. Tray Delivered Fluoride Agents

▶ A tray delivery system can be used to apply a 2% neutral sodium fluoride solution.

▶ Select trays of adequate height and fill with sufficient fluoride agent to cover the cervical areas of each tooth.

B. Fluoride Varnish

▶ A 5% sodium fluoride varnish maintains prolonged contact with the tooth surface by serving as a reservoir to release fluoride ions in response to pH changes in saliva and biofilm.[38]

▶ Does not require a dry tooth surface, which is advantageous since drying the tooth can be a painful procedure for a patient with dentin hypersensitivity.

▶ Use a microbrush to apply the varnish to the exposed dentin surface.

▶ Instruct the patient to avoid oral hygiene self-care for several hours to allow the fluoride to stay in contact with the tooth surface for as long as possible, preferably overnight.

C. 5% Gluteraldehyde

▶ Use a microbrush to apply to the affected tooth surface.

▶ Prevent excess flow into soft tissues with cotton roll isolation since contact with soft tissues may cause gingival irritation.

D. Oxalates

▶ Oxalate preparations are applied (burnished) to a dried tooth surface.

▶ May provide immediate and short- rather than long-term relief.

E. Unfilled or Partially Filled Resins

▶ Used to cover patent dentinal tubules.

▶ Resins are applied following an acid etch step that may remove the smear layer, and cause discomfort.

▶ The tooth surface must be dehydrated before resin application, which can create discomfort.

▶ Use of local anesthetic may facilitate patient comfort during this procedure.

F. Dentin-Bonding Agents

▶ Obturates the tubule opening and does not require use of acid etch or dehydration; a single application may protect against further erosion for 3–6 months.

▶ Methylmethacrylate polymer is a common dentin sealer.

G. Composite/Glass Ionomer

▶ Glass ionomer may be placed in the presence of moisture, which eliminates the need for drying the tooth.

▶ In addition to the glass ionomer restoration physically blocking the dentinal tubule, there is an added benefit of slow fluoride release.

H. Soft Tissue Grafts

▶ Surgical placement of soft tissue grafts to cover a sensitive dentinal surface.

I. Lasers

▶ Nd:YAG laser treatment can obliterate dentinal tubules through a process called "melting and resolidification." When used with an appropriate protocol, there is no resulting damage to the pulp or dentin surface cracking.[39,40]

▶ Long-term, in vivo studies are needed to establish safety and efficacy of laser treatment for dentin hypersensitivity. The Food and Drug Administration (FDA) has not approved these devices for this therapeutic modality.

VI. Additional Considerations

A. Periodontal Debridement Considerations

▶ *Preprocedure*
  - Explain potential for sensitivity resulting from calculus removal and/or instrumentation of teeth with areas of exposed cementum or dentin.
  - Patients are likely to respond more favorably to treatment when prepared for what might occur.
  - When multiple teeth in the same treatment area are hypersensitive during scaling and root planing procedures, local anesthetics and/or nitrous oxide analgesia can be utilized.
  - Desensitizing agents that are marketed for immediate relief from severe hypersensitivity can be used.

EVERYDAY ETHICS

Marcy, the dental hygienist, practices with Dr. Goldman, who only schedules time to examine a patient at alternate dental hygiene visits unless requested for special needs. Mrs. Stuart arrives for her dental hygiene appointment but is not scheduled to see Dr. Goldman until her next visit. She is complaining of discomfort "on the lower back teeth" when she chews and when she eats or drinks something cold. The pain may last up to an hour.

When she completes the scaling and debridement, Marcy determines that Dr. Goldman is running behind schedule. She knows it will be difficult to get him to come to her treatment room to examine her patient in a timely manner. Marcy gives Mrs. Stuart a sample of desensitizing toothpaste and suggests they will see how it is at the next appointment. Marcy then advises Mrs. Stuart to "Call if it gives you more trouble." The patient is not classified

as having a periodontal condition, is considered low-to-medium risk for dental caries. Her next visit will be in 4 months.

Questions for Consideration

1. How do each of the core values (Table II-1, Section II Introduction) apply in this event? Does the issue of informed consent enter this discussion? Explain why or why not.

2. What ethical issues can arise if Marcy and Dr. Goldman do not take time during this appointment to thoroughly assess Mrs. Stuart's situation to establish a differential diagnosis?

3. Answer the questions provided in the "Questions to Ask" column of Table VI-1 (Section VI Introduction) to determine at least two ethical alternative actions Marcy could have taken.

▶ *Postprocedure*
- Professionally applied desensitization agents can be used.
- Patient is instructed in daily oral health behavior changes and use of self-applied desensitizing agents.

B. Research Developments

▶ The search for the ideal desensitizing agent is ongoing.
▶ Evidence-based scientific research is indicated as new products are developed; *in vivo* research protocols are needed to support clinical application.

C. Tooth Whitening–Induced Sensitivity

Tooth whitening agents, such as hydrogen peroxide and carbamide peroxide, may contribute to increased dentinal hypersensitivity.

▶ Thought to result from by-products of 10% carbamide peroxide (3% hydrogen peroxide and 7% urea) readily passing through the enamel and dentin into the pulp, the reversible pulpitis caused from the dentin fluid flow and pulpal contact of the hydrogen peroxide without apparent harm to the pulp.[41]
▶ Hypersensitivity may dissipate over time, lasting from a few days to several months.
▶ Exposed dentin and pre-existing dentin hypersensitivity increase hypersensitivity risk secondary to whitening.
▶ Some whitening products contain fluoride or potassium nitrate to eliminate or minimize the effects of sensitivity.
▶ Recommendations outlined in Table 46-3, Chapter 46 to prevent or reduce tooth whitening–induced sensitivity include:

- Use of a potassium nitrate, fluoride, or other desensitization product before, or concurrently with whitening.
- Some take home whitening gels incorporate, 5% potassium nitrate, fluoride and amorphous calcium phosphate.
- Home-use whitening products are usually less concentrated than professionally applied in-office treatment options, with less hypersensitivity risk.
- Allow for a "recovery period" between whitening sessions during which desensitizing agents are used. Decrease frequency of use by whitening every second or third day.

DOCUMENTATION

The permanent record for a patient with a history of tooth sensitivity needs to include at least the following information:

▶ Medical and dental history, vital signs, extra- and intraoral examinations, consultations, and individual progress notes for each appointment and maintenance appointments.
▶ For dentin hypersensitivity: identify teeth involved, differential diagnosis, and all treatments, along with patient instruction for ideal oral self-care, diet, and other for preventive recommendations.
▶ Outcomes and posttreatment directions.
▶ A progress note example for the patient with hypersensitive dentin may be reviewed in Box 44-5.

BOX 44-5

Example Documentation: Patient with Dentin Hypersensitivity

S–Patient complains of pain when eating/drinking cold foods/beverages that disappears immediately after.

O–Generalized facial gingival recession of 1–2 mm on all teeth in the mandibular arch.

A–Based on patient symptoms, exposed roots, and no other evidence of dental disease, the working diagnosis is dentin hypersensitivity.

P–Applied fluoride varnish and gave post-op instructions; advised patient to avoid acidic beverages: or not to brush immediately after ingestion of citrus fruits or beverages; also advised rinse with fluoridated water to buffer acidic conditions (to raise pH). Recommended purchase and use of an OTC potassium nitrate-containing dentifrice. Explained that relief from the dentifrice can take between 2 and 4 weeks. Advised to recontact the office if pain persists or worsens.

Next Steps: Follow-up at next visit.

Signed _____, RDH

Date _____

Factors To Teach The Patient

▷ Etiology and prevention of gingival recession.

▷ Factors contributing to dentin hypersensitivity.

▷ Mechanisms of dentin tubule exposure, which can allow various stimuli to trigger pain response.

▷ Natural desensitization mechanisms that may lessen sensitivity over time.

▷ Appropriate oral hygiene self-care techniques, such as using a soft toothbrush and avoiding a vigorous brushing technique that may contribute to gingival recession and subsequent abrasion of root surfaces.

▷ Connection between an acidic diet and dentin sensitivity; need to eliminate specific foods and beverages that can trigger sensitivity.

▷ Toothbrushing is not recommended immediately after consumption of acidic foods or beverages.

▷ The challenges of managing hypersensitivity, hierarchy of treatment measures, and variable effect of treatment options.

References

1. Addy M. Etiology and clinical implications of dentine hypersensitivity. *Dent Clin North Am.* 1990;34(3):503–514.

2. Absi EG, Addy M, Adams D. Dentine hypersensitivity: the development and evaluation of a replica technique to study sensitive and non-sensitive cervical dentine. *J Clin Periodontol.* 1989;16(3):190–195.

3. Frank RM. Attachment sites between the odontoblast process and the intradental nerve fibre. *Arch Oral Biol.* 1968;13(7):833–834.

4. Thomas HF, Carella P. Correlation of scanning and transmission electron microscopy of human dentinal tubules. *Arch Oral Biol.* 1984;29(8):641–646.

5. Dufour LA, Bissell HS. Periodontal attachment loss induced by mechanical subgingival instrumentation in shallow sulci. *J Dent Hyg.* 2002;76(3):207–212.

6. Absi EG, Addy M, Adams D. Dentine hypersensitivity: the effect of toothbrushing and dietary compounds on dentine in vitro. *J Oral Rehabil.* 1992;19(2):101–110.

7. Prati C, Montebugnoli L, Supp P, et al. Permeability and morphology of dentin after erosion induced by acidic drinks. *J Periodontol.* 2002;74(4):428–436.

8. Staninec M, Nalla RK, Hilton JF, et al. Dentin erosion simulation by cantilever beam fatigue and pH change. *J Dent Res.* 2005;84(4):371–375.

9. Litonjua LA, Andreana S, Bush OJ, et al. Wedged cervical lesions produced by toothbrushing. *Am J Dent.* 2004;17(4):237–240.

10. Estafan A, Furnari PC, Goldstein G, et al. In vivo correlation of noncarious cervical lesions and occlusal wear. *J Prosthet Dent.* 2005;93(3):221–226.

11. Sarode GS, Sarode CS. Abrraction: a review. *J Oral Maxillofac Pathol.* 2013;17(2):222–227.

12. Brannstrom M, Linden LA, Astrom A. The hydrodynamics of the dental tubule and of pulp fluid: a discussion of its significance in relation to dentinal sensitivity. *Caries Res.* 1967;1(4):310–317.

13. Eldarrat AH, High AS, Kale GM. In vitro analysis of "smear layer" on human dentine using ac-impedance spectroscopy. *J Dent.* 2004;32(7):547–554.

14. Cunha-Cruz J, Wataha JC, Heaton LJ, et al. The prevalence of dentin hypersensitivity in general dental practices in the northwest United States. *J Am Dent Assoc.* 2013;144(3):288–296.

15. Taani Q, Awartani F. Clinical evaluation of cervical dentin sensitivity (CDS) in patients attending general dental clinics and periodontal specialty clinics (PSC). *J Clin Periodontol.* 2002;29(2):118–122.

16. Addy M, Pearce N. Aetological, predisposing and environmental factors in dentine hypersensitivity. *Arch Oral Biol.* 1994;39 (Suppl):33S–38S.

17. Kassaba MM, Cohen RE. The etiology and prevalence of gingival recession. *J Am Dent Assoc.* 2003;134(2):220–225.

18. Gillam DG, Aris A, Bulman JS, et al. Dentine hypersensitivity in subjects recruited for clinical trials: clinical evaluation, prevalence and intraoral distribution. *J Oral Rehabil.* 2002;29(3):226–231.

19. Addy M. Dentine hypersensitivity: new perspectives on an old problem. *Int Dent J.* 2002;52 (Suppl 1):367–375.

20. Orchardson R, Gillam DG. The efficacy of potassium salts as agents for treating dentin hypersensitivity. *J Orofac Pain.* 2000;14(1):9–19.

21. Correa FO, Sampaio JE, Rossa C, et al. Influence of natural fruit juices in removing the smear layer from root surfaces—an in vitro study. *J Can Dent Assoc.* 2004;70(10): 697–702.

22. Orchardson R, Gilla DC. Managing dentin hypersensitivity. *J Am Dent Assoc.* 2006;137(7):990–998.

23. Kawasaki A, Ishikawa K, Sug T, et al. Effects of plaque control on the patency and occlusion of dentine tubules in situ. *J Oral Rehabil.* 2001;28(5):439–449.

24. Van Der Weijden GA, Timmerman MF, Reijerse E, et al. Toothbrushing force in relation to plaque removal. *J Clin Periodontol.* 1996;23(8):724–729.

25. Pashley DH, Leibach JG, Horner JA. The effects of burnishing NaF/kaolin/glycerin paste on dentin permeability. *J Periodontol.* 1987;58(1):19–23.

26. Suge T, Ishikowa K, Kawasaki A, et al. Effects of fluoride on the calcium phosphate precipitation method for dentinal tubule occlusion. *J Dent Res.* 1995;74(4):1079–1085.

27. Ritter AV, de L Dias W, Miguez P, et al. Treating cervical dentin hypersensitivity with fluoride varnish: a randomized clinical study. *J Am Dent Assoc.* 2006;137(7):1013–1020.

28. Cunha-Cruz J, Wataha, JC, Zhou, L, et al. Treating dentin hypersensitivity, therapeutic choices made by dentists of the Northwest PRECEDENT network. *J Am Dent Assoc.* 2010;141(9):1097–1105.

29. Haywood VB. Dentine hypersensitivity: bleaching and restorative considerations for successful management. *Int Dent J.* 2002;52 (Suppl 1):376.

30. Pashley DH, Kalathoor S, Burnham D. The effects of calcium hydroxide on dentin permeability. *J Dent Res.* 1986;65(3):417–420.

31. Featherstone JD. The continuum of dental caries-evidence for a dynamic disease process. *J Dent Res.* 2004;83 (Spec No C):C39–C42.

32. Karlinsey RL, Mackey AC, Walker ER, et al. Surfactant-modified B-TCP: structure, properties, and in vitro remineralization of subsurface enamel lesions. *J Mater Sci Mater Med.* 2010;21(4):2009–2020.

33. Chow L, Wefel JS. The dynamics of de-and remineralization. *Dimensions Dent Hyg.* 2009;7(2):42–46.

34. Giniger M, MacDonald J, Ziemba S, et al. The clinical performance of professionally dispensed bleaching gel with added amorphous calcium phosphate. *J Am Dent Assoc.* 2005;136(3):383–392.

35. Yengopal V, Mickenautsch S. Caries-preventive effect of casein phosphopeptide-amorphous calcium phosphate (CPP-ACP): a meta-analysis. *Acta Odontol Scand.* 2009;21:1–12.

36. Pradeep AR, Sharma A. Comparison of clinical efficacy of a dentifrice containing calcium sodium phosphosilicate to a dentifrice containing potassium nitrate and to a placebo on dentinal hypersensitivity: a randomized clinical trial. *J Periodontol.* 2010;81(8):1167–1173.

37. Karlinsey RL, Mackey AC, Walker ER, et al. Preparation, characterization and in vitro efficacy of an acid-modified β-TCP material for dental hard-tissue remineralization. *Acta Biomater.* 2010;6(3):969–978.

38. Shen C, Autio-Gold J. Assessing fluoride concentration uniformity and fluoride release from 3 varnishes. *J Am Dent Assoc.* 2002;133(2):176–182.

39. Kara C, Orbak R. Comparative evaluation of Nd:YAG laser and fluoride varnish for the treatment of dentinal hypersensitivity. *J Endod.* 2009;35(7):971–974.

40. Lopes AO, Aranha ACC. Comparative evaluation of the effects of Nd:YAG laser and a densensitizer agent on the treatment of dentin hypersensitivity: a clinical study. *Photomed Laser Surg.* 2013;31(3):132–138.

41. Li Y, Greenwall L. Safety issues of tooth whitening using peroxide-based materials. *Br Dent J.* 2013;215(1):29–34.

ENHANCE YOUR UNDERSTANDING

the**Point**® **DIGITAL CONNECTIONS**
(see the inside front cover for access information)

- **Audio glossary**
- **Quiz bank**

SUPPORT FOR LEARNING
(available separately; visit lww.com)

- *Active Learning Workbook for Clinical Practice of the Dental Hygienist, 12th Edition*

prepU **INDIVIDUALIZED REVIEW**
(available separately; visit lww.com)

- **Adaptive quizzing with *prepU for Wilkins' Clinical Practice of the Dental Hygienist***

45

Extrinsic Stain Removal

Caren M. Barnes, RDH, BS, MS

CHAPTER OUTLINE

After studying this chapter, the student will be able to:

1. Describe the difference between a cleaning agent and a polishing agent.

2. Explain the basis for selection of the grit of polishing paste for each individual patient.

3. Discuss the rationale for avoiding polishing procedures on areas of demineralization.

4. Explain the effect abrasive particle shape, size, and hardness have on the abrasive qualities of a polishing paste.

5. Explain the types of powdered polishing agents available and their use to remove tooth stains.

6. Explain patient conditions that contraindicate the use of air-powder polishing.

INTRODUCTION

After treatment by scaling, root planing, and other dental hygiene care, the teeth are assessed for the presence of remaining dental stains.

▶ The cleaning or polishing agents used must be *selected* based on the patient's individual needs such as the type and amount of stain present and whether or not restorations are present.

▶ Preliminary examination of each tooth will reveal that the surfaces to be treated may be tooth structure (enamel, or with recession cementum or dentin) or when restored, a variety of dental materials (metal or esthetic, tooth-color restorations).

▶ *Preservation of the surfaces of both the teeth and the restorations is of primary importance during all cleaning and polishing procedures.*

▶ Stain removal will require the use of prophylaxis polishing agents that contain various abrasive grits. The smallest, least abrasive grit is used.

▶ Some patients will not consider their teeth "cleaned" unless they have been polished. This situation is ideal for a *cleaning agent* that will not abrade the dental hard tissues, but will remove dental biofilm and the patient's teeth will have the same clean feeling as they would if an abrasive prophylaxis paste were used.

▶ *One size grit prophylaxis paste is not appropriate for every patient and is unethical and clinically the wrong choice. To use such a practice is to ignore a patient's individual needs, can worsen hypersensitivity, and cause significant damage to esthetic restorations.*

▶ The longevity, esthetic appearance, and smooth surfaces of dental restorations depend on appropriate care by the dental hygienist and the daily personal care by the patient.

▶ It is a responsibility of the dental hygienist to be current in knowledge of the procedures to prevent damage to the restorations during professional health-care appointments.

▶ The dental hygienist is responsible for educating the patient about proper daily oral self-care that will contribute to the maintenance of the restorations, such as recommending the least abrasive dentifrices.[1,2]

▶ Terms related to extrinsic stain removal are defined in Box 45-1.

PURPOSES FOR STAIN REMOVAL

Stains on the teeth are not etiologic factors for oral disease or destructive process.

▶ The removal of stains is for esthetic, not for therapeutic or health, reasons.

• Stain removal procedures have been an integral part of the oral prophylaxis since the inception of tooth cleaning procedures and patients have come to expect to have their teeth polished as a part of the oral prophylaxis.

▶ The American Dental Hygienists' Association and the Academy of Periodontology include tooth polishing in their definitions of the term "oral prophylaxis."[3,4]

▶ Key words related to stain removal, polishing, instruments, coronal polishing, air-powder polishing, cleaning agent, prophylaxis polishing agent, tribiology, two-body abrasion and three-body abrasion are defined in Box 45-1.

SCIENCE OF POLISHING

▶ Polishing is intended to produce intentional, selective and controlled wear. Within the science of tribiology, polishing is considered to be two-body or three-body abrasive polishing.

BOX 45-1   KEY WORDS AND ABBREVIATIONS: Extrinsic Stain Removal

Abrasion: wearing away of surface material by friction.

Abrasive: a material composed of particles of sufficient hardness and sharpness to cut or scratch a softer material when drawn across its surface; available in various particle sizes.

Air-powder polisher: air-powered device using air and water pressure to deliver a controlled stream of specially processed sodium bicarbonate slurry through the handpiece nozzle; also called air abrasive, airpolishing, air-powered abrasive, or airbrasive.

Binder: substance used to hold abrasive particles together; examples are ceramic bonding used for mounted abrasive points, electroplating for binding diamond chips for rotary instruments, and rubber or shellac for soft discs.

Coronal polishing: polishing of the anatomic crowns of the teeth to remove dental biofilm and extrinsic stains; does not involve calculus removal.

Glycerin: clear, colorless, syrupy fluid used as a vehicle and sweetening agent for drugs and as a solvent and vehicle for abrasive agents.

Grit: with reference to abrasive agents, grit is the particle size.

Polishing: the production, especially by friction, of a smooth, glossy, mirrorlike surface that reflects light; a very fine agent is used for polishing after a coarser agent is used for cleaning.

psi: pounds per square inch.

rpm: revolutions per minute.

Slurry: thin, semi-fluid suspension of a solid in a liquid.

Three-body abrasion: involves loose abrasive particles that move in the interface space between the surface being polished and the polishing application device.

Two-body abrasion: involves abrasive particles attached to a medium (polishing application device) that move directly against the surface being polished.

Tribiology: tribiology incorporates the study and application of the principles of friction, lubrication, and wear as they apply to polishing.

- Two-body abrasive polishing involves the abrasive particles attached to a medium, such as a rubber cup impregnated with abrasive particles that would not require a prophylaxis polishing paste.
- Three-body abrasive polishing is the type most commonly used by dental hygienists, in which loose abrasive particles (the abrasive particles in prophylaxis polishing paste) move in the interface space between the surface being polished and the polishing application device (rubber cup or brush).[6–8]

EFFECTS OF CLEANING AND POLISHING

Attention is given to the positive and negative effects of polishing so that evidence-based decisions can be made for the treatment of each patient. *Professional judgment based on a patient's needs and requests determines when a service is to be included in a dental hygiene care plan, and if services are warranted, they should be selected carefully.*

I. Precautions

▶ As with all gingival manipulation with instruments, including a toothbrush,[9,10] bacteremia can be created during the use of power-driven stain removal instruments. Rotation of the rubber cup can force microorganisms into the tissues.

▶ An inflammatory response can be expected, and bacteria may gain access to the bloodstream to create a bacteremia.

▶ The response is a normal expectation and not of concern in healthy patients.

▶ It is a concern for a patient who requires prophylactic antibiotic coverage before dental treatment; another reason why the medical history is such an essential part of patient assessment and is recorded before all treatments.

▶ The medical history is reviewed and updated at each succeeding appointment.

▶ For patients at risk, particularly those with damaged or abnormal heart valves, prosthetic valves, and other conditions listed in Chapter 10 (Box 10-2) may require antibiotic prophylaxis as specified by the patient's cardiologist.

II. Environmental Factors

A. Aerosol Production

▶ Aerosols are created during the use of all rotary instruments, including a prophylaxis handpiece with a rubber cup to hold polishing paste, the air and water sprays used during rinsing, and air-polishing.[11]

▶ The biologic contaminants of aerosols stay suspended for long periods and provide a means for disease transmission to dental personnel, as well as to other patients.

▶ Use of power-driven instruments is limited when a patient is known to have a communicable disease, a serious or chronic respiratory disease, or is immunocompromised.

▶ Standard personal protective procedures are used.

B. Spatter

▶ Protective eyewear is needed for all dental team members and for the patient.

▶ Serious eye damage has occurred because of spatter from polishing paste or from instruments.[12]

III. Effect on Teeth

A. Removal of Tooth Structure

▶ Polishing with coarse abrasive prophylaxis pastes may remove a few micrometer of the outer enamel. This is justification for using the least abrasive prophylaxis paste necessary to meet the patient's needs for polishing procedures.

▶ The fluoride-rich outer surface of the enamel is necessary for protection against dental caries[13] and care is taken for it to be preserved. The use of a cleaning agent in place of an abrasive prophylaxis polishing agent will prevent any removal of the outermost layer of enamel.

B. Areas of Demineralization

▶ *Demineralization*: Polishing demineralized white spots of enamel is contraindicated. More surface enamel is lost from abrasive polishing over demineralized white spots than over intact enamel.[14]

▶ *Remineralization*: Demineralized areas of enamel can remineralize as these areas are exposed to fluoride from saliva, water, dentifrices, and professional fluoride applications.

  • Since remineralization cannot be detected visually, it is necessary to remember that polishing procedures can interrupt enamel surface remineralization.

C. Areas of Thin Enamel, Cementum, or Dentin

▶ Areas of thin enamel are contraindicated for polishing.

  • Amelogenesis imperfecta is an example of thin enamel resulting from imperfect tooth development in Chapter 22.

▶ *Exposure of dentinal tubules*: cementum and dentin are softer and more porous than enamel, so greater amounts of their surfaces can be removed during polishing than from enamel. When cementum is exposed because of

gingival recession, polishing of the exposed surfaces is avoided.

▶ Smear layer could be removed and dentinal tubules exposed.[15]

▶ When surface structure is removed, unnecessary tooth sensitivity can result.[16]

D. Care of Restorations and Implants

▶ Use of coarse abrasives may create deep, irregular scratches in restorative materials. Figure 45-1 shows a scanning electron photomicrograph of the damaged surface of a composite restoration polished with a rubber cup and coarse prophylaxis paste.

▶ Microorganisms collect and colonize on a rough surface much more rapidly than on a smooth surface.[17]

▶ It is imperative that prophylaxis polishing agents are not used on restorative materials. Polishing pastes not intended for use on restorative materials can destroy the surface integrity of the dental material.[18]

  • Select a cleaning agent or a polishing agent recommended by the manufacturer of the restorative materials.[18,19]

E. Heat Production

▶ Steady pressure with a rapidly revolving rubber cup or bristle brush and a minimum of wet abrasive agent can create sufficient heat to cause pain and discomfort for the patient.

▶ The pulps of children are large and may be more susceptible to heat.

▶ The rules for the use of cleaning or polishing agents are:
  • Use light pressure, slow speed of the rubber cup.
  • Use a moist agent.
  • Cleaning or polishing agents are never to be used as dry powders applied directly on teeth.

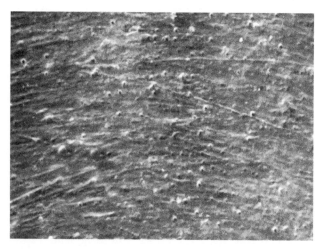

FIGURE 45-1 **Scanning Electron Photomicrograph of A Composite Restoration Polished with Coarse Prophylaxis Paste.**

IV. Effect on Gingiva

▶ Trauma to the gingival tissue can result, especially when the prophylaxis angle is run at a high speed with heavy pressure and the rubber cup is applied for an extended period adjacent to gingival tissues.

▶ Stain removal after gingival and periodontal treatments, including scaling and root planing, is not recommended on the same day. The diseased lining of the pocket usually has been removed during scaling and incidental curettage, leaving the pocket wall wide open ready to receive abrasive particles and microorganisms that can become embedded out of reach of the most careful irrigation and rinsing.

INDICATIONS FOR STAIN REMOVAL

I. Removal of Extrinsic Stains

A. Patient Instruction

▶ Discuss source of stain and how it can be prevented.

▶ Encourage patient to make necessary habit changes, especially to seek counseling for smoking cessation if that is the cause of the patient's stain. Tobacco cessation is described in Chapter 34.

▶ Practice toothbrushing to remove stains incorporated in dental biofilm.

  • For example: The patient can be taught that chlorhexidine stain can be prevented and/or lessened with dental biofilm removal during personal oral care procedures. The less dental biofilm the patient has, the less chlorhexidine may stain the teeth.

B. Scaling and Root Planing

▶ In addition to the use of cleaning or polishing agents during polishing procedures, stains can also be removed during scaling and root planing instrumentation.

  • Example: Black line stain has been compared to calculus because it may be elevated from the tooth surface and may need to be removed by instrumentation. It is described in Chapter 22.[20]

II. To Prepare the Teeth for Caries-Preventive Procedures

A. Placement of Pit and Fissure Sealant

▶ Follow manufacturer's directions. Sealants vary in their requirements.

▶ Avoid commercial oral prophylaxis pastes that contain glycerin, oils, flavoring substances, or other agents. Glycerin and oils can prevent an optimum acid-etch and interfere with the adherence of the sealant to the tooth surface, causing the sealant to fail.

▶ Air-powder polishing is one method of choice for preparing tooth surfaces for sealants (see Chapter 37).[21,22]

▶ An alternative is the use of a plain, fine pumice mixed with water when precleaning is determined to be necessary.

  • After the use of pumice, the tooth surface(s) needs to be rinse thoroughly to remove the particles.

B. Professional Application of Fluoride Varnishes, Solutions, or Gels

▶ Tooth polishing is not necessary before fluoride application.[23]

  • Biofilm and debris removal can be accomplished adequately by the patient using a toothbrush and dental floss, after complete calculus removal.

▶ The pellicle on the tooth surface does not act as a barrier to fluoride, and fluoride uptake in the enamel from a fluoride application is similar whether the teeth are brushed by the patient or polished with a cleaning or polishing agent.[23]

III. To Contribute to Patient Motivation

Removal of biofilm is a *daily* procedure to be carried out *by the patient*. When accomplished thoroughly at least twice daily and for some patients three times daily, infection can be controlled, the sanitation of the mouth maintained, and staining can be minimized or prevented.

A. Development of Biofilm

▶ It is known that pellicle returns to cover the teeth within minutes after complete polishing.

▶ Biofilm begins to collect on the pellicle within 1 or 2 hours, increasing in thickness until, by 12–24 hours, biofilm is thick enough to show clearly when a disclosing agent is applied.

▶ Undisturbed, biofilm may begin to calcify within a few days in a calculus-susceptible patient.

B. Motivation

Smooth polished tooth surfaces may contribute in part to the following effects:

▶ Help the patient to obtain more satisfactory results from oral self-care procedures. A smooth surface can be easier to achieve once the patient understands what a biofilm and debris-free mouth feels like after having the teeth professionally polished with a cleaning or polishing agent.

▶ Show the patient the appearance and feeling of a clean mouth for motivational purposes. The change in behavior, or the true learning, can be obtained through patient participation in the use of a disclosing agent and personal visualization of the biofilm followed by removal of the biofilm with floss and toothbrush.

CLINICAL APPLICATION OF STAIN REMOVAL

The decision to polish teeth is based on the individual patient's needs.

I. Summary of Contraindications for Polishing

The following list suggests some of the specific instances in which polishing either can be performed with a cleaning agent or is contraindicated.

A. No Unsightly Stain

▶ Polishing is a procedure based on the patient's individual needs. If no stain is present, polishing with an abrasive polishing agent is not necessary; however, this is an ideal situation for using a cleaning agent.

▶ If cleaning agents will not remove the stain that is present, the choice is the least abrasive polishing agent that will remove the stain.

▶ Appearance is important to patients, but maintaining the integrity of the tooth surface for disease prevention is more important.

▶ When the abrasive paste is a medium, coarse, or extra coarse paste, those pastes need to be followed by the use of the next least abrasive paste in succession until the final paste used is fine paste.

B. Characteristics of Patients at Risk for Dental Caries

▶ Patients at risk for dental caries need extra fluoride to protect their tooth surfaces and fluoride-rich enamel surfaces need to be preserved. Examples include:
- Rampant caries, nursing caries, root caries, all ages
- Noncavitated dental caries in early stages of demineralization
- Xerostomia, from any reason.

C. Patients with Respiratory Problems

Polishing procedures typically require rinsing of the patient's mouth several times throughout the procedure.

▶ Care is taken to minimize the spray from the air–water syringe as much as possible as the aerosols are contraindicated for such conditions as asthma, emphysema, cystic fibrosis, lung cancer, patients requiring oxygen, or when breathing is a problem.

▶ This caution also applies to the use of air-powder polishers and spatter from prophylaxis polishing pastes.

D. Tooth Sensitivity

▶ Abrasive agents can uncover ends of dentinal tubules in areas of thin cementum or dentin.

▶ The polishing of dentin and cementum is contraindicated and needs to be avoided to every extent possible.

E. Restorations

▶ Restorations and titanium implants may be scratched by abrasive prophylaxis polishing pastes.
- However, a cleaning agent will not scratch restorative materials or titanium implants.[19]

▶ Tooth-colored restorations need to be polished with a cleaning agent, a polishing paste specifically formulated for use on esthetic restorations, or the paste recommended by the manufacturer of the restorative material.[18]

F. Conditions that Require Postponement for Later Evaluation

▶ When instruction for personal biofilm removal (daily care) has not yet been given or when the patient has not demonstrated adequate biofilm control.

▶ Soft spongy tissue that bleeds on brushing or gentle instrumentation.

▶ Communicable disease potentially disseminated by aerosol.

II. Suggestions for Clinic Procedure

A. Give Instruction First

▶ Daily dental biofilm removal to assist in dental stain control.

▶ Explain to the patient that drinking coffee, tea, and color-added soft drinks and/or use of tobacco is responsible for most dental stains.

▶ Patients need information about the types of dentifrices that are safe for stain control and those that are contraindicated due to excessive abrasiveness or chemical harshness.

▶ Tobacco cessation introduction when stain is primarily from tobacco use (Chapter 34).

B. Remove Stain by Scaling

▶ Whenever possible, stains can be removed during scaling, root planing, and debridement.

▶ Assist in planning a preventive plan for stain control.

C. Stain Removal Techniques

▶ Cleaning agent or low-abrasion oral prophylaxis paste.

▶ Use the lightest pressure necessary for stain removal.

▶ Low-speed handpiece.

▶ Minimal heat production.

▶ Soft rubber cup at 90° to tooth surface with intermittent light applications.

CLEANING AND POLISHING AGENTS

There are two distinct types of agents used for "polishing" teeth: one is a cleaning agent, and the other is a polishing agent.[1]

I. Polishing Agents

▶ Traditionally, abrasive agents have been applied with polishing instruments to remove extrinsic dental stains and leave the enamel surface smooth and shiny.

▶ Polishing agents act by producing scratches in the surface of the tooth or restoration created by the friction between the abrasive particle and the softer tooth or restorative surface.

▶ The cleaning and polishing process progresses from coarse abrasion to fine abrasion until the scratches are smaller than the wavelength of visible light, which is 0.05 μm.[1]

▶ When scratches this size are created, the surface appears smooth and shiny—the smaller the scratches, the shinier the surface.

▶ Unless the abrasive agent has been specially formulated for esthetic restorative surfaces, the use of prophylaxis polishing pastes is contraindicated for application to any esthetic restorative surfaces.[19,24]

II. Cleaning Agents

▶ Unlike polishing agents, cleaning agents are round, flat, nonabrasive particles, and do not scratch surface material but produce a higher luster than polishing agents.

▶ The most readily available cleaning agent (ProCare, Young Dental Mfg. Earth City, MO) is made of a combination of feldspar, alkali (sodium and potassium) and aluminum silicates. This feldspar, sodium–aluminum silicate cleaning agent is formulated into a powder and can be mixed with water or sodium fluoride to make a paste for cleaning.[25,26]

▶ Because of the extremely low level of abrasion, cleaning agents can be used on any tooth surface, restorative surface, or implant surface without fear of creating deep scratches.

▶ Cleaning agents will not harm restorative surfaces and any other polishing agent selected for restorative surfaces is selected based on the formulation and appropriateness for the restorative material.[27]

▶ Dental hygienists must be mindful that many esthetic restorations are virtually undetectable due to color and surface match; therefore, it is imperative that the patient's dental chart and radiographs be examined to locate the esthetic restorations before applying polishing agents.

III. Factors Affecting Abrasive Action with Polishing Agents

During polishing, sharp edges of abrasive particles are moved along the surface of a material, abrading it by producing microscopic scratches or grooves. The rate of abrasion, or speed with which structural material is removed from the surface being polished, is governed by hardness and shape of the abrasive particles, as well as by the manner in which they are applied.

A. Characteristics of Abrasive Particles

▶ *Shape*: Irregularly shaped particles with sharp edges produce deeper grooves and thus abrade faster than do rounded particles with dull edges.

▶ *Hardness*: Particles must be harder than the surface to be abraded; harder particles abrade faster.

• Many of the abrasives used in prophylaxis polishing pastes are 10 times harder than the tooth structure to which they are applied.[27]

• Table 45-1 provides a comparison of the Mohs hardness value of dental tissues compared to agents commonly used in prophylaxis polishing pastes and substances used in cleaning agents.

▶ *Body strength*: Particles that fracture into smaller sharp-edged particles during use are more abrasive than those that wear down during use and become dull.

TABLE 45-1	Mohs Hardness Value of Dental Tissues Compared to Commonly Used Polishing Abrasive Particles
	MOHS HARDNESS VALUE
DENTAL TISSUES	
Enamel	5
Dentin	3.0–4.0
Cementum	2.5–3.0
ABRASIVE AGENTS IN POLISHING PASTES	
Zirconium silicate	7.5–8.0
Pumice	6.0–7.0
Silicone carbine	9.5
Boron	9.3
Aluminum oxide	9
Garnet	8.0–9.0
Emery	7.0–9.0
Zirconium oxide	7
Perlite	5.5
Calcium carbonate	3
Aluminum silicates	2
Sodium	0.5
Potassium	0.4

The Mohs hardness value of enamel, cementum, and dentin compared to the Mohs hardness value of abrasive materials commonly used in prophylaxis polishing pastes. The Mohs hardness value is indicative of a material's resistance to scratching. Diamonds have a maximum Mohs value of 10; talc has a minimum of Mohs hardness of 1.

▶ *Particle size (grit)*

- The larger the particles, the more abrasive they are and the less polishing ability they have.
- Finer abrasive particles achieve a glossier finish.
- Abrasive and polishing agents are graded from coarse to fine based on the size of the holes in a standard sieve through which the particles will pass.
- The finer abrasives are called powders or flours and are graded in order of increasing fineness as F, FF, FFF, and so on.
- Particles embedded in papers are graded 0, 00, 000, and so on.

B. Principles for Application of Abrasives

▶ *Quantity applied:* The more particles applied per unit of time, the faster the rate of abrasion.

- Particles are suspended in water or other vehicles for frictional heat reduction.
- Dry powders or flours represent the greatest quantity that can be applied per unit of time.
- Frictional heat produced is proportional to the rate of abrasion; therefore, the use of *dry agents* is *contraindicated* for polishing natural teeth because of the potential danger of thermal injury to the dental pulp.

▶ *Speed of application:* The greater the speed of application, the faster the rate of abrasion.

- With increased speed of application, pressure must be reduced.
- *Rapid abrasion* is *contraindicated* because it increases frictional heat.

▶ *Pressure of application:* The heavier the pressure applied, the faster the rate of abrasion.

- *Heavy pressure* is *contraindicated* because it increases frictional heat.

▶ *Summary:* When cleaning and polishing are indicated after patient evaluation, the following are observed:

- Use wet agents.
- Apply a rubber polishing cup, using low speed.
- Use a light, intermittent touch.

IV. Abrasive Agents

The abrasives listed here are examples of commonly used agents. Some are available in several grades, and the specific use varies with the grade.

- For example, while a superfine grade might be used for polishing enamel surfaces and metallic restorations, a coarser grade would be used only for laboratory purposes.

Abrasives for use daily in a dentifrice necessarily are of a finer grade than those used for professional polishing accomplished a few times each year.

A. Silex (Silicon Dioxide)

▶ *XXX Silex:* Fairly abrasive.

▶ *Superfine Silex:* Can be used for heavy stain removal from enamel.

B. Pumice

▶ Powdered pumice is of volcanic origin and consists chiefly of complex silicates of aluminum, potassium, and sodium.

▶ Pumice is the primary ingredient in commercially prepared prophylaxis pastes. The specifications for particle size are listed in the *National Formulary*[28] as follows:

- *Pumice flour or superfine pumice:* Least abrasive, and may be used to remove heavy stains from enamel.
- *Fine pumice:* Mildly abrasive.
- *Coarse pumice:* Not for use on natural teeth.

C. Calcium Carbonate (Whiting, Calcite, Chalk)

▶ Various grades are used for different polishing techniques.

D. Tin Oxide (Putty Powder, Stannic Oxide)

▶ Polishing agent for teeth and metallic restorations.

E. Emery (Corundum)

Not used directly on the enamel.

▶ *Aluminum oxide (alumina):* The pure form of emery. Used for composite restorations and margins of porcelain restorations.

▶ *Levigated alumina:* Consists of extremely fine particles of aluminum oxide, which may be used for polishing metals but are destructive to tooth surfaces.

F. Rouge (Jeweler's Rouge)

▶ Iron oxide is a fine red powder sometimes impregnated on paper discs.

▶ It is useful for polishing gold and precious metal alloys in the laboratory.

G. Diamond Particles

▶ Constituent of diamond polishing paste for porcelain surfaces.

V. Cleaning Ingredients

▶ Particles for cleaning agents differ from abrasive agents in shape and hardness.

▶ Particles used for cleaning agents include feldspar, alkali, and aluminum silicate.

A. Clinical Applications

Numerous commercial preparations for dental prophylactic cleaning and polishing preparations are available. Clinicians need more than one type available to meet the requirements of individual restorative materials.

B. Packaging

▶ Commercial preparations are in the forms of pastes or powders.

‣ Some are available in measured amounts contained in small plastic or other individual packets that contribute to the cleanliness and sterility of the procedure.

‣ Selection of a preparation is based on qualities of abrasiveness, consistency for convenient use, or flavor for patient pleasure.

C. Enhanced Prophylaxis Polishing Pastes

Additives are included in prophylaxis polishing pastes to provide a specific function, such as enhancing the mineral surface of enamel, diminishing dentin hypersensitivity, or tooth whitening.

‣ *Fluoride prophylaxis pastes*

- Application of fluoride by use of fluoride-containing prophylaxis polishing pastes **cannot** be considered a substitute for or the equivalent of a conventional topical fluoride treatment.
- There is no scientific evidence that the amount of fluoride in prophylaxis paste is sufficient to have a preventive effect for dental caries. The fluoride ions in the prophylaxis paste mix with the saliva; fluoride is not burnished into enamel with prophylaxis paste.
- *Enamel surface*: The greatest benefit of fluoride as a prophylaxis polishing paste additive occurs when the fluoride ions in the prophylaxis paste are released into the saliva.
    ◦ The fluoride ions that become mixed in the saliva may become incorporated into the hydroxyapatite structure of the tooth, thus aiding in the remineralizing of the tooth and improving enamel hardness.
- *Clinical application*: Use only an amount sufficient to accomplish stain removal to prevent a child patient from swallowing unnecessary fluoride. The paste may contain 4,000–20,000 ppm fluoride ion.[29]

‣ *Amorphous calcium phosphate and other forms of calcium and phosphate*

- Amorphous calcium phosphate and other formulations of calcium and phosphate, as an additive to prophylaxis polishing pastes, have been shown to hydrolyze the tooth mineral to form apatite.
- When these additives are included in oral prophylaxis paste, the benefit is not solely from burnishing them into the tooth surface.
- When prophylaxis polishing pastes containing calcium and phosphate become mixed with saliva, the mineral ions may become incorporated into the hydroxyapatite structure of the tooth, thus aiding in remineralizing the tooth and improving enamel hardness.
- Polishing agents containing amorphous calcium phosphate have the potential to enhance tooth smoothness and the luster of the enamel surface.[30,31]

‣ *Fluoride, calcium, and phosphate*

- Fluoride, calcium, and phosphate prophylaxis pastes have an edge over those pastes that contain only calcium

and phosphate, in that there are three minerals that can be incorporated into the tooth surface. Just as with the pastes that contain amorphous calcium and phosphate, the mineral ions, including the fluoride ions, may become incorporated into the hydroxyapatite structure of the tooth, thus aiding in remineralization to improve enamel hardness.

‣ *Tooth whitening*

- In addition to removing extrinsic stains, there are commercially available prophylaxis polishing pastes that contain 35% hydrogen peroxide to provide a whitening benefit.
- A hydrogen peroxide gel is applied to the tooth and then "polished" into the tooth surface with a rubber cup and prophylaxis polishing paste.[32]
- Prophylaxis polishing pastes with the hydrogen peroxide additive are not intended to be a primary delivery system for professional tooth whitening but can be used as an aid to maintain whitening results.

‣ *Dentin hypersensitivity*

- Topical desensitizing products work either by occluding dentinal tubules thereby blocking fluid flow or by interfering with nerve transmission.
- Topical products that occlude dentinal tubules do so by physically occluding the tubules.
- The desensitizing products that block nerve transmission utilize the active ingredient 5% potassium nitrate (KNO_3). Nerve transmission is blocked by KNO_3 by penetration of dentinal tubules and depolarization the nerve.[33–35]
- Dentifrices for patients that have dentinal hypersensitivity have long been available and some prophylaxis polishing pastes have been formulated for this purpose.
- Prophylaxis polishing pastes that contain arginine, calcium, and bicarbonate/carbonate have the purpose of minimizing dentin hypersensitivity. Mixing these ingredients produces arginine bicarbonate and calcium carbonate. When applied with a rubber cup these adjunctive ingredients can aid in sealing the dentinal tubules.[36] However, the sealing of the dentinal tubules is not permanent.

PROCEDURES FOR STAIN REMOVAL (CORONAL POLISHING)

I. Patient Preparation for Stain Removal

A. Instruction and Clinical Procedures

‣ Review medical history to determine premedication requirements.

‣ Review intraoral charting and radiographs. The intraoral chart and radiographs need review before any polishing procedures to locate all restorations. Some tooth-colored restorations are so artfully created and color matched that they are almost impossible to detect.

▸ After review, a plan for polishing can be made that includes the appropriate polishing agents for the restorations that are present.

▸ Practice biofilm control.

▸ Complete scaling, root planing, and overhang removal.

▸ Inform the patient that polishing is a cosmetic procedure, not a therapeutic one.

▸ After scaling and other periodontal treatment, an evaluation is made to determine the need for stain removal of teeth, polishing restorations, and dental prostheses.

▸ Check all restorations to ensure that the correct polishing agent has been selected.

▸ Explain the difference between cleaning and polishing agents.

B. Explain the Procedure

▸ Describe the noise, vibration, and grit of the polishing paste.

▸ Explain the frequent use of rinsing and evacuation with the saliva ejector.

C. Provide Protection for Patient

▸ Safety glasses worn for scaling are kept in place to prevent eye injury or infection.

▸ Fluid-resistant drape over patient to keep moisture from skin and clothing.

D. Patient Position

▸ The patient is positioned for maximum visibility.

E. Patient Breathing

▸ Encourage the patient to breath only through the nose.

▸ Reduce potential for aspiration of oral pathogens into the lungs.

▸ Allow water to pool for evacuation with saliva ejector.

▸ Less fogging of mouth mirror.

▸ Enhanced patient comfort.

II. Environmental Preparation

Environmental factors are described in Chapter 6.

A. Procedures to Lessen the Extent of Contaminated Aerosols

▸ Flush water through the tubing for 2 minutes at the beginning of each work period and for 30 seconds after each appointment.

▸ Request the patient rinse with an antimicrobial mouthrinse to reduce the numbers of oral microorganisms before starting instrumentation.

▸ Use high-velocity evacuation.

B. Protective Barriers

▸ Protective eyewear and bib are necessary for the patient.

▸ The clinician wears the standard barrier protection, namely, eyewear, mask, gloves, and clinic gown to cover clothing.

HISTORIAL PERSPECTIVE: THE PORTE POLISHER

▸ *Design*

• The porte polisher is a manual instrument designed especially for extrinsic stain removal or application of treatment agents such as for hypersensitive areas.

• It is constructed to hold a wood point at a contra-angle. The wood points may be cone or wedge shaped and made of various kinds of wood, preferably orangewood. Figure 45-2 illustrates a typical porte polisher.

▸ *Grasp:* The instrument is held in a modified pen grasp, Figure 39-16, or palm grasp, as shown in Figure 39-17 in Chapter 39.

▸ *Application:* The wood point is applied to the tooth surface using firm, carefully directed, massaging, circular or linear strokes to accommodate the anatomy of each tooth.

• A firm finger rest and a moderate amount of pressure of the wood point provide protection for the gingival margin and efficiency in technique.

▸ *Features*

• The porte polisher is useful for instrumentation of difficult-to-access surfaces of the teeth, especially malpositioned teeth.

• No heat generation, no noise compared with powered handpieces, and minimal production of aerosols.

• The porte polisher is readily portable and therefore is useful in any location, for example, for a bed bound patient.

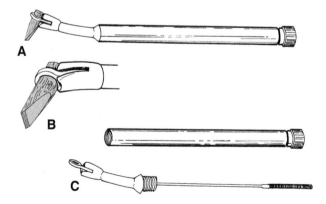

FIGURE 45-2 **Porte Polisher. A:** Assembled instrument shows position of wood point ready for instrumentation. **B:** Working end shows wedge-shaped wood point inserted. **C:** Disassembled, ready for autoclave.

THE POWER-DRIVEN INSTRUMENTS

I. Handpiece

▶ A handpiece is used to hold rotary instruments.

▶ The three basic designs are straight, contra-angle, and right angle.

▶ Instruments have been classified according to their rotational speeds, designated by revolutions per minute (rpm) as high speed and low (or slow) speed.

▶ Handpiece must be maintained and sterilized according to manufacturer's directions.

A. Ultra or High Speed

▶ *Speed*: 100,000–800,000 rpm; air driven.

▶ *Uses*: For cavity preparation and other restorative preparations.

▶ *Fiberoptic light*: Better visibility is provided when a fiberoptic light is built into the head of the handpiece. The beam of light is projected onto the field of operation when the handpiece is activated.

▶ Ultra and high-speed handpieces operate at very high speeds and therefore are *not* used for cleaning or polishing teeth with a prophylaxis angle and rubber cup.

B. Low Speed

▶ *Speed*: Typical range is up to 5,000 rpm for low-speed handpieces manufactured for dental hygienists. Other low-speed handpieces may have a higher range of rpms; air driven.

▶ Low speed handpieces are used for cleaning or polishing the teeth with a prophylaxis angle and rubber cup.

II. Types of Prophylaxis Angles

▶ Types of prophylaxis angles are described in Table 45-2.

▶ Contra- or right-angle attachments to the handpiece for which polishing devices (rubber cup, bristle brush) are available.

▶ Contra-angle prophylaxis angles may have a longer shank and a wider angle between the rubber cup and shank to allow for greater reach when polishing posterior teeth and surfaces.

▶ Disposable with rubber cup impregnated with polishing agent abrasive particles embedded in the rubber cup.[1]

▶ Stainless steel with hard chrome, carbon, steel, or brass bearings.

▶ Figure 45-3 shows examples of disposable for one-time use[37] contra-angle and right-angle prophylaxis angles and a stainless steel prophylaxis angle.

▶ Stainless steel prophylaxis angles that are sealed will not allow saliva and debris into the head of the angle nor will they allow grease and debris to leak out of the head of the angle.[38,39]

▶ Unless they are disposable, only instruments that can be sterilized are selected.

TABLE 45-2	Types of Prophylaxis Polishing Angles

Comparison of disposable prophylaxis angles and stainless steel prophylaxis angles[a]

TYPE OF ANGLE	DISPOSABLE PROPHYLAXIS ANGLE	DISPOSABLE ANGLE WITH ABRASIVE IMPREGNATED RUBBER CUP	STAINLESS STEEL PROPHYLAXIS ANGLE
Maintenance and care	One-time use, discard	One-time use, discard	Requires maintenance, sterilization
Attachments	Supplied with rubber cup from the manufacturer	Supplied with rubber cup from the manufacturer that is impregnated with one type of abrasive	Accepts variety of attachments: cups, brushes, and cone-shaped rubber points
Screw-in or snap-on rubber cups	Usually screw-in type cup		Will accept screw-in or snap-on cups and brushes
Advantages	Requires no maintenance or sterilization	Requires no additional prophylaxis paste	Can be used hundreds of times if maintained properly
Disadvantages	Not package with other attachments Creates refuse that is not biodegradable	Must have water and/or saliva as lubricant Creates refuse that is not biodegradable	Does require time to clean and maintain

[a]A comparison of the features of a disposable prophylaxis angle to a disposable prophylaxis angle with abrasive-impregnated rubber cup and a sterilizable stainless steel prophylaxis angle.

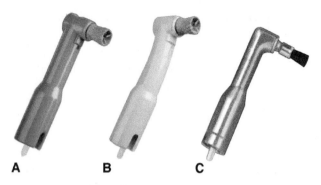

FIGURE 45-3 **Prophylaxis Angles. A:** Disposable right-angled prophylaxis angle with rubber cup attached. **B:** Disposable contra-angled prophylaxis angle with an attached rubber cup impregnated with a polishing agent (abrasive particles). **C:** Sterilizable stainless steel prophylaxis angle holding a cleaning or polishing brush on a mandrel.

- Stainless steel or any other type of metal autoclavable prophylaxis angle must be sterilized after every use and the manufacturer's instructions followed for the proper maintenance and care as well as the correct sterilization procedures.

III. Prophylaxis Angle Attachments

A. Rubber Polishing Cups

▶ *Types:* Figure 45-4 shows several types of rubber polishing cups from which to choose. The internal designs and sizes have the same purpose, which is to aid in holding the prophylaxis polishing paste in the rubber cup while polishing. The ideal rubber cup design retains the prophylaxis polishing paste in the cup and will release the paste at a steady rate.
  - *Slip-on (snap-on):* with ribbed cup to aid in holding polishing agent.

FIGURE 45-4 **Rubber Cup Attachments. A:** Slip-on or snap-on for button-ended prophylaxis angle. **B:** Threaded for direct insertion in right angle. **C:** Mandrel stem for latch-type prophylaxis angle.

- *Threaded (screw type):* with plain ribbed cup or flange (webbed) type.
- Mandrel mounted.
▶ *Materials*
  - *Natural rubber:* more resilient; adapts readily to fit the contours of the teeth.
  - *Synthetic:* stiffer than natural rubber.

B. Bristle Brushes

▶ *Types*
  - *For prophylaxis angle:* slip-on or screw type.
  - *For handpiece:* Mandrel mounted.
▶ *Materials:* synthetic.

C. Rubber Polishing Points

▶ Figure 45-5 shows an example of a rubber point that screws into a prophylaxis angle.
▶ *Material*
  - *Natural rubber:* Flexible so that tip adapts to proximal surfaces, embrasures, and around orthodontic bands and brackets.
▶ *Use:* Because the ribs for holding the prophylaxis polishing paste onto the rubber polishing point are on the external surface, the polishing paste will have to be reapplied frequently.

IV. Uses for Attachments

A. Handpiece with Straight Mandrel

▶ Dixon bristle brush (type C, soft) for polishing removable dentures.
▶ Rubber cup on mandrel for polishing facial surfaces of anterior teeth.

B. Prophylaxis Angle with Rubber Cup, Brush, or Rubber Point

▶ *Rubber cup:* for removal of stains from the tooth surfaces and polishing restorations.
▶ *Brush:* for removing stains from deep pits and fissures and enamel surfaces away from the gingival margin. A brush is contraindicated for use on exposed cementum or dentin.
▶ *Rubber polishing point:* for removing stains and biofilm from proximal surfaces, embrasures, and around orthodontic bands and brackets.

FIGURE 45-5 **Flexible Rubber Point has Screw Connection for a Prophylaxis Angle.** Made with ribs or grooves to carry cleaning or polishing agent to difficult-to-reach areas.

USE OF THE PROPHYLAXIS ANGLE

I. Effects on Tissues: Clinical Considerations

▶ Can cause discomfort for the patient if care and consideration for the oral tissues are not exercised to prevent unnecessary trauma.

▶ Tactile sensitivity of the clinician while using a thick, bulky handpiece is diminished and unnecessary pressure may be applied inadvertently.

▶ The greater the speed of application of a polishing agent, the faster the rate of abrasion. Therefore, the handpiece is applied at a low rpm.

▶ Trauma to the gingival tissue can result from too high a speed, extended application of the rubber cup, or use of an abrasive polishing agent.

▶ Tissue damage and the need for antibiotic premedication for risk patients are described in Chapter 10.

II. Prophylaxis Angle Procedure

▶ Apply the polishing agent only where it is needed, that is, where there is unsightly stain. See section Contraindications.

▶ As with all oral procedures, a systematic order is followed.

A. Instrument Grasp

▶ Modified pen grasp (Figure 39-16).

B. Finger Rest

▶ Establish a fulcrum firmly on tooth structure or use an exterior rest.

▶ Use a wide rest area when practical to aid in the balance of the large instrument. For example, place cushion of rest finger across occlusal surfaces of premolars while polishing the molars.

▶ Avoid use of mobile teeth as finger rests.

C. Speed of Handpiece

▶ Use lowest available speed to minimize frictional heat.

▶ Adjust rpm as necessary.

D. Use of Rheostat

▶ Apply steady pressure with foot to produce an even, low speed.

E. Rubber Cup: Stroke and Procedure

▶ Observe where stain removal is needed to prevent unnecessary rubber cup application.

▶ Fill rubber cup with polishing agent, and distribute agent over tooth surfaces to be polished before activating the power.

▶ Establish finger rest and bring rubber cup almost in contact with tooth surface before activating power source.

▶ Using slowest rpm, apply revolving cup at a 90° angle lightly to tooth surfaces for 1 or 2 seconds. Use a light pressure so that the edges of the rubber cup flare slightly. The rubber cup needs to flare slightly underneath the gingival margin and onto the proximal surfaces.

▶ Move cup to adjacent area on tooth surface; use a patting or brushing motion.

▶ Replenish supply of polishing agent frequently.

▶ Turn handpiece to adapt rubber cup to fit each surface of the tooth, including proximal surfaces and gingival surfaces of fixed partial dentures.

▶ Start with the distal surface of the most posterior tooth of a quadrant and move forward toward the anterior; polish only the teeth that require stain removal. For each tooth, work from the gingival third toward the incisal third of the tooth.

▶ When two polishing agents of different abrasiveness are to be applied, use a separate rubber cup for each.

▶ Rubber cups, polishing points, and polishing brushes cannot be sterilized and are used only for one patient and then discarded.

F. Rubber Polishing Points (Figure 45-5)

▶ Rubber polishing points can be used around orthodontic bands and brackets, on fixed bridges and in wide interproximal spaces or embrasures.

▶ Rubber points are loaded with the cleaning or polishing agent in the grooves around the sides. The rubber points will need to be replenished frequently with paste after use on every 1–2 teeth.

G. Bristle Brush

▶ Bristle brushes are used selectively and limited to occlusal surfaces.

▶ Lacerations of the gingiva and grooves and scratches in the tooth surface, particularly the roots and restorations can result when the brush is not used with caution.

▶ Soak stiff brush in hot water to soften bristles.

▶ Distribute mild abrasive polishing agent over occlusal surfaces of teeth to be polished.

▶ Place fingers of nondominant hand in a position that both retracts and protects cheek and tongue from the revolving brush.

▶ Establish a firm finger rest and bring brush almost in contact with the tooth before activating power source.

▶ Use slowest rpm as the revolving brush is applied lightly to the occlusal surfaces only. Avoid contact of the bristles with the soft tissues.

▶ Use a short stroke in a brushing motion; follow the inclined planes of the cusps.

▶ Move from tooth to tooth to prevent generation of excessive frictional heat. Avoid overuse of the brush. Replenish supply of polishing agent frequently.

H. Irrigation

▶ Irrigate teeth and interdental areas thoroughly several times with water from the syringe to remove abrasive particles. Avoid heavy water pressure to prevent forcing particles into the tissue.

▶ The rotary movement of the rubber cup or bristle brush tends to force the abrasive into the gingival sulci, thereby creating a potential source of irritation to the soft tissues.

POLISHING PROXIMAL SURFACES

▶ Care must be exercised in the use of floss, tape, and finishing strips.

▶ Understanding the anatomy of the interdental papillae and their relationship to the contact areas and proximal surfaces of the teeth is prerequisite to the prevention of tissue damage.

▶ As much polishing as possible of accessible proximal surfaces is accomplished during the use of the rubber cup in the prophylaxis angle.

▶ This can be followed by the use of dental tape with polishing agent when indicated.

▶ Finishing strips are used only in selected instances, when all other techniques fail to remove a stain.

I. Dental Tape and Floss

A. Features

▶ Floss and tape are described in Chapter 29.

▶ The wax covering affords some protection for the tissues, facilitates the movement of the floss or tape, prevents excessive absorption of moisture, and helps prevent shredding.

▶ Dental tape is flat and has relatively sharp edges, whereas floss is round. Either floss or tape may injure the tissue when used incorrectly or carelessly.

▶ The use of dental floss or tape for dental biofilm control on proximal tooth surfaces is an essential part of self-care by the patient.

B. Uses During Cleaning and Polishing

▶ Techniques for tape and floss application are described in Chapter 29 and illustrated in Figures 29-4, 29-5, and 29-6.

▶ The same principles apply whether the patient or the clinician is using the floss.

▶ Finger rests are used to prevent snapping through contact areas.

▶ *Stain removal with dental tape*: Polishing agent is applied to the tooth, and the tape is moved gently back and forth and up and down curved over the area where stain was observed.

▶ *Cleaning gingival surface of a fixed partial denture*: A floss threader is used to position the floss or tape over the gingival surface. Floss threaders are described and illustrated in

Chapter 32 in Figure 32-3. The agent is applied under the pontic, and the floss or tape is moved back and forth with contact on the bridge surface.

▶ *Flossing*: Particles of abrasive agent can be removed by rinsing and by using a clean length of floss applied in the usual manner.

▶ *Rinsing and irrigation*: Irrigate with water-spray syringe to clean out all abrasive agent.

II. Finishing Strips

A. Description

▶ Finishing strips are thin, flexible, and tape shaped.

▶ Available in four widths: extra narrow, narrow, medium, and wide.

▶ Available in extra fine, fine, medium, and coarse grit. *Only extra narrow or narrow strips with extrafine or fine grit are suggested for stain removal, and then only with discretion.*

▶ Most finishing strips are now made of plastic; however, linen abrasive strips are available. Finishing strips have one side that is smooth and the other side serves as a carrier for abrasive agents bonded to that side.

▶ "Gapped" strips are available with an abrasive-free portion to permit sliding the strip through a contact area without abrading the enamel.

▶ Finishing strips are available with two different grits on one strip. One-half of the strip may have fine abrasives and the other one-half will have medium grit abrasives. These strips are available in several different combinations.

B. Use

▶ *For stain removal on proximal surfaces of anterior teeth; when other techniques are unsuccessful.*

▶ *Precautions for use*
  • Edge of strip is sharp and may cut gingival tissue or the lip.
  • Use of a finishing strip is limited to enamel surfaces and some restorative materials, such as composite. It is of upmost importance to ensure the finishing strip selected has an appropriate grit abrasive for the surface to be polished. Manufacturers make finishing strips intended for use solely on composites or porcelain; other types of finishing strips are available for use on enamel.

C. Technique for Finishing Strip

▶ *Grasp and finger rest*
  • A strip no longer than 6 inches is most conveniently applied.
  • Grasp and finger rest must be well controlled.
  • Protection of the lip by retraction with the thumb and index finger holding the strip is a helpful safety measure.

▶ *Positioning*

- Direct the abrasive side of the strip toward the proximal surface to be treated as the strip is worked slowly and gently between the teeth with a slight sawing motion.

- Bring strip just through the contact area. If the strip breaks, immediately use floss to remove abrasive particles that may have separated from the finishing strip.

- When a space is clearly visible through an embrasure and the interdental papilla is missing, a narrow finishing strip may be threaded through. Prepare strip by cutting the end on a diagonal to facilitate threading.

▶ *Stain removal*

- Press abrasive side of strip against tooth. Draw back and forth in a 1/8-inch arc two or three times, rocking on the established fulcrum.

- Remove strip. Do not attempt to turn the strip while it is in the interdental area.

▶ *Dental floss:* Follow each application of a finishing strip with dental floss to remove abrasive particles.

AIR-POWDER POLISHING

▶ Principles of selective stain removal are applied to the use of the air-powder polishing system. After biofilm control instruction, instrumentation, and periodontal debridement are completed, follow with an evaluation of need for stain removal.

I. Principles of Application

▶ Air-powder systems manufactured by several companies are efficient and effective methods for mechanical removal of stain and biofilm.[40,41]

▶ Air-powder polishing systems use air, water, and specially formulated powders to deliver a controlled spray that propels the particles to the tooth surface.

- Only powders approved by each air-powder polishing manufacturer are used in each brand of air-powder polishing unit. The use of an unapproved powder in an air-powder polishing unit could void the warranty on the unit.[42]

▶ The equipment is operated using inlet air pressure between 40 and 100 psi and inlet water pressure between 20 and 60 psi. Internal air polishing unit air and water pressures will vary according to manufacturer and are not to be adjusted from their original settings.

▶ The handpiece nozzle is moved in a constant circular motion, with the nozzle tip 4–5 mm away from the enamel surface.

▶ The spray is angled away from the gingival margin.

▶ The periphery of the spray may be near the gingival margin, but the center is directed at an angle less than 90° away from the margin.

▶ Complete directions for care of equipment and preparation for use of the device are provided by the individual manufacturer.

II. Specially Formulated Powders for Use in Air-Powder Polishing

Several manufacturers make and sell air-powder polishing powders.

▶ The abrasiveness of one brand of powder may differ from another brand, even though it is the same type of powder.[43]

A. Sodium Bicarbonate[42]

▶ Sodium bicarbonate is the original powder used in air-powder polishing.

▶ It is specially formulated with scant amounts of calcium phosphate and silica to keep it free flowing.

▶ The Mohs hardness number for sodium bicarbonate is 2.5 and the particles average 74 μm in size.

▶ Warning: over-the-counter sodium bicarbonate cannot be used in airpolishing equipment as it will clog the unit.

▶ The *only* type of sodium bicarbonate that can be used in air-powder polishing units is the type specially formulated for air-powder polishing.

▶ Sodium bicarbonate air-powder is available with flavorings. However, the patient will taste the salt and smell the flavor.

B. Aluminum Trihydroxide

▶ Aluminum trihydroxide was the first air-powder developed as an alternative to sodium bicarbonate for patients who are sodium bicarbonate intolerant.[44]

▶ Aluminum trihydroxide has a Mohs hardness value of 4 and the particles range in size from 80 to 325 μm.

C. Glycine

▶ Glycine is an amino acid. For use in powders, glycine crystals are grown using a solvent of water and sodium salt.

▶ Glycine particles for use in airpolishing have a Mohs hardness number of 2 and are 20 μm in size.

D. Calcium Carbonate

▶ Calcium carbonate is a naturally occurring substance that can be found in rocks.

▶ It is a main ingredient in antacids, and is also used as filler for pharmaceutical drugs.

▶ Calcium carbonate has a Mohs number of 3.[42]

E. Calcium Sodium Phosphosilicate (Novamin)

▶ Calcium sodium phosphosilicate (Novamin) is a bioactive glass and has a Mohs hardness number of 6, making it the hardest air polishing particle used in air-powder polishing powders.[42] The particles vary from 25 to 120 μm in size.

▶ Since calcium sodium phosphosilicate was first introduced, research on the effects of this air polishing powder has determined that it is highly abrasive and destructive to enamel, hybrid composites, and glass ionomers. The investigators concluded this powder should not be used on any tooth structure or restorative material.[44]

III. Uses and Advantages of Air-Powder Polishing

▶ Requires less time, is ergonomically favorable to the clinician, and generates no heat.[40–42,45]

▶ Sodium bicarbonate is less abrasive than traditional prophylaxis pastes, which makes the air-powder polisher ideal for stain and biofilm removal. However, some air-polishing powders are much more abrasive than sodium bicarbonate and should only be used on surfaces that they will not damage.[42]

▶ Removal of heavy, tenacious tobacco stain and chlorhexidine-induced staining.[40–42,45]

▶ Stain and biofilm removal from orthodontically banded and bracketed teeth[45,46,47] and dental implants.[48,49]

▶ Before sealant placement or other bonding procedures.[21,22]

▶ Root detoxification for periodontally diseased roots by the periodontist during open periodontal surgery.[50,51]

IV. Technique

Proper angulation of the air-powder polishing handpiece is essential to reduce the amount of inherent aerosols created[52–54] and to remove stain and biofilm without iatrogenic soft tissue trauma.

A. For Anterior Teeth

▶ Place the handpiece nozzle at a 60° angle to the facial and lingual surfaces of anterior teeth (Figure 45-6A).

B. For Posterior Teeth

▶ Place the handpiece nozzle at an 80° angle to the facial and lingual surfaces (Figure 45-6B).

C. For Occlusal Surfaces

▶ Place the handpiece nozzle at a 90° angle to the occlusal plane (Figure 45-6C).

D. Incorrect Angulation

▶ Incorrect angulation of the handpiece is probably the single most common cause of excess aerosol production.

▶ The handpiece nozzle is never directed into the gingival sulcus or into a periodontal pocket with little bony support remaining, as this could result in facial emphysema[42] (also known as a subcutaneous emphysema).

▶ Facial emphysemas occur due to the abnormal introduction of air into subcutaneous tissues or interstitial spaces.[42]

▶ Facial emphysemas can be prevented by avoiding the use of high-speed handpieces during third molar extractions,[55] air/water syringes near extraction or surgical sites or lacerations,[56–59] and airpolishing[60,61] spray in these areas.

▶ Facial emphysemas exhibit symptoms such as facial swelling, a "crackling" sensation of the face and neck area when touched, tenderness, and pain. If detected early, patients with facial emphysemas usually require observation, antibiotics, and analgesia.[42]

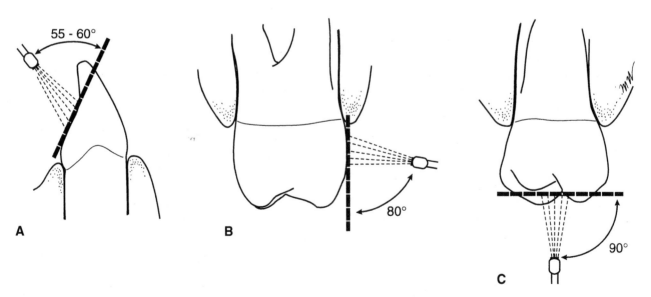

FIGURE 45-6 Air-Powder Polishing. Direct the aerosolized spray for **A:** the anterior teeth at a 60° angle. **B:** The posterior teeth facial and lingual or palatal at an 80° angle. **C:** The occlusal surfaces at a 90° angle to the occlusal plane.

BOX 45-2

Sequelae that Can Develop as a Result of Compressed Air Forced into Soft Tissues of the Head and Neck

Bilateral pneumothorax
Cerebral air embolism
Cervicofacial emphysema
Facial emphysema
Mediastinal emphysema
Pneumediastinum
Pneumothorax
Retropharyngeal emphysema

BOX 45-3

Sequelae that Can Develop as a Result of Facial Emphysema

Bilateral pneumothorax
Cerebral air embolism
Embolism
Pneumediastinum
Pneumothorax
Thrombosis

- Box 45-2 Contains a list of the sequelae that can develop as a result of compressed air forced into soft tissues of the head and neck.
- Box 45-3 contains a list of sequelae that can develop as a result of a facial emphysema.
- The closer the nozzle is held to the enamel, the more spray will deflect back into the direction of the clinician.
- When a clinician directs the handpiece at a 90° angle toward a facial, buccal, and some lingual surfaces, the result is an immediate reflux of the aerosolized spray back onto the clinician.
- Changing the angle of incidence to the proper angulations of 60° and 80° will result in a change in the angle of the reflection, thus reducing the amount of reflux of aerosolized spray.

V. Recommendations and Precautions

A. Aerosol Production

A copious spray containing oral debris and microorganisms is produced. As with all contaminated aerosols, a health hazard can exist. Suggestions for minimizing contamination and the effects of the aerosols include the following:

- Patient uses a preprocedural antibacterial mouthrinse.[62]
- High-volume evacuation is needed, using a wide tip held near the tooth where the spray is released from the nozzle or using a high-volume scavenger attachment for a high-volume evacuation suction tip or saliva ejector.[52–54]

B. Protective Patient and Clinician Procedures

- Use protective eyewear, protective gown, and hair cover.
- Lubricate patient's lips to prevent drying effect of the sodium bicarbonate using a nonpetroleum lip lubricant.
- Do not direct the spray on the gingiva, directly into the gingival sulcus or other soft tissues, which can create patient discomfort, undue tissue trauma, or more seriously, a facial emphysema.
- Avoid directing the spray into periodontal pockets with bone loss or into extraction sites as a facial emphysema can be induced.

VI. Risk Patients: Air-Powder Polishing Contraindicated

The information from the patient's medical history is used and appropriate applications made. Antibiotic premedication is indicated for all the same patients who are at risk for any dental hygiene procedure (Chapter 10).

A. Contraindications[42]

- Physician-directed sodium-restricted diet (only for sodium bicarbonate powder).
- Respiratory disease or other condition that limits swallowing or breathing, such as chronic obstructive pulmonary disease.
- Patients with end-stage renal disease, Addison's disease or Cushing's disease.
- Communicable infection that can contaminate the aerosols produced.
- Immunocompromised patients.
- Patients taking potassium, antidiuretics, or steroid therapy.
- Patients who have open oral wounds, such as tooth sockets, from oral surgery procedures.

B. Other Contraindications

- *Root surfaces:* Avoid routine polishing of cementum and dentin.
  - There is some evidence they can be removed readily during air-powder polishing.[63]
  - However, much more research on the effect of air polishing and the removal of cementum and dentin needs to be conducted.
- *Soft, spongy gingiva:* The air-powder can irritate the free gingival tissue, especially if not used with the recommended technique.
  - When heavy stain calls for the use of an air-powder polisher, instruct the patient in daily bacterial biofilm removal.
  - Following scaling and periodontal debridement, postpone the stain removal until soft tissue has healed.

TABLE 45-3	Recommendations for Use of Air Polishing on Restorative Materials	
	POLISHING POWDER CONTAINING	
RESTORATIVE MATERIAL	**SODIUM BICARBONATE**	**ALUMINUM TRIHYDROXIDE**
Amalgam	Yes	No
Gold	Yes[a]	No
Porcelain	Yes[a]	No
Hybrid composite	No	No
Microfilled composite	No	No
Glass ionomer	No	No
Compomer	No	No
Luting agents	No	No

[a]Only if margin is avoided.

> *Restorative materials:* The use of air-powder polishing on composite resins, cements, and other nonmetallic materials can cause removal or pitting.[18,19,25,63]
>
> - Table 45-3 provides a guide as to which restorative materials can be safely treated with air-powder polishing agents, the sodium bicarbonate powder, and the aluminum trihydroxide powder.[37]
> - Significant damage to margins of dental castings has been shown.[50]

BOX 45-4

Example Documentation: Selection of Polishing Agent for a Patient with Esthetic Restorations

S–A 36-year-old male patient presents for regular maintenance appointment, grinning to show that his new implant crown and other esthetic restorations are not distinguishable from the color of his teeth. Updated medical history, medications, no changes.

O–Blood pressure (115/75); extra-intraoral exams no findings periodontal examination with complete probing localized 3–4 mm, with BOP in 4 mm pockets in molar areas with supragingival calculus mand ant.; minimal biofilm with sparse and isolated areas of yellowish staining.

A–Checked his dental records for the material used for the various restorations and found that the patient has porcelain crowns on teeth numbers #2, 14, and anterior microhybrid composite restorations in teeth numbers #6, 7, 8, 10, and 11. Patient has an implant and porcelain crown on #9. Note: Microhybrid composite restorations and implant crown match the patient's natural teeth to the extent that it is difficult to identify the restorations.

P–Gave patient new toothbrush with tongue cleaner on back, and demonstrated the tongue cleaner. Went over places he had been missing on his teeth and gingiva. Calculus removal. Avoided use of airpolishing with sodium bicarbonate (the only powder I have available) and also avoided prophy paste. Selected a cleaning agent to remove biofilm and isolated areas of yellowish staining.

Next regular appointment 4 months made at front desk.

Signed _____, RDH

Date _____

EVERYDAY ETHICS

Mr. Jackson, the 62-year-old chief executive officer of a major oil company, presents for his routine 3-month maintenance with Carol, his dental hygienist of several years. Mr. Jackson is meticulous about his appearance and is always handsomely dressed. He is well-known internationally and frequently seen in the news media being interviewed and having pictures taken for news articles.

Mr. Jackson had a complete cosmetic restoration of his teeth a year ago. Previously his teeth had been stained by the numerous cups of tea he drank every day. He has had porcelain veneers placed on his maxillary anterior teeth, and all restorations are now tooth colored. The color match of the restorations to his teeth is perfect. Unfortunately, Mr. Jackson has not cut back on drinking tea and during her assessment, Carol notes that generalized stain is starting to discolor most of the new restorations. Before the cosmetic restorations were placed, Carol used a coarse prophy paste to eliminate the tea stains and now Mr. Jackson asks her to "just use that gritty stuff again." He states that he absolutely does not want his teeth to appear stained.

Questions for Consideration

1. What role does each of the dental hygiene core values play as Carol contemplates a course of action to take in this situation?

2. What alternative actions are available that would respect Mr. Jackson's rights as well as allow Carol to provide treatment that meets standards of care?

3. What financial or legal considerations will Carol need to consider as she determines her course of action?

DOCUMENTATION

Documentation for a patient receiving tooth stain removal as part of the dental hygiene care plan for a maintenance appointment would include a minimum of the following:

▶ Review patient medical history with questions to determine health problems, recent medical examinations and treatments, and changes in medications.

▶ *Current clinical examination findings*: intraoral, extraoral, periodontal, and dental.

▶ *With dental charting*: identification of dental materials used in restorations that can influence choice of polishing agents. Identification would require use of radiographs and the intraoral dental charting.

▶ Dental hygiene examination for state of patient's personal daily self-care, calculus and biofilm deposits, sources for dental stains, products used for oral care, and dietary factors influencing the dentition and all oral tissues: questions answered about best choices for various products.

▶ A sample progress note may be reviewed in Box 45-4.

 Factors to Teach the Patient

▷ How dental biofilm and stains form on the natural teeth and their replacements.

▷ The meaning of selective polishing and why it is not necessary to polish all teeth at every appointment when daily care is effective.

▷ Stains and biofilm removed by polishing can return promptly if biofilm is not removed faithfully on a schedule of two or three times each day.

▷ Polishing agents used during professional coronal polishing are too abrasive for daily home use.

References

1. Barnes CM. The science of polishing. *Dimensions Dent Hyg.* 2009;7(11):18–20, 22.
2. Liljeborg A, Tellefsen G, Johannsen G. The use of a profilometer for both quantitative and qualitative measurements of toothpaste abrasivity. *Int J Dent Hyg.* 2010;8(3):237–243.
3. American Academy of Periodontology. *Glossary of Periodontal Terms.* 3rd ed. Chicago, IL: American Academy of Periodontology; 1992:40.
4. American Dental Hygienists' Association. *Position Paper on the Oral Prophylaxis.* Chicago, IL: ADHA; 1998. www.adha.org/profissues/prophylaxis.htm.
5. Jeffries SR. Abrasive finishing and polishing in restorative dentistry: a state-of-the-art review. *Dent Clin North Am.* 2007;51(2):379–397.
6. Hutchings IM. Abrasion process in wear and manufacturing. *Proc Inst Mech Eng Part J: J Eng Tribol.* 2002;216(2):55–62.
7. Rémond G, Nockolds C, Phillips M, et al. Implications of polishing techniques in quantitative x-ray microanalysis. *J Res Natl Inst Stand Technol.* 2002;107(6):639–662.
8. Williams JA. Wear and wear particles: some fundamentals. *Tribiol Int.* 2005;38(10):863–870.
9. Fine DH, Furgang D, McKiernan M, et al. An investigation of the effect of an essential oil mouthrinse on induced bacteraemia: a pilot study. *J Clin Periodontol.* 2010;37(9):840–847.
10. Lucas V, Roberts GJ. Odontogenic bacteremia following tooth cleaning procedures in children. *Pediatr Dent.* 2000;22(2):96–100.
11. Cristina ML, Spagnolo AM, Sartini M, et al. Investigation of organizational and hygiene features in dentistry: a pilot study. *J Prev Med Hyg.* 2009;50(3):175–180.
12. Farrier SL, Farrier JN, Gilmour AS. Eye safety in operative dentistry: a study in dental practice. *Br Dent J.* 006;200(4):218–223.
13. Featherstone JD. Prevention and reversal of dental caries: role of low level fluoride. *Community Dent Oral Epidemiol.* 1999;27(1):31–40.
14. Honório HM, Rios D, Abdo RC, et al. Effect of different prophylaxis methods on sound and demineralized enamel. *J Appl Oral Sci.* 2006;14(2):117–123.
15. Kubinek R, Zapletalova Z, Vujtek M, et al. Examination of dentin surface using AFM and SEM. In: Méndez-Vilas A, Díaz J, eds. *Modern Research and Educational Topics in Microscopy,* Vol. 2. Zurbarán, Spain: Formatex; 2007:593–598.
16. Miglani S, Aggarwal V, Ahuja B. Dentin hypersensitivity: recent trends in management. *J Conserv Dent.* 2010;13(4):218–224.
17. Anusavice KJ. Finishing and polishing materials. In: Anusavice KJ, ed. *Phillips' Science of Dental Materials.* 11th ed. St Louis, IL: Saunders; 2003:352.
18. Barnes CM. Polishing esthetic restorative materials. *Dimensions Dent Hyg.* 2010;8(1):24, 26–28.
19. Barnes CM. Care and maintenance of esthetic restorations. *J Prac Hyg.* 2004;14:19–22.
20. Essex GA. Predilection for polishing. *Dimensions Dent Hyg.* 2005;3(3):36, 38.
21. Scott L, Greer D. The effect of an air polishing device on sealant bond strength. *J Prosthet Dent.* 1987;58(3):384–387.
22. Ahovuo-Saloranta A, Hiiri A, Nordblad A, et al. Pit and fissure sealants for preventing dental decay in the permanent teeth of children and adolescents. *Cochrane Database Syst Rev.* 2008;4:CD001830. Review.
23. Azarpazhooh A, Main PA. Efficacy of dental prophylaxis (rubber cup) for the prevention of caries and gingivitis: a systematic review of literature. *Br Dent J.* 2009;207(7):E14.
24. Barnes CM, Covey DA, Walker MP, et al. Essential selective polishing: the maintenance of aesthetic restorations. *J Prac Hyg.* 2003;12(5):18–24.
25. Putt MS, Kleber CJ, Davis JA, et al. Physical characteristics of a new cleaning and polishing agent for use in a prophylaxis paste. *J Dent Res.* 1975;54(3):527–534.
26. Putt MS, Kleber CJ, Muhler JC. Enamel polish and abrasion by prophylaxis pastes. *J Dent Hyg.* 1982;56(9):38, 40–43.
27. Barnes CM. Adapting polishing procedures to maintain aesthetic restorations. *J Prac Hyg.* 2005;15:22.
28. United States Pharmacopeia. *The National Formulary.* Rockville, MD: United States Pharmacopeia Convention; 1995:1342.
29. Burrell KH, Chan JT. Fluorides. In: *American Dental Association, Council on Scientific Affairs: ADA Guide to Dental Therapeutics.* 3rd ed. Chicago, IL: ADA; 2003:238.

30. Tung MS, Eichmiller FC. Amorphous calcium phosphates for tooth mineralization. *Compend Contin Educ Dent.* 2004;25 (9, Suppl 1):9–13.

31. Tung M, Malerman R, Huang S, et al. Reactivity of prophylaxis paste containing calcium phosphate and fluoride salts. *J Dent Res.* 2005;84 (Special Issue A). Abstract #2156, IADR Abstracts, 2005.

32. Daniels A. Professionally applied enhanced polishing agents. *J Prac Hyg.* 2006;15:26.

33. Wolff MS, Kleinberg I. Duration of reduction of dentinal hypersensitivity after prophylaxis with a calcium/arginine bicarbonate carbonate paste. *J Dent Res.* 2003;82 (Special Issue A). Abstract 180.

34. Canadian Advisory Board on Dentin Hypersensitivity. Consensus-based recommendations for the diagnosis and management of dentin hypersensitivity. *J Can Dent Assoc.* 2003;69(4):221–226.

35. Addy M. Dentine hypersensitivity: new perspectives on an old problem. *Int Dent J* 2002;52 (5, Suppl 1):367–375.

36. Mattana D. Reducing dentin Hypersensitivity. *J Prac Hyg.* 2006;15:24.

37. Barnes CM, Fleming LS. An in vitro evaluation of commercially available disposable prophylaxis angles. *J Dent Hyg.* 1991;65(9):438–441.

38. Barnes CM, Anderson NA, Li Y, et al. Effectiveness of steam sterilization in killing spores of *Bacillus stearothermophilus* in prophylaxis angles. *Gen Dent.* 1994;42(5):456–458.

39. Barnes CM, Anderson NA, Michalek SM, et al. Effectiveness of sealed dental prophylaxis angles inoculated with *Bacillus stearothermophilus* in preventing leakage. *J Clin Dent.* 1994;5(2):35–37.

40. Gutmann ME. Air polishing: a comprehensive review of the literature. *J Dent Hyg.* 1998;72(3):47–56.

41. Weaks LM, Lescher NB, Barnes CM, et al. Clinical evaluation of the Prophy-Jet as an instrument for routine removal of tooth stain and plaque. *J Periodontol.* 1984;55(8):486–488.

42. Barnes CM. An in-depth look at air polishing. *Dimensions Dent Hyg.* 2010;8(3):32, 34–36.

43. Barnes CM, Covey DA, Walker MP, et al. An in vitro evaluation of the effects of aluminum trihydroxide delivered via the Prophy Jet on dental restorative materials. *J Prosthet Dent.* 2004;13(3):166–172.

44. Barnes CM, Covey DA, Watanabe H, et al. An in vitro comparison of the effects of various airpolishing powders on enamel and selected esthetic restorative materials. *J Clin Dent.* 2014;25(4):76-87.

45. Orton GS. Clinical use of an air-powder abrasive system. *Dent Hyg.* 1987;61(11):513–518.

46. Barnes CM, Russell CM, Gerbo LR, et al. Effects of an air-powder polishing system on orthodontically bracketed and banded teeth. *Am J Orthod Dentofac Orthop.* 1990;97(1):74–81.

47. Shultz PH, Brockmann-Bell SL, Eick JD, et al. Effects of air-powder polishing on the bond strength of orthodontic bracket adhesive systems. *J Dent Hyg.* 1993;67(2):74–80.

48. Barnes CM, Fleming LS, Mueninghoff LA. An SEM evaluation of the in-vitro effects of an air-abrasive system on various implant surfaces. *Int J Oral Maxillofac Implants.* 1991;6(4):463–469.

49. Barnes CM, Toothaker RW, Ross J. Polishing dental implants and dental implant restorations. *J Prac Hyg.* 2005;14(8):6–8.

50. Berkstein S, Reiff RL, McKinney JF, et al. Supragingival root surface removal during maintenance procedures utilizing an air-powder abrasive system or hand scaling: an in vitro study. *J Periodontol.* 1987;58(5):327–330.

51. Agger MS, Hörsted-Bindslev P, Hovgaard O. Abrasiveness of an air-powder polishing system on root surfaces in vitro. *Quintessence Int.* 2001;32(5):407–411.

52. Barnes CM. The management of aerosols with airpolishing delivery systems. *J Dent Hyg.* 1991;65(6):280–282.

53. Harrel SK, Barnes JB, Rivera-Hidalgo F. Aerosol reduction during air polishing. *Quintessence Int.* 1999;30(9):623–628.

54. Worrall SF, Knibbs PJ, Glenwright HD. Methods of reducing bacterial contamination of the atmosphere arising from use of an air-polisher. *Br Dent J.* 1987;163(4):118, 119.

55. Davies DE. Pneumomediastinum after dental surgery. *Anaesth Intensive Care.* 2001;29(6):638–641.

56. Tan WK. Sudden facial swelling: subcutaneous facial emphysema secondary to use of air/water syringe during dental extraction. *Singapore Dent J.* 2000;23 (1, Suppl):42–44.

57. Josephson GD, Wambach BA, Noordzji JP. Subcutaneous cervicofacial and mediastinal emphysema after dental instrumentation. *Otolaryngol Head Neck Surg.* 2001;124(2):170, 171.

58. Yang SC, Chiu TH, Lin TJ, et al. Subcutaneous emphysema and pneumomediastinum secondary to dental extraction: a case report and literature review. *Kaohsiung J Med Sci.* 2006;22(12):641–645.

59. Heyman SN, Babayof I. Emphysematous complications in dentistry, 1960–1993: an illustrative case and review of the literature. *Quintessence Int.* 1995;26(8):535–543.

60. Arai I, Aoki T, Yamazaki H, et al. Pneumomediastinum and subcutaneous emphysema after dental extraction detected incidentally by regular medical checkup: a case report. *Oral Surg Oral Med Oral Pathol Oral Radiol Endod.* 2009;107(4):e33–e38.

61. Finlayson RS, Stevens FD. Subcutaneous facial emphysema secondary to use of the Cavi-Jet. *J Periodontol.* 1988;59(5):315–317.

62. Fine DH, Mendieta C, Barnett ML, et al. Efficacy of preprocedural rinsing with an antiseptic in reducing viable bacteria in dental aerosols. *J Periodontol.* 1992;63(10):821–824.

63. Atkinson DR, Cobb CM, Killoy WJ. The Effect of an air-powder abrasive system on in vitro root surfaces. *J Periodontol.* 1984;55(1):13–18.

ENHANCE YOUR UNDERSTANDING

thePoint° DIGITAL CONNECTIONS
(see the inside front cover for access information)

- **Audio glossary**
- **Quiz bank**

SUPPORT FOR LEARNING
(available separately; visit lww.com)

- ***Active Learning Workbook for Clinical Practice of the Dental Hygienist, 12th Edition***

prepU INDIVIDUALIZED REVIEW
(available separately; visit lww.com)

- **Adaptive quizzing with *prepU for Wilkins' Clinical Practice of the Dental Hygienist***

46

Tooth Bleaching

Pamela S. Kennard, BSN, CRDH, MA

CHAPTER OUTLINE

LEARNING OBJECTIVES

After studying this chapter, the student will be able to:

1. Discuss the mechanism, safety, and efficacy of tooth bleaching agents.

2. Identify specific tooth conditions and staining responses to tooth bleaching.

3. Discuss reversible and irreversible side effects associated with the tooth bleaching process.

4. List appropriate interventions for tooth bleaching side effects.

INTRODUCTION

Patients of all ages have concerns about the appearance of their teeth and expect their dental hygienists to provide information to guide them in their esthetic choices. Because there are many causes of tooth discoloration, a review of Chapter 22 is recommended.

▶ Tooth bleaching may improve a patient's appearance and contribute to a patient's self-confidence.

▶ A whiter smile may motivate the patient to maintain improved oral health, which is a significant benefit.

I. Bleaching Versus Whitening

The terms bleaching and whitening have been used interchangeably, but two separate descriptions can define them more accurately.[1]

▶ Tooth whitening refers to use of abrasive agents contained in a dentifrice to remove extrinsic stain.

▶ Bleaching involves free radicals and the breakdown of pigment, which occurs in the tooth bleaching procedures.

▶ Key words and abbreviations are defined in Box 46-1.

II. Vital Tooth Bleaching Versus Nonvital Tooth Bleaching

▶ External tooth bleaching is used for both vital and nonvital teeth.

▶ Vital teeth can be stained intrinsically and extrinsically.

▶ Agents for bleaching are applied to the external surfaces of the teeth.

▶ Color change can extend into the dentin to produce a whitened tooth.

▶ Nonvital teeth become intrinsically stained by blood breakdown products, or agents from root canal therapy.[1]

▶ Nonvital tooth bleaching is a procedure performed by a dentist after root canal therapy using rubber dam or other type of isolation.

● The bleaching agents are introduced into the pulp chamber.

● The color of a single tooth is lightened to help it blend with the adjacent teeth.

III. History

A. Nonvital Tooth Bleaching History

▶ Bleaching of discolored, nonvital teeth was first described as early as 1864.[2,3]

BOX 46-1 | KEY WORDS: Tooth Bleaching

Bleaching: a cosmetic dental procedure that uses free radicals and breakdown of pigments to whiten teeth.

Block-out resins: light-cured resin materials that can be used as a rubber dam substitute during bleaching procedure or on study models to create space to hold bleaching material on custom trays.

Color: a phenomenon of light or visual perception that enables the differentiation of otherwise identical objects. Usually determined visually by measurement of hue, saturation, and luminous reflectance of light.

Esthetic: pertaining to the study of beauty and the sense of beautiful; objectifies beauty and attractiveness, elicits pleasure.

Extrinsic: external, extraneous, as originating from or on the outside.

Iatrogenic: resulting from the activity of a clinician; disorders induced in a patient by the clinician.

Intrinsic: from within, incorporation of a colorant within a material.

Laser bleaching and ultraviolet light system: dental office procedure that uses light in combination with hydrogen peroxide to activate bleaching materials and reduce the time necessary to produce a lighter color of teeth; use of

rubber dam or protective light-cured resin on soft tissue required during use, as well as eye protection.

Microabrasion: a proven method for treating tooth discolorations by microreduction of superficial enamel through various methods of mechanical and/or chemical actions.

NGVB: acronym for night guard vital bleaching, which requires development of a custom tray that allows for administration and containment of tooth bleaching material such as carbamide peroxide or hydrogen peroxide.

Potassium nitrate: active ingredient in many antisensitivity dentifrices.

Psoralen: a compound that absorbs ultraviolet radiation, and is used to treat skin problems such as psoriasis, eczema, or alopecia.

Synergism: when the combined effect of the interaction of elements produces a greater total effect than the sum of the individual elements.

Surfactant: a wetting agent.

Translucency: having the appearance between complete opacity and complete transparency; partially opaque.

Whitening: use of abrasive agents in the dentifrice that results in whitening of teeth. Has also been used to describe the process of bleaching.

- In 1961, the "walking bleach" method was introduced. The "walking bleach" method sealed a mixture of sodium perborate and water into the pulp chamber and retained it there between the patient's visits.[4]
- By 1963 the "walking bleach" was modified using water and 30%–35% hydrogen peroxide instead of the sodium perborate and water. Result: improved lighter color of nonvital teeth.[2]

B. Vital Tooth Bleaching History

- In the 1960s, tooth lightening was observed after orthodontic patients used an antiseptic that contained carbamide peroxide to promote tissue healing due to gingivitis.[2,5]
- In the 1980s lighter tooth color was noted after advising patients to use carbamide peroxide in customized trays for antiseptic purposes following periodontal surgery.[5]
- In 1989 the use of carbamide peroxide for the primary purpose of tooth bleaching was introduced.[6]
  - A custom tray was used to maintain the bleaching gel on the tooth surface for an extended time.
  - The procedure was known as nightguard vital bleaching (NGVB).
- No significant, long-term oral or systemic health risks have been associated with professional at-home tooth bleaching materials containing 10% carbamide peroxide or 3.5% hydrogen peroxide when professionally supervised.[7]

VITAL TOOTH BLEACHING

The bleaching process is being studied and still is not fully understood. The color of the teeth is influenced by thickness of enamel and underlying color of dentin.

I. Mechanism of Bleaching Vital Teeth

- Bleaching products penetrate enamel and dentin reaching the pulp within 5–15 minutes.[7,8]
- Bleaching products break down larger pigmented organic molecules into smaller, less pigmented constituents that are locked in the enamel matrix and dentinal tubules.
- Oxygen released from bleaching products changes the optical qualities of the tooth color.[9]

II. Tooth Color Change with Vital Tooth Bleaching

- Color of both dentin and enamel are changed; primarily the dentin color is changed.[10]
- Dentin color is either yellow or gray and transilluminates through the enamel.

- Darker teeth take more time to lighten.
- Each tooth reaches a maximum color change. Additional bleaching product or contact time will not necessarily result in a lighter color.[10]
- Bleaching products cause teeth to become dehydrated immediately during and after product administration. A lighter shade can result temporarily.
- Color will stabilize approximately 2 weeks after bleaching.[9,10]

III. Materials Used for Vital Tooth Bleaching

- Both hydrogen peroxide and carbamide peroxide are used to lighten vital teeth.
- Hydrogen peroxide is approximately three times stronger than carbamide peroxide.[5]
- Hydrogen peroxide has a short working time; carbamide peroxide has an extended working time.[8] Figure 46-1 compares the release or duration time of carbamide peroxide with that of hydrogen peroxide.
- The chemicals are used alone or in combination with each other.
- Bleaching materials need an appropriate viscosity to flow over the tooth surface but not so excessive as to spread onto gingival and other oral tissues.

A. Hydrogen Peroxide

- Active agent in most bleaching systems in a 15%–35% concentration.
- Used directly or produced through a chemical reaction when carbamide peroxide breaks down.[10] See Figure 46-2.

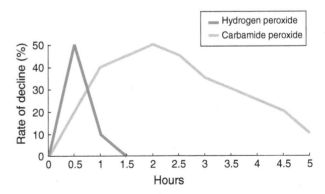

FIGURE 46-1 **Release Time of Carbamide Peroxide Compared to Hydrogen Peroxide.** Hydrogen peroxide has a much shorter working time than carbamide peroxide and causes more sensitivity. Hydrogen peroxide releases all of the peroxide within 1.5 hours. Carbamide peroxide releases the peroxide over a much longer time. Hydrogen peroxide is approximately three times stronger than carbamide peroxide. (Figures courtesy of Dr. Van Haywood. Reprinted from Haywood VB. Treating sensitivity during tooth whitening. *Compend Contin Educ Dent.* 2005;28(9, Suppl 3):11–20. © 2005, AEGIS Publications, LLC. Used with permission.)

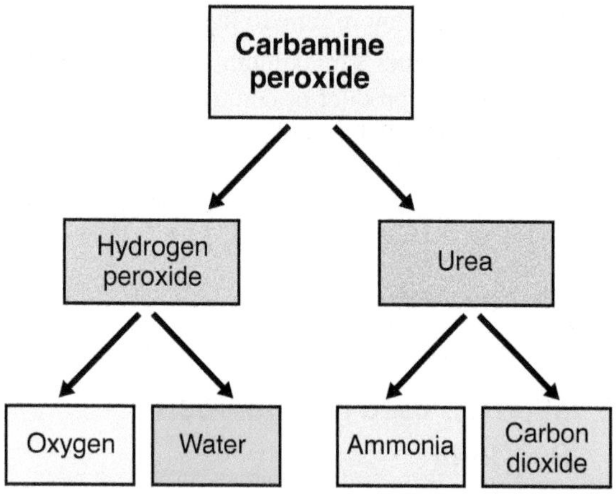

FIGURE 46-2 **Hydrogen Peroxide and Carbamide Peroxide Product Breakdown.** Flowchart to show breakdown of bleaching products. Hydrogen peroxide breaks down into oxygen and water; carbamide peroxide breaks down into hydrogen peroxide and urea, which further break down as shown.

▶ Has a lower pH than carbamide peroxide, which may result in demineralization when used for longer treatment times than recommended.

▶ Takes less time per day, but more days to change tooth color effectively.[7]

▶ Has high acidic nature; may result in dentin changes which never recover.[11]

B. Carbamide Peroxide

▶ Breaks down into hydrogen peroxide and urea. As shown in the flowchart (Figure 46-2), urea may further break down into ammonia with high pH to facilitate bleaching.

▶ Has slow release: 50% of peroxide released in 2–4 hours and remainder of peroxide in 2–6 hours resulting in less sensitivity.[8] In Figure 46-1 the release time is shown for carbamide peroxide compared with hydrogen peroxide.

▶ At neutral pH, 10% solution is both safe and effective as a bleaching agent.[12]

▶ Takes fewer days but more contact time.[1]

C. Desensitizers

▶ Materials to reduce the sensitivity side effect of bleaching are added to bleaching systems.

▶ Materials can be:
  • incorporated into the bleaching gel
  • applied to teeth before bleaching
  • given for use in trays before, during, and after treatment.

▶ Material used:
  • Potassium nitrate creates a calming effect on pulp by affecting the transmission of nerve impulses.[8]
  • Sodium fluoride.

• Calcium phosphate and amorphous calcium phosphate aid in remineralization.[8]

D. Other Ingredients

▶ Carbopol: A water-soluble resin used as a thickening agent, which:
  • prolongs the release of hydrogen peroxide from carbamide peroxide
  • promotes quicker results.

▶ Glycerin: A gel to thicken and control the flow of bleaching agent to prevent overextending onto gingival tissues.

▶ Sodium hydroxide: A chemical base.

▶ Surfactants help to lift and remove extrinsic stains.

▶ Flavoring.

E. Interactions with Bleaching Agents[1]

▶ Coffee and tea may compromise treatment. Advise patient to avoid.

▶ Tobacco may compromise treatment; may have additive carcinogenic effect when combined with hydrogen peroxide. Advise patient to avoid.

IV. Vital Tooth Bleaching Safety

A. Tooth Structure

▶ Both hydrogen peroxide 3.5% and carbamide peroxide 10% are considered safe to lighten the color of teeth when professionally monitored.[7]

▶ Up to two-thirds of patients will experience transitory mild-to-moderate tooth sensitivity.[7]

▶ Higher concentrations of hydrogen peroxide may result in:
  • greater sensitivity
  • greater color relapses after termination of bleaching.[11]

▶ Hydrogen peroxide at concentrations of 30% or higher may:
  • remove the enamel matrix
  • create microscopic voids that scatter light
  • Result: increase in whiteness until remineralization occurs and color partly relapses.[1]

▶ Carbamide peroxide 10% will cause fewer changes in the enamel matrix.[1]

▶ Pulpal necrosis was noted when material combined with excessive heat or trauma.[12]

B. Soft Tissue

▶ Hydrogen peroxide is caustic and may cause burning and bleaching of the gingiva and any exposed oral tissue.[2]

▶ Hydrogen peroxide 10% concentration or higher has greater incidence of gingival irritation.[7]

▶ Ill-fitting or overfilled tray may cause product spillage onto soft tissues resulting in tissue burning.

C. Restorative Materials

▶ Restorative material color such as porcelain or composite materials will not be changed by bleaching.

▶ After bleaching, new restorative procedures need to be delayed for 2 weeks to allow for color stabilization.[12]

▶ Bonding needs to be delayed for 2 weeks due to significantly reduced bonding strength associated with recently bleached tooth surface.[11]

▶ Bleaching chemicals containing hydrogen peroxide may:
  • Have a negative effect on restorations and restorative materials due to lower pH, although impact does not require the renewal of the restoration.[9]
  • Increase mercury release from amalgam restorations giving off a green hue.[9]
  • Increase solubility of some dental cements.[13]

D. Systemic Factors

▶ The use of tooth-bleaching products containing hydrogen peroxide or carbamide peroxide has not been proven to increase the risk of oral cancer in the general population, including those persons who are alcohol abusers and/or heavy cigarette smokers.[7]

▶ Accidental ingestion of small amounts of the product may cause sore throat, nausea, vomiting, abdominal distention, and ulcerations of the oral mucosa, esophagus, and stomach.[2]

▶ Drugs that may be associated with photosensitivity and hyperpigmentation when light-activated whitening agents are used are listed in Box 46-2.

E. Cautions and Contraindications Associated with Vital Tooth Bleaching

1. *Personal factors that affect acceptance for treatment*
  • Teeth at an acceptable shade, which is subjective.
  • Patients with unrealistic personal expectations.
  • Patients who are unable to be compliant with treatment will not achieve optimal results.
  • Patients with tooth conditions that do not respond favorably to vital tooth bleaching.

2. *Children and adolescents*
  • The American Academy of Pediatric Dentistry[14] discourages full-arch cosmetic bleaching for patients with a mixed dentition, but encourages judicious use of vital and nonvital bleaching due to the negative self-image that may arise from a discolored tooth or teeth.
  • Current American Dental Association recommendations for children and adolescent use include:
    ○ Delaying treatment until after permanent teeth have erupted.
    ○ Use of a custom-fabricated tray to limit amount of bleaching gel.
    ○ Close supervision.[7]

3. *Contraindications*
  • Bleaching products are contraindicated for pregnant and lactating women.
  • Patients taking photosensitive medications. See Box 46-2.
  • Laser light/power bleaching contraindicated for some patients as described in Box 46-3.

V. Factors Associated with Efficacy[1,9]

▶ Some tooth conditions will not respond to tooth bleaching; other tooth conditions will respond slowly (Table 46-1).

▶ The initial color of the teeth and type of stain present will affect the final color change.

▶ Specific indications for bleaching and methods of treatments are listed in Table 46-2.

▶ Patient age: Attrition, incisal, and occlusal wear through enamel exposes the darker underlying dentin.

▶ Concentration of bleaching agent.

▶ Ability of agent to reach the stain molecules.

▶ Duration of contact of the active bleaching agent: longer duration, the greater the degree of bleaching.

▶ Number of types the agent is applied to obtain desired results: darker teeth tend to require more treatment applications.

BOX 46-2

Drugs Associated with Potential Photosensitivity and Hyperpigmentation

▷ Acne medications
▷ Anticancer drugs
▷ Antidepressants
▷ Antiparasitics
▷ Antipsychotics
▷ Diuretics
▷ Hypoglycemics
▷ Nonsteroidal anti-inflammatory drugs

BOX 46-3

Issues Associated with Light-Activated Bleaching

All contraindications noted are for bleaching with a light. Contraindicated for patients who are:
▷ Light sensitive
▷ Taking a photosensitive medication
▷ Receiving photochemotherapeutic drugs or treatments such as psoralen and ultraviolet radiation.
Exposure to ultraviolet radiation produced by some lights is avoided by those at increased risk for or have a history of skin cancer, including melanoma.

TABLE 46-1	Decision Making for Tooth Bleaching	
TOOTH CONDITION	**RESPONSE TO TOOTH WHITENING**	**SPECIAL CONSIDERATIONS**
Yellow color	Normally excellent.	Resistant yellow may be tetracycline stain.
Enamel white spots	Do not bleach well or may get lighter during whitening.	<ul><li>Eventually background color lightens resulting in less noticeable white spots.</li><li>Goes through splotchy stage before background color whitens.</li><li>Microabrasion may lessen white spots if less than one-third through enamel.</li></ul>
Brown fluorosis stains	Respond 80% of the time.	Microabrasion techniques done after whitening and color stabilization may improve final result.
Nicotine stains	Require longer treatment.	May take 2–3 mo of nightly application.
Tetracycline stains	Multicolored band may not respond well. <ul><li>Gray most difficult.</li><li>Dark grays only get lighter.</li><li>Dark cervical has poorest prognosis.</li></ul>	Requires 2–12 mo of daily whitening.
Minocycline stains	Will respond; will take longer than yellow stain.	<ul><li>Type of tetracycline stain.</li><li>Gives gray hue.</li></ul>
Root exposure	Does not respond to whitening.	Better treated with periodontal coverage.
Dentinogenesis imperfecta and amelogenesis imperfecta	No significant improvement with bleaching.	Inherited condition resulting in defective dentin and enamel, respectively.
Microcracks	Become whiter than rest of tooth.	Bright light or magnification required during assessment to view; may appear streaky during whitening process.
Anterior lingual amalgams	Become more visible after bleaching.	Replacement with very light composite restoration before bleaching.
Dental caries	Not to be bleached.	Decay removal; temporary restoration followed by bleaching and final restoration after color stabilization; carbamide peroxide will increase sensitivity and is bactericidal.
Dark canines	Require longer bleaching.	Isolated canine treatment until color match.
Attrition	Incisal edges do not respond.	Composite restorations added to incisal edges after bleaching.
Aging	Excellent.	More youthful appearance; root surfaces exposure likely.
Translucent teeth	Bleaching will increase translucency at incisal.	Translucent areas will appear darker after whitening due to contrast.

TABLE 46-2	Indications for Tooth Bleaching and Methods of Treatment
INDICATION	**METHOD TO TREAT**
Discolored, endodontically treated tooth	Internal bleaching; in-office or walking.
Single or multiple discolored teeth	External bleaching: in-office 1–3 visits or custom trays worn 2–6 wk.
Surface staining	Brushing with whitening dentifrice.
Isolated brown or white discoloration, shallow depth in enamel	Microabrasion followed by neutral sodium fluoride applications.
White discoloration on yellowish teeth	Microabrasion followed by custom tray whitening.

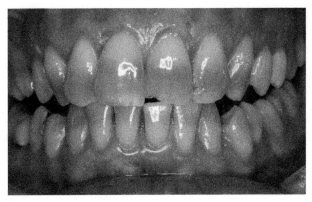
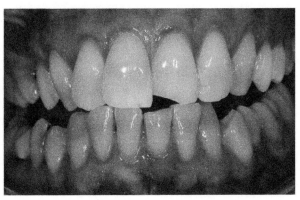

A   **B**

FIGURE 46-3 **Before and after Bleaching of Brown Tetracycline-Stained Teeth. A:** Patient before treating. **B:** Patient treated with 10% carbamide peroxide for 2 months. Some tetracycline-stained teeth will require up to 12 months to achieve improved results. Those with severe gray stain or banded staining may require porcelain veneers to achieve an acceptable cosmetic result. (Images courtesy of Dr. Van Haywood. Reprinted from Haywood VB. The "bottom line" on bleaching 2008. *Inside Dent.* 2008;4(2):2–5. © 2008, AEGIS Publications, LLC. Used with permission.)

▶ Temperature of agent: heat will result in faster oxygen release, but speed of color change may not be altered.

A. Intrinsic

1. Tetracycline and minocycline staining

- Tetracycline particles incorporate into dentin calcium during mineralization of unerupted teeth. Result: discolored dentin resistant to bleaching.[15]
- Minocycline, a derivative of tetracycline, can discolor erupted teeth.[13]
- Tetracycline and minocycline staining severity varies. A comparison of before and after bleaching of brown tetracycline staining is shown in Figure 46-3.
  - *First category staining*: Light-yellow to light-gray responds to bleaching.
  - *Second category staining*: darker, more extensive yellow-gray responds to extended bleaching time.
  - *Third category staining*: intense dark gray-blue banding stains. Severe third category staining may require porcelain veneers for satisfactory esthetic result.

- Some tetracycline stains will require 1–12 months to achieve a satisfactory result.

2. Fluorosis

- Fluorosis results from ingesting excessive fluoride during tooth development resulting in white or brown spots on teeth.
- Bleaching does not change white spots, but lightens the background color, making the contrast less noticeable.
- White spots go through a splotchy stage during bleaching but will return to baseline.[12]
- Amorphous calcium phosphate may be effective in lessening the white spots if lesion is less than one-third through enamel.[12]
- Brown discoloration responsive to bleach 80% of the time.[12]

3. Nicotine

- Nicotine stains: require 1–3 months of nightly treatment due to the tenacity of the stain.

B. Longevity of Results

▶ Relapse of shade occurs almost immediately as newly bleached, dehydrated teeth rehydrate.

▶ As months and years pass, teeth may discolor and darken again, especially if stain-inducing activities continue.

▶ To maintain shade, periodic bleaching procedures are performed or repeated.

C. Additional Benefits of Bleaching

▶ Hydrogen peroxide used in bleaching has temporary additional effects, which include an antimicrobial action that may lead to a reduction in biofilm and improved gingival health.[16]

▶ Improved motivation to have higher standards of personal daily oral hygiene while participating in bleaching procedures.

▶ Carbamide peroxide may assist with caries control due to raising pH levels to 8 during application.[17]

▶ Carbamide peroxide has been shown to be bacteriocidal to cariogenic bacteria, which benefits elderly xerostomic patients, and orthodontic patients.

VI. Reversible Side Effects of Vital Bleaching: Sensitivity

The most common side effects of bleaching are tooth tingling and sensitivity. Aching sensation can occur because of insult of peroxide on nerves: a reversible pulpitis.[8]

▶ Primarily occur in the first 2 weeks of treatment and may last days to months after cessation of bleaching.

▶ Side effects resolve completely as teeth become accustomed to bleaching.

▶ Not correlated with increased wear time.[8]

▶ Lower concentrations have been used for up to 12 months and do not exhibit greater sensitivity.[8]

▶ Patients with prior history of tooth sensitivity may be more at risk to develop sensitivity during bleaching.

▶ Vulnerable tooth surfaces include:

- Exposed root surfaces and dentin appear to increase risk of developing sensitivity and need to be protected from bleaching material.
- Teeth with unrestored abfraction lesions (see Figure 44-3, Chapter 44) tend to have more sensitivity.

▶ Addition of desensitizing materials decreases sensitivity.

▶ Treatments to reduce tooth sensitivity are listed in Table 46-3.

VII. Irreversible Tooth Damage[1]

A. Root Resorption

▶ Can occur after bleaching, particularly after intracoronal, nonvital tooth bleaching when heat is applied during the technique.

▶ Internal and external resorption may become apparent several years after bleaching.

▶ Occurs usually in cervical third of the tooth.

▶ Cause may be related to a history of trauma.

TABLE 46-3	Desensitization Procedures for Bleaching
Pretreatment	■ Brush on or use with tray a desensitizing toothpaste containing potassium nitrate, without sodium lauryl sulfate, which removes smear layer from dentin, beginning 2 wk before whitening. ■ Use toothpaste with prescription strength sodium fluoride. ■ Use toothpaste that includes calcium carbonate.
During treatment	■ Continue to use desensitizing toothpaste, which includes sodium fluoride or potassium nitrate, daily between treatments. ■ Increase time intervals between treatments. ■ Reduce exposure time of bleaching materials. ■ Limit the amount in tray to prevent tissue contact.
Postbleaching	■ Sensitivity diminishes with time. ■ Continue daily use of desensitizing dentifrice. ■ Have professional fluoride varnish application. ■ Avoid foods and beverages with temperature extremes or that contain acidic elements.

▶ May lead to tooth loss.

▶ Bleaching agents are not placed on exposed cementum to avoid complications.

B. Tooth Fracture

▶ May be related to removal of tooth structure or reduction of the microhardness of dentin and enamel.

▶ May lead to tooth loss.

C. Demineralization

▶ Patient with over-the-counter product may not seek or follow professional advice and attempt to get the teeth whiter by using the product more than recommended.

▶ Demineralization with slight surface pitting can result.

▶ Remineralization may be possible if started early enough.

▶ Remineralization protocols are described in Chapter 27.

VIII. Modes of Vital Tooth Bleaching

▶ A comparison of the advantages and disadvantages of professionally applied and professionally dispensed/professionally monitored systems and the over-the-counter systems is listed in Table 46-4.

▶ The different methods of tooth bleaching can achieve similar, effective results, although the mode of delivery, length of treatment, and ease of treatment vary.

A. Professionally Applied

▶ Professionally applied bleaching is performed with high concentrations of 30%–40% hydrogen peroxide or 35%–44% carbamide peroxide.

▶ Some systems use activation or enhancement with a light or heat source.

▶ Teeth are not anesthetized in order to monitor heat-provoked sensitivity.

▶ Heat applied or produced by the use of light may cause an adverse effect such as necrosis of the pulp of the tooth.

▶ The additional issues associated with the use of a light-activated whitening are listed in Box 46-3.

▶ Treatment may take one to six applications for preferred results.

▶ Time for each application varies between different products; ranges from 30- to 60-minute treatment.

▶ Bleaching gels are administered in a professional treatment room. They are not for at-home use.

▶ Rubber dam or an equivalent technique, such as a liquid light-cured resin dam, is applied to isolate the caustic agents from contact with soft tissues.

▶ Care is taken to assure the liquid light-cured resin dam is in the interproximal spaces to protect gingival tissue.

▶ Improvements in paint-on rubber dams, cheek, lip retractors, and lower concentrations of peroxide

have made in-office bleaching safer for patient and dentist.

▶ Laser-safe/ultraviolet light protection of eyes for all in treatment room is required.

▶ Gingival sensitivity or irritation may occur.

▶ Laser/power bleaching treatment plan may also involve use of trays for home use.

B. Professionally Dispensed/Professionally Monitored

▶ Also called NGVB, external bleaching, at-home bleaching.

▶ Tray preparation:
  • An impression of the teeth is taken to prepare the cast for fabrication of the tray.
  • Thin, vacuum-formed custom trays are made for each dental arch to be bleached.
  • Trays are fitted to the patient and adjusted to ensure bleaching material will not come into contact with soft tissues.
  • As shown in Figure 46-4, trays are either scalloped at gingival margin or unscalloped and trimmed at mucogingival line.
  • Nonscalloped trays seal better, use less material, and are more comfortable.

▶ Patient instruction:
  • Patient is given instructions and bleaching materials for use in the trays at home.
  • Once or twice daily application for 1–2 weeks is usually recommended if lack of sensitivity and other side effects permit. Maximum color change obtained with consistent compliance. See Figure 46-5.

▶ Patient retains the trays after completion of bleaching to reuse for touch-ups as needed.

▶ Professionally dispensed bleaching products are commonly recommended after professionally applied bleaching procedures to maintain and promote results.

C. Over-the-Counter Products

▶ Also called "at-home" or "self-directed" products.

▶ When asked about use of the self-directed product, a dental hygienist may stress the need for professional examination and supervision; the products can cause harm if misused, may irritate tissues, or cause systemic illness if ingested.

▶ May be recommended to help maintain results of professionally applied and professionally dispensed methods of bleaching.

▶ Patient informs dental professional of proposed use to discuss risks and possible interaction with any proposed dental treatment.

▶ Patient is advised to have thorough oral evaluation before use of the products, as well as appropriate dental

TABLE 46-4	Comparisons of Modes of Tooth Bleaching Systems	
METHODS	**ADVANTAGES**	**DISADVANTAGES**
Professionally applied utilizing laser/ ultraviolet light system procedure	■ Comprehensive ■ Treatment may be combined with trays and professional grade home bleaching materials ■ Product selection ■ Patient education ■ Follow-up, evaluation of effectiveness ■ Sensitivity treatment ■ Compliance guaranteed ■ Quickest result	■ Higher cost
Professionally dispensed includes professional grade product and trays	■ Comprehensive ■ Dental examination ■ Appropriate patient ■ Selection ■ Product selection ■ Patient education ■ Follow-up, evaluation of effectiveness ■ Sensitivity treatment ■ Choice of comfortable time and place for application ■ Quicker result	■ Cost ■ Longer time to whiten than professionally applied
Over the counter	■ Lowest cost ■ Immediate start ■ Easier access to purchase	■ No comprehensive exam ■ Slowest whitening ■ Noncustomized delivery ■ Results and tissue response not monitored ■ Over-the-counter products have short exposure times, which limit effects ■ Unsupervised ■ Compliance issues

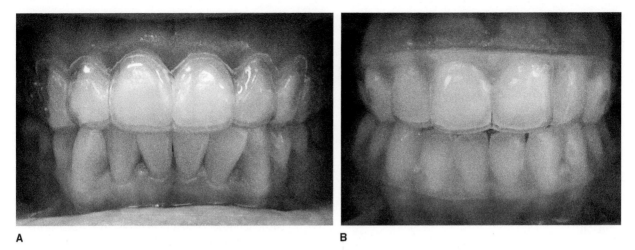

A   **B**

FIGURE 46-4 **Scalloped and Unscalloped NGVB Tray Designs.** Either scalloped or unscalloped trays may be used. **A:** Scalloped trays aim to protect the gingiva and exposed root surfaces. **B:** Unscalloped trays are more comfortable and take less preparation time. Patients need to be warned to avoid overfilling trays.

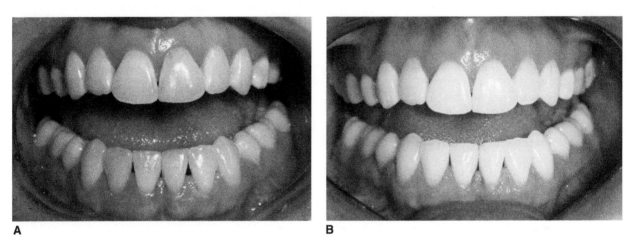

A   **B**

FIGURE 46-5 (A) Before and (B) After Home Tray Bleaching Treatment. (Photo courtesy of Gordon J. Christensen DDS MSD PhD. Used with permission.)

and periodontal treatment including calculus, stain, and biofilm removal.

▸ Delivered through various packaging, viscosities, and flavors (Box 46-4).

NONVITAL TOOTH BLEACHING

▸ Also called "walking bleach" procedure, internal bleaching.

▸ Bleaching of a single, endodontically treated tooth that is discolored can be accomplished by nonvital tooth bleaching procedures.

▸ Alternative to more invasive correction, such as a post and core with crown, or single, discolored, endodontically treated tooth.

▸ Performed by a dentist.

▸ Requirements for procedure:
  • Healthy periodontium.
  • Successfully obturated root canal filling.

• Root canal filling is sealed off with a restorative material before treatment to prevent bleaching agent from reaching periapical tissue.

▸ Hydrogen peroxide and/or sodium perborate is placed in the pulp chamber, sealed, and left for 3–7 days, as outlined in Box 46-5.

▸ Hydrogen peroxide and sodium perborate may be synergistic and very effective in bleaching the tooth.

▸ The process is repeated until a satisfactory result is obtained.

▸ Once satisfactory result is obtained, the pulp chamber is sealed with glass ionomer cement.

▸ Appoint patient 2 weeks later to place permanent, bonded, composite-resin restoration in access cavity to allow dissipation of residual oxygen that would interfere with efficacy of bonding agent.

▸ If unsuccessful after repeated attempts, techniques for vital tooth bleaching can be tried or an alternative restorative procedure, such as a post and core, with crown.

BOX 46-4

Over-the-Counter Bleaching Preparations

Strips

▷ Hydrogen peroxide is delivered on polyethylene film strips.

▷ Strips are placed on the teeth up to two times per day for 30 minutes for about 2 weeks.

Prefabricated Trays

▷ Thin membrane tray loaded with bleaching agent is adapted to maxillary or mandibular arch.

▷ Usually worn 30–60 minutes daily for 5–10 days.

Paint-on

▷ Carbamide peroxide is incorporated into a thick gel that is painted on the teeth selected to be bleached.

▷ An advantage to this method is that individual teeth may be bleached.

Dentifrice

▷ Used to help keep teeth cleaner, and therefore look whiter.

▷ Some have more abrasive materials to remove extrinsic stains.

▷ Owing to short exposure time, the bleaching agent in the dentifrice has little effect on staining.

▷ Some contain hydrogen peroxide; others contain agents that may deter further attachment of stains to the teeth.

Mouthrinse

▷ Content of alcohol is avoided in selection of mouthrinse.

BOX 46-5

Procedure for Nonvital Tooth Bleaching

Periodontally healthy, endodontically treated tooth:
1. Photograph of the tooth to be bleached with shade guide.
2. Provide dental hygiene services to remove extrinsic stain and calculus.
3. Probe circumferentially to determine the outline of the cementoenamel junction.
4. Rubber dam isolation is applied to prevent contamination of root canal therapy.
5. Prepare access cavity. Remove all endodontic obturation material, sealer, cement, and necessary restorative material without removing more dentin than necessary.
6. Remove 2–3 mm of obturation material from the root canal to level below the crest of the gingival margin.
7. Irrigate access cavity with copious amount of water and dry well without desiccating.
8. Root canal therapy is sealed off, commonly with glass ionomer cement or other filling material.
9. Medicament is placed in pulp chamber.
10. Pulp chamber is sealed with a temporary restoration.
11. Patient returns in 3–7 days for evaluation.
    Aforementioned procedure is repeated several times until desired result is obtained.

To finalize procedure:
1. Rubber dam isolation.
2. Temporary restoration on medicament is removed.
3. Pulp chamber is irrigated thoroughly with water.
4. Coronal restoration is placed; generally a composite material.
5. Photograph tooth with corresponding shade guide for records.

▶ Results usually last longer than external tooth bleaching.

▶ There is no universal standard for what is considered acceptable esthetics.

▶ Personal background, culture, and society's and patient's image of esthetics are factors.

▶ The dentist initially may not identify a patient's esthetic issues in the same way that the patient identifies them.

▶ Care is taken to communicate and agree about the course of treatment and the expected result of treatment before the start of bleaching.

DENTAL HYGIENE PROCESS OF CARE

I. Patient Assessment

▶ Review of medical history; identify any contraindications for bleaching.

▶ Complete dental assessment including the following:
  - Complete extraoral and intraoral examination including oral cancer screening.

- Updated radiographs.
- The presence of cavitated dental caries is a contraindication for bleaching.
- A lesion is prepared and restored with a temporary restoration to be replaced with permanent matching restoration upon completion of bleaching.
- Updated radiographs to identify abscesses or nonvital teeth, which would require endodontic therapy before bleaching.
- Periodontal examination including areas of recession. Cementum needs to be protected from bleaching material to avoid potential internal and/or external resorption.
- Obtain photographic record of tooth shade without lipstick or strong clothing colors that may interfere with accurate assessment. Use canine for base color. Color will be gray or yellow. Confirm with patient. Figure 46-6 illustrates using a shade guide.

▶ Identify those factors that would lead to a guarded prognosis for bleaching such as:
  - History or presence of sensitive teeth.

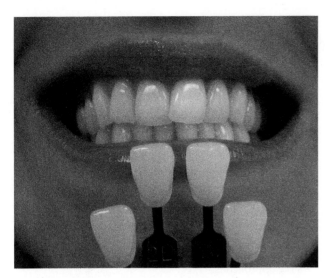

FIGURE 46-6 Digital Photographic Record of Tooth Shade. Patient's shade taken, recorded, and photographed in natural light or color-corrected lighting after extrinsic stain removal before bleaching. Several manufacturers provide color ranges with as many as 29 shades. Electronic digital shade guides provide objective records. Patient's shade and photograph are recorded at each visit while in bleaching treatment. (Photo courtesy of author.)

- Extremely dark gingival third of tooth visible during a smile.
- Extensive white spots that are very visible.
- Temporomandibular joint dysfunction or bruxism that would make wearing NGVB uncomfortable and potential for aggravating condition.
- Very translucent teeth that would become less esthetic due to increased translucency.

▶ Identify contraindications for at-home whitening including the following:
  - Unrealistic expectations of the patient.
  - Unwillingness or inability to comply with at-home treatment routines.
  - Excessive existing restorations not requiring replacement.
  - Inability to tolerate the taste of the product.
  - Pregnancy or lactation.

II. Dental Hygiene Diagnosis

Deficit in wholesome body image as evidenced by patient statement related to dissatisfaction of tooth color.

III. Dental Hygiene Care Plan

▶ *Dental hygiene therapy* with complete removal of all supra- and subgingival calculus and stain along with personal care instruction.

▶ *Patient education*
  - Procedure, product chosen based on patient need.
  - Tooth sensitivity treatment and sensitivity prevention.
  - Emphasis on the following:

- Effective daily biofilm removal before bleaching material use to prevent additional extrinsic stain accumulation.
- Use of nonabrasive whitening dentifrice.
- Removal of excess bleaching material after use.
- Avoidance of over-filling tray to protect soft tissue and exposed cementum.
- Avoidance of foods that stain teeth, coffee, alcohol, and use of tobacco to maximize results.
- Avoidance of swallowing bleaching material due to irritation of materials to mucosa.

▶ Choose appropriate bleaching method.
  - Discussion of procedure, risks, and realistic results.
  - Plan with patient for anticipated needs after bleaching, such as replacement of existing tooth-colored restorations that will not match after bleaching.
  - Obtain informed consent listing procedure and risks with patient's signature (see Chapter 25).

IV. Implementation

▶ Review instructions for use and patient education items previously listed.

▶ *Dental hygiene therapy*: removal of all calculus deposits, and extrinsic stains.

▶ Pretreatment desensitization when indicated. Recommended procedures for pretreatment, during treatment, and postbleaching are listed in Table 46-3.

▶ Premedication with anti-inflammatory pain medication when indicated for sensitivity.

▶ Preparation of trays; impression and construction.
  - Wet teeth before taking impression to ensure teeth are not dehydrated.
  - Monitoring appointments as needed to assess patient compliance, results, sensitivity.

V. Evaluation, Planning for Maintenance

▶ At routine appointments, compare tooth color with tooth color guide. Take follow-up photos as appropriate for records.

▶ Tooth color from bleaching relapses with time.

▶ Plan for repeat of bleaching process at appropriate intervals.

DOCUMENTATION

Documentation in the patient's permanent record when planning tooth bleaching includes a minimum of the following:

▶ Current oral conditions.

▶ Consent to treat related to tooth whitening.

▶ Services provided including necessary records for tooth shade.

▶ Impressions and preparation of the trays.

EVERYDAY ETHICS

Julia is a 12-year-old dental hygiene patient who is quite verbal about the appearance of her "dark front tooth." As part of the oral care instructions, Theresa, the dental hygienist, begins to discuss possible options of nonvital bleaching to lighten the tooth. Julia becomes visibly excited and wants to whiten the tooth right away. Following Dr. Leonard's examination, Theresa brings Julia's mother in to discuss the possibility of whitening. The mother quickly tells Julia "You don't want to do that, it's probably too expensive."

Questions for Consideration

1. Is it ethical to discuss treatment options with a child patient before informing the parent or guardian who will make the decision for treatment? Explain.

2. Consider the steps in resolving an issue or a dilemma (Box 1-10 in Chapter 1). What are the rights of each of the individuals involved in this situation? Are there any conflicts of interest that Theresa must identify as she works through the steps in resolving this issue?

3. What financial, legal, or cultural factors need consideration if Theresa is to identify an alternative approach that will lead to a positive outcome? Describe her possible approaches.

▶ Demonstration of tray filling, positioning, timing, and cleaning.

▶ Instructions given to patient.

▶ Planned follow-up care and appointments.

▶ Patient problems or complaints expressed.

▶ An example documentation is shown in Box 46-6.

BOX 46-6

Example Documentation: Patient Receiving Vital Tooth Bleaching

S –Patient states she is unhappy with the color of teeth. Patient states she has sensitive teeth.

O –Tooth shade: C-1; appears to have only yellow stain. Patient's medical and dental histories present no contraindications for tooth bleaching. Radiographs and dental examination reveal absence of cavitated caries.

A –Patient presents with a deficit in wholesome body image as evidenced by her statement she is self-conscious of tooth color.

P –Consent for treatment signed and copy given to patient. Completed prophy with all extrinsic stain removed. Intraoral photographs obtained to document tooth color. Impressions and preparation of NGVB trays. Dispensed three syringes of carbamide peroxide 10%. Patient instructed to brush with potassium nitrate product for 2 weeks before beginning bleaching process; after beginning bleaching use of carbamide peroxide 10% every other day.

Patient demonstrated dispensing correct amount of bleaching gel into tray. Patient states: tray provides comfortable fit; understanding of sensitivity treatment; and willingness to return for follow-up appointment.

Next steps: Patient scheduled for follow-up appointment 2 weeks after bleaching process initiated.

Signed _____, RDH

Date _____

Factors To Teach The Patient

▷ Why a complete oral cancer screening and dental examination, including radiographs and periodontal evaluation, is performed before any form of whitening is initiated.

▷ During bleaching, teeth and gingival tissues may become sensitive for a period of time.

▷ If sensitivity is experienced, use a desensitizing product, discontinue bleaching, or delay next treatment.

▷ Regardless of method, color relapse occurs in a relatively short period of time.

▷ Excessive use of bleaching products may be harmful. Follow manufacturer's directions.

▷ Existing tooth-colored restorations will not change color, and therefore may not match and may need to be replaced after bleaching.

References

1. Byrne BE, McIntyre F. Chapter 12: Bleaching agents. In: *ADA/PDR Guide to Dental Therapeutics*. 5th ed. Chicago, IL: American Dental Association; 2009:351.

2. Dahl JE, Pallesen U. Tooth bleaching—a critical review of the biological aspects. *Crit Rev Oral Biol Med*. 2003; 14(4):292–304.

3. Truman J. Bleaching of non-vital discolored anterior teeth. *Dent Times*. 1864;1:69–72.

4. Spasser HF. A simple bleaching technique using sodium perborate. *NY State Dent J*. 1961;27:332.

5. Mokhlis GR, Matis BA, Cochran MA, et al. A clinical evaluation of carbamide peroxide and hydrogen peroxide whitening agents during daytime use. *J Am Dent Assoc*. 2000;131(9):1269–1277.

6. Haywood VB, Heymann HO. Nightguard vital bleaching. *Quintessence Int*. 1989;20(3):173–176.

7. ADA Council on Scientific Affairs. *Tooth Whitening/Bleaching Treatment Considerations for Dentists and Their Patients*. Chicago, IL: American Dental Association; 2009:12.

8. Haywood VB. Treating sensitivity during tooth whitening. *Compend Contin Educ Dent.* 2005;26(9, Suppl 3):11–20.

9. Sweeney MR. Tooth whitening. In: Gladwin M, Bagby M, eds. *Clinical Aspects of Dental Materials.* Philadelphia, PA: Lippincott, Williams & Wilkins; 2009:212–222.

10. Haywood VB. Chapter 1: Diagnosis and treatment planning for bleaching. In: *Tooth Whitening Indications and Outcomes of Nightguard Vital Bleaching.* Chicago, IL: Quintessence; 2007:1–26.

11. Haywood VB. The "bottom line" on bleaching 2008. *Inside Dent.* 2008;4(2):2–5.

12. Matis BA, Wang Y, Eckert GJ, et al. Extended bleaching of tetracycline stained teeth: a 5-year study. *Oper Dent.* 2006;31(6):643–651.

13. Basting RT, Rodrigues AL Jr, Serra MC. The effect of 10% carbamide peroxide, carbopol and/or glycerin on enamel and dentin microhardness. *Oper Dent.* 2005;30(5):608–616.

14. American Academy of Pediatric Dentistry Council on Clinical Affairs. Policy on dental bleaching for child and adolescent patients. *Pediatric Dent.* 2005–2006; 27(7, Suppl):46–48.

15. Mello HS. The mechanism of tetracycline staining in primary and permanent teeth. *J Dent Child.* 1967; 34(6):478–487.

16. Marshall K, Berry TG, Woolum J. Tooth whitening: current status. *Compend Contin Educ Dent.* 2010;31(7):486–492, 494–495.

17. Haywood VB. Bleaching and caries control in elderly patients. *Aesthet Dent Today.* 2007;1(4):42–44.

ENHANCE YOUR UNDERSTANDING

the**Point**® **DIGITAL CONNECTIONS**
(see the inside front cover for access information)

- **Audio glossary**
- **Quiz bank**

SUPPORT FOR LEARNING
(available separately; visit lww.com)

- *Active Learning Workbook for Clinical Practice of the Dental Hygienist, 12th Edition*

prepU **INDIVIDUALIZED REVIEW**
(available separately; visit lww.com)

- **Adaptive quizzing with** *prepU for Wilkins' Clinical Practice of the Dental Hygienist*